CUBA

Recent Titles in
Bibliographies and Indexes in World History

Iran Media Index
Hamid Naficy, compiler

Serial Bibliographies and Abstracts in History: An Annotated Guide
David Henige, compiler

An Annotated Bibliography of the Holy Roman Empire
Jonathan W. Zophy, compiler

War Crimes, War Criminals, and War Crimes Trials: An Annotated Bibliography
and Source Book
Norman E. Tutorow, compiler

Jewish-Polish Coexistence, 1772-1939: A Topical Bibliography
George J. Lerski and Halina T. Lerski, compilers

Primary Sources in European Diplomacy, 1914-1945: A Bibliography
of Published Memoirs and Diaries
Frederic M. Messick, compiler

Strengthening the United Nations: A Bibliography on U.N. Reform and
World Federalism
Joseph Preston Baratta, compiler

An Annotated Bibliography of the Napoleonic Era: Recent Publications,
1945-1985
Jack Allen Meyer, compiler

Irish Research: A Guide to Collections in North America, Ireland,
and Great Britain
DeeGee Lester, compiler

CUBA

An Annotated Bibliography

Compiled by
Louis A. Pérez, Jr.

Bibliographies and Indexes in World History, Number 10

GREENWOOD PRESS
New York • Westport, Connecticut • London

Library of Congress Cataloging-in-Publication Data

Cuba : an annotated bibliography / compiled by Louis A. Pérez, Jr.
   p.   cm. — (Bibliographies and indexes in world history, ISSN
0742-6852 ; no. 10)
  Bibliography: p.
  Includes index.
  ISBN 0-313-26162-8 (lib. bdg. : alk. paper)
  1. Cuba—Bibliography. I. Pérez, Louis A., 1943-
II. Series.
Z 1511.C83 1988
[F1758]
016.97291—dc19   87-28017

British Library Cataloguing in Publication Data is available.

Library of Congress Catalog Card Number: 87-28017
ISBN: 0-313-26162-8
ISSN: 0742-6852

First published in 1988

Greenwood Press, Inc.
88 Post Road West, Westport, Connecticut 06881

Printed in the United States of America

The paper used in this book complies with the
Permanent Paper Standard issued by the National
Information Standards Organization (Z39.48-1984).

10 9 8 7 6 5 4 3 2 1

For Eddie, Quique, Patrick, and the memory of Freddie:

the best stoop ball team ever.

Contents

viii   Contents

Introduction

The reader with an interest in things Cuban has a truly vast and varied body of literature from which to select reading materials. Much of this literature is the result of a remarkable surge of interest in Cuba following the triumph of the revolution in 1959. The revolution brought the island world-wide attention, attention which has remained more or less constant for almost three decades and which contributed to the development of a corpus of literature of prodigious proportions. Indeed, as the bibliographical entries in this volume suggest, the preparation of bibliographies and research guides to keep pace with this expanding literature has become an enterprise of no small dimensions.

It is also true, however, that international interest in Cuba is historic, with origins dating back to the sixteenth century. Geo-political factors conferred a value to the island well out of proportion to its intrinsic importance. Cuba's location at the maritime crossroads of the Gulf of Mexico and the Caribbean situated the island along the vital shipping lanes of the Spanish New World empire. Commercial and strategic considerations were also the source of United States preoccupation with the status of Cuba during much of the nineteenth and twentieth centuries. The geographic position of the island in the New World middle latitudes, further, made Cuba an obligatory port of call for untold numbers of travellers and tourists visiting the Western Hemisphere. Indeed, travel accounts provide one of the richest sources of information about Cuba in both the nineteenth and twentieth centuries.

The result was the accumulation of an extraordinarily rich body of literature, spanning several centuries, and dealing with a vast range of subjects. One of the more difficult aspects in the preparation of this bibliography was to limit the number of useful entries to manageable proportions. This guide is designed to assist two principal groups of readers: generalists seeking an introduction to the full range of the literature on Cuba and scholars interested in fields outside of their immediate specialties.

The bibliography seeks to identify the major written works on Cuba in a wide variety of fields. In pursuit of this objective, a number of criteria were employed. Most important, effort was made to include those materials that are at once comprehensive treatments of the subject, representative of the field and "state of the art," and suggestive of additional literature, either by way of notes and/or bibliography. When appropriate and adequate, preference was given to English-language works, though this was not always possible or desirable, particularly with some of the more specialized fields, where the literature was almost entirely in Spanish. At the other extreme, for some categories the literature in both languages is voluminous. In these instances, preference was given to English-language materials, particularly if the notes and bibliographies of the entries cited provided useful additional references for further reading and research. The section on José Martí, for example, is one such an instance. The corpus of the literature on Martí assumes truly vast proportions. In the section on Martí, the entries were limited largely to English-language titles and a few of the better representative works in Spanish. One last general consideration influenced the type of materials included. Only titles that are generally available to readers were included. Publications not available outside of Cuba were omitted. All the materials cited, as far as can be determined, are likely to be owned either by most general libraries or by the better research facilities in the United States.

This bibliography also strives to present a balanced compilation of the literature about Cuba: between pre-revolutionary and post-revolutionary, between Cuban and non-Cuban. Effort was made to provide balance among the various categories included in the volume. Some topics are of comparatively little interest outside of Cuba. This is not to suggest that the subject was ignored, but rather that the material that does exist is of such a specialized nature and so difficult to obtain that their inclusion would be of little value to the general reader. All the materials in each chapter are organized alphabetically by titles with the exception of travel accounts. These are arranged in the chronological order of their original writing, subsequent re-publication notwithstanding, so as to facilitate the identification of works for specific periods.

In the course of several years during which this bibliography was in preparation, I received courteous cooperation and assistance from the staffs of a number of libraries and research centers, including the Library of Congress, the Bibioteca Nacional "José Martí," the New York Public Library, the Center for Cuban Studies, University of Pittsburgh Library, University of Florida Library, and most of all, the University of South Florida Library.

Several persons need to be acknowledged for their part in making this volume possible, for it is entirely possible that without their assistance this book could not have been completed. I owe a particular debt of gratitude to Sylvia Wood, who worked with some of the early draft material, made sense out of a vast and varied mass of notes, and assisted with the preparation of the index. Nita Desai helped throughout, but especially during numerous "crises" as the project neared completion. In this regard, I am enormously in the debt of Cecile Pulin, who saw the manuscript through all of its phases. She did a splendid job, and I fall deeper into her debt.

CUBA

The Country and Its People

1. Alrededor de nuestra psicología.
    Manuel Márquez Sterling.
    Havana: Imprenta Avisador Comercial, 1906. 237p.
    An investigation into the national character of Cuba within
    a larger context of Latin America. The study attempts to
    trace the development of the Cuban personality to the
    primacy of sugar monoculture.

2. Area Handbook for Cuba.
    Jan Knippers Black (et al.).
    Washington, D.C.: Government Printing Office, 1976. 550p.
    bibliog. A comprehensive look at Cuba examining a wide
    range of topics, including physical environment, history,
    population, economy, agriculture, government and
    administration, labor, foreign policy, education, culture,
    commerce, and the armed forces.

3. "Aspectos censurables del carácter cubano."
    Mario Guiral Moreno.
    Cuba Contemporánea, vol. 4, no. 2 (Feb. 1914), p. 121-33.
    In this critical study of Cuban character, the author
    singles out what he perceives to be "censurable" national
    personality traits, including the lack of discipline,
    informality, pessimism and frivolity.

4. Background to Revolution.
    Edited by Robert Freeman Smith.
    New York: Knopf, 1966. Reprinted, Huntington, New York:
    Krieger Publishing Company, 1979. 244p. bibliog.
    A collection of twenty-six essays designed to provide an
    historico-cultural context for the Cuban revolution. The

topics examined include nationalism, historiography, U.S.-Cuban relations, economic development, race and slavery, political parties, labor, agriculture, and class structures.

5.   Cuba.
Irene A. Wright.
New York: The MacMillan Company, 1910. 512p. maps.
One of the better first-person accounts of Cuba. The author was an historian and long-time resident of Cuba, and an astute and critical observer of developments on the island. At times the work can be overbearing and patronizing, but generally it provides a trenchant analysis of Cuban society during the early twentieth century.

6.   Cuba and the Cubans.
Raimundo Cabrera.
Translated from the Spanish by Laura Guiteras.
Philadelphia: The Levytype Company, 1896. 442p.
This general survey of social, economic, and political conditions in late nineteenth century Cuba serves as a basis for the author's case for Cuban independence. The volume also contains several appendices consisting of official Spanish proclamations and edicts.

7.   Cuba and Porto Rico; with the Other Islands of the West Indies. Their Topography, Climate, Flora, Products, Industries, People, Political Conditions, etc.
Robert Thomas Hill.
London: T. Fisher Unwin, 1898. 429. maps.
Surveys general economic, political, and social conditions in the Caribbean at the end of the nineteenth century. Cuba is discussed on p. 33-144.

8.   Cuba in Pictures.
Nathan A. Haverstock and John P. Hoover.
New York: Sterling Publishing Company, 1974. 64p.
A collection of photographs depicting life in socialist Cuba. The book is organized with a thematic text covering the land, history, government, people, and economy, with each topic being accompanied by appropriate photographs.

9.   Cuba, Island of Paradox.
R. Hart Phillips.
New York: McDowell, Obolensky, 1959. map.
This fascinating first person provides a portrait of Cuban society from the early 1930s through 1959. The author served as the resident New York Times correspondent in Havana for most of these years, a position that provided a unique vantage point from which to observe and record conditions on the island. The book is an enormously useful

source for the period, particularly for the years of Gerardo Machado's presidency during the 1930s and the Batista period of the 1950s.

10. Cuba, la isla fascinante.
Juan Bosch.
Santiago de Chile: Editorial Universitario, 1955.   252p.
A well written description of Cuba by the former president of the Dominican Republic, this work includes an historical survey as well as perceptive comments about conditions in Cuba during the 1940s and 1950s.

11. Cuba, the Land of Opportunity.
George Clarke Musgrave.
London: Simpkin, Marshall, Hamilton, 1919.   103p.
A discussion of economic, political, social, and cultural conditions in Cuba. This dated but still interesting book was designed primarily to assist British travellers and investors.

12. Cuba, Old and New.
Albert Gardner Robinson.
New York: Longmans, Green and Company, 1915.   264p.
While providing a general account of Cuban life in the early years of the twentieth century, the book deals largely with conditions in the capital and passing attention to the provinces. Emphasis is placed on the economy, population, politics, and agriculture.

13. Cuba: Population, History and Resources, 1907.
Victor H. Olmstead and Henry Gannett.
Washington, D.C.:   United States Bureau of the Census, 1909.   275p.
Prepared by the directors of the Cuban census of 1907, this work is a useful synthesis of the findings of that year's census.   The volume deals principally with demography, population, economy, climate, communications, and transportation.

14. Cuba, Prophetic Island.
Waldo Frank.
New York: Marzani and Munsell, Inc., 1961.   191p. bibliog.
A well-written and evocative portrayal of Cuba in the twentieth century. The account is unabashedly sympathetic with the Cuban struggle for social justice and self-determination, and these concerns lead the author to look upon the early phase of the revolution (1959-1961) with favor and support.

15. Cuestiones cubanas.

Emilia Bernal.
Madrid: Imprenta G. Hernández y Galo Saíz, 1928. 316p.
bibliog.
A general socio-political impressionistic view of Cuba.
The value of the book is in the survey discussion of Cuban
literature, with particular emphasis on the works of José
María Heredia, Gabriel de la Concepción Valdés, Juan
Clemente Zenea, and Gertrudis Gómez de Avellaneda.

16. De la factoría a la colonia.
     Francisco de Arango y Parreño.
     Havana: Cultural, S.A., 1936. 168p.
     This reprint of the classic nineteenth century study of
     economic conditions in the colony, deals principally with
     population, agriculture, and commerce.

17. De los vicios y defectos del criollo y de su remedio.
     Cristobal de la Guardia.
     Havana: Imprenta Masip y Soles, 1941. 2nd ed. 159p.
     An examination of Cuban national character, the work is
     generally critical of what are perceived as the moral
     deficiencies and cultural shortcomings of the "creole
     personality."

18. Entre cubanos: psicología tropical.
     Fernando Ortiz Fernández.
     Paris: P. Ollendorff, 1913, 230p.
     The study represents an interesting attempt by one of
     Cuba's most prominent ethnologists to formulate a coherent
     theory of the nature of Cuban character. It is both an
     entertaining and informative treatment of the "tropical
     psychology."

19. Humanismo (Mexico), vol. 7, nos. 53-54 (Jan.-April 1959).
     The essays in this special double issue devoted to Cuba
     examine colonial and republican history, economic
     development, industry, nationalism, science, literature,
     plastic arts, theater, and music. Also included is
     material dealing with the early phase of the Cuban
     revolution, including essays on the rebel army, agrarian
     reform, education, women, and early revolutionary
     legislation.

20. Military Notes on Cuba. 1909.
     United States War Department. General Staff.
     Washington, D.C.: Government Printing Office, 1909. 757p.
     A useful compendium of vast data on Cuba compiled during
     the Second U.S. Intervention (1906-1909). While dealing
     with general themes of geography, fauna and flora, geology,
     transportation, population, agriculture, and mineral
     resources, the book also contains detailed description of

conditions in each province.

21. **Libro de Cuba.**
    Havana: Publicaciones Unidas, 1954. 956p.
    A massive over-sized tome celebrating the fiftieth
    anniversary of the founding of the republic, the book deals
    with virtually all aspects of Cuban national life,
    including history, art, literature, theater, dance,
    industry, commerce, agriculture, education, foreign policy,
    social structure, living conditions, and religion.

22. **Problems of the New Cuba.**
    Commission on Cuban Affairs.
    New York: Foreign Policy Association, 1935. 523p. maps.
    One of the most comprehensive appraisals of conditions in
    Cuba in the aftermath of the economic depression, political
    upheavals, and social dislocations of the late 1920s and
    early 1930s. The work covers a wide range of subjects,
    including economics, politics, population, family, public
    health, education, social welfare, labor, agriculture,
    commerce, finances, public utilities, soil and forestry,
    and diversification.

23. **Twentieth Century Cuba.**
    Wyatt McGaffey and Clifford R. Barnett.
    Garden City, New York: Anchor Books, 1965. 462p. map.
    bibliog.
    A useful reference work on Cuba published soon after the
    revolution. Successive chapters deal with early history,
    ethnic influences and social patterns, economics, political
    processes, labor, education and welfare, foreign trade,
    relations with the U.S., banking and finance, religion,
    intellectuals and artists, the revolutionary struggles of
    the 1950s, the victory of Fidel Castro and the
    consolidation of power, and foreign relations.

24. **Twentieth Century Impressions of Cuba: its History,**
    People, Commerce, Industries, and Resources.
    Reginald Lloyd (et al.).
    London: Unwin Brothers, Ltd. 1913. 520p. maps.
    A comprehensive over-sized book dealing with nearly all
    aspects of early twentieth century Cuba. Among the topics
    discussed include economy, climate, fauna, flora, geology,
    history, education, music, sports, and public health. In
    addition, the book contains several shorter essays written
    by residents and specialists which deal with specific
    issues within many areas. An enormously useful and richly
    illustrated book.

B. CURRENT EVENTS

25. Areíto.
    New York: Areíto, Inc. 1974-1984. trimester.
    This periodical offered an informative review of
    developments in Cuba and the Cuban expatriate community.
    Each issue ranges over a variety of subjects and covered
    current developments concerning literature, art, theater,
    politics, U.S.-Cuba relations, religion, and history.

26. Cuba Resource Center Newsletter.
    New York: Cuba Resource Center. 1971-1973. bi-monthly.
    An informative bi-monthly report dealing with political,
    economic, social, religious, and diplomatic issues.

27. Cuba Review.
    New York: Cuba Resource Center, 1974-1978. quarterly.
    A continuation of the Cuba Resource Center Newsletter,
    dealing with similar themes on a quarterly basis.

28. Cuba Times.
    New York: Cuba Resource Center, 1984-. bi-monthly.
    A bi-monthly publication in the form of a news digest
    dealing with current developments in Cuba. News briefs are
    supplemented by longer feature articles dealing with
    various social, economic, political, religious, and foreign
    policy issues.

29. Cuba Update.
    New York: Center for Cuban Studies, 1979-. bi-monthly.
    Provides an informative review of Cuban developments and
    presents translations of major speeches and news summaries
    from Cuba.

30. Latin America.
    New York: Facts on File, 1973-79. annual.
    Published annually between 1972 and 1979, each annual issue
    provides a summary of the year's principal news stories.

31. Latin American Perspectives.
    Riverside, California: Latin American Perspectives.
    1974-. quarterly.
    This journal contains a wide variety of articles, many
    dealing with Cuba. Thematic issues deal with imperialism,
    dependency, and revolutionary struggle, and of particular
    interest is number 4 (vol. II, supplemental 1975) devoted
    entirely to the Cuban revolution.

32. U.S.-Cuba Bulletin.   Washington, D.C.:   Cuban-American
    Committee. 1982-. quarterly.
    A newsletter given specifically to reporting current
    developments affecting U.S.-Cuba relations and matters
    relative to the Cuban exile community.

Geography

A. GENERAL SURVEYS

33. Apuntes biográficos y bibliografía de Mario Sánchez Roig.
    Alfredo de la Torre y Callejas.
    Havana: Academia de Ciencias de Cuba, 1943. 81p.
    A biography of the Cuban geographer Mario Sánchez Roig
    which includes a bibliographical compilation of his
    principal works.

34. Diccionario geográfico de la isla de Cuba.
    José de Jesús Márquez.
    Havana: Imprenta Pérez, Sierra y Cía., 1926. 170p.
    A compilation of the principal geographical features,
    paying specific attention to geological developments,
    natural resources, flora and fauna, and geographic sites.

35. Elementos de geografía de Cuba.
    Rolando Espinosa Carballo.
    Miami, Florida: Editorial AIP, 1967. 116p. maps.
    bibliog.
    Provides a general survey of Cuban geography, emphasizing
    natural resources, climate, soil, public health,
    communications, and transportation.

36. Geografía de Cuba.
    Delia Díaz de Villar.
    Miami, Florida: Roger's Printers, 1965. 228p. maps.
    bibliog.
    A geographical work dealing generally with regional
    variations, flora and fauna, industry, ranching,
    agriculture, climate, coastal features, and resources
    administration.

37. Geografía de Cuba.
     Levi Marrero.
     Havana: Alfa, 1951. 736p. plates. bibliog.
     One of the standard surveys of Cuban geography providing
     separate coverage of each of the six provinces. The topics
     examined include geology, climate, soil, coastal
     development, flora and fauna, population, agriculture,
     mining, forestry, fishing, and economic development.

38. Geografía de Cuba.
     Antonio Núñez Jiménez.
     Havana: Editorial Lex, 1959.   2nd ed.   624p.   maps.
     plates. bibliog.
     This   comprehensive   volume   examines   the   major
     characteristics of Cuban geography and covers such topics
     as physical geography, natural resources, and economic
     geography. The six provinces are examined region by
     region.

39. Geografía de la isla de Cuba.
     Esteban Pichardo y Tapia.
     Havana: D.M. Soler, 1854-1855. 4 vols.
     A detailed geographical survey of Cuba, one that was
     remarkably well conceived in the nineteenth century. The
     volume deals with water resources, mines and mining,
     topography, and geographic statistics.

40. Historia de la geografía de Cuba.
     José Alvarez Conde.
     Havana: n.p., 1961. 574p. maps. bilbiog.
     Provides a geographic history of Cuba, stressing ethnology,
     archaeology, and natural history. Biographical sketches of
     the leading geographers of the island are also included.

41. Indicador-guía de la isla de Cuba, geografía política.
     José López Fernández.
     Havana: Editorial Guerrero, 1949. 183p. maps.
     A guide to the administrative and geo-political divisions
     of the island, with further information on the organization
     of   the   postal   system   and   the   nature   of   the
     telecommunications network.

42. Introducción a la geografía de Cuba.
     Salvador Massip and Sarah A. Ysalque de Massip.
     Havana: n.p., 1942. 250p. maps. plates. bibliog.
     This   survey   of   Cuban   physical   geography,   includes
     information on cartography, geological origins, coasts,
     climate, and zoological aspects of Cuban geography.

43. La liberación de las islas.
     Antonio Núñez Jiménez.

Havana: Editorial Lex, 1959. 623p.
A collection of articles, essays, and speeches by one of
Cuba's most prominent geographers. The work includes
material dealing with a range of issues related to
agriculture, agrarian reform, and land tenure.

44. Nomenclatura geográfico y toponímico de Cuba.
    Ernesto de los Ríos.
    Havana: Biblioteca Nacional "José Martí," 1970. 159p.
    A catalogue of Cuban geographic names, places, and
    features.

B. REGIONAL GEOGRAPHY

45. Geografía económica de Cuba.
    Francisco A. Pardeiro.
    Havana: López y Fradraga, 1957. 3 vols.
    This study of the regional economy of the island examines
    the natural resources, topography, and population of each
    of the six provinces of Cuba.

46. Geology and Paleontology of Central Camagüey, Cuba.
    Aart Van Wessem.
    Utrecht, The Netherlands: J. Van Boekhoven, 1943. 91p.
    maps.
    One of the few works in English on the paleontology of the
    eastern region of Cuba.

47. "The High Sierra Maestra."
    B.E. Fernow.
    Bulletin of the American Geographical Society, vol. 39, no.
    5 (1907), p. 257-268.
    An older but still very useful description of the
    southeastern mountain range. The article deals with
    topography, geology, climate, plant geography, and animal
    life.

C. CLIMATE

48. Aclimatación e higiene de los europeos en Cuba.
    Ramón Hernández Poggio.
    Cádiz: Imprenta de la Revista Médica, 1874. 128p.
    A study of the climate of Cuba and its effects on
    Europeans. The emphasis of the work falls on tropical
    diseases and hygiene.

49. Climate of Cuba.
    William F.R. Phillips.
    Washington, D.C.: United States Department of Agriculture,

1898. 23p.
Examines the varieties of weather conditions in Cuba.

50. Hidrología y climatología médicas.
Víctor Santamarina.
Havana: "La Propagandista," 1937. 296p. maps. bibliog.
This informative series of essays examines the relationship
between climate and health. The central themes involve two
basic considerations: climate as a source of illness and
climate as a cure for illness.   The book emphasizes the
salutary aspects of the Cuban climate, specifically the
effects of temperature, rainfall, wind currents, and
atmospheric pressure.

51. Los recursos climáticos de Cuba, su utilización en la
economía nacional.
F.F. Davitaya and I.I. Trusov.
Havana: Academia de Ciencias de Cuba, 1965. 68p.
A study of climatic conditions, paying particular attention
to their potential implication for agricultural production.

D. GEOLOGY AND NATURAL RESOURCES

52. Contribución a la geología de Cuba.
Edited by Yuri M. Puscharosky.
Havana: Academia de Ciencias de Cuba, 1974.   183p.
bibliog.
This collection of essays and lectures deals with geology,
mines, and mineral resources in Cuba. Summaries in English
are provided.

53. "Estudio geológico de los suelos de la provincia de La
Habana."
Jesús Francisco de Albear.
Revista Bimestre Cubana, vol. 48, no. 2 (July-Dec. 1941),
p. 398-424.
A study of the variety of soils of Havana province. The
article examines the historical formation of the region,
the chemical composition and texture of soils, and
drainage.

54. Geografía económica.
Andrés Ateaga Menesis.
Havana: P. Fernández y Cía., 1939. 304p.
A general survey of economic geography of the island,
including an appraisal of promise and prospects for the
development of Cuban natural resources.

55. Geología de Cuba.
Gustavo Furrazola-Bermúdez.

Havana: Editora del Consejo Nacional de Universidades, 1964. 239p. maps. bibliog.
A general geological survey of Cuba, including information on mineral resources, land formation, and water management.

56. Historia de la geología, minerología y paleontología en Cuba.
José Alvarez Conde.
Havana: Junta Nacional de Arqueología y Etnología, 1957. 248p. maps.
The study is organized into several sections, including a brief historical survey, achievements of the most prominent geologists and paleontologists, and a description of geological conditions of the island.

57. Notas sobre los cocodrilos de Cuba y descripción de una nueva especie del pleistoceno.
Luis S. Varona.
Havana: Instituto de Biología, 1966.   34p.   bibliog.
Examines crocodile fossils during the Pleistocene age. A summary in English is provided.

58. La pesca en Cuba.
Mario Sánchez Roig and Federico de la Maza.
Havana: Ministerio de Agricultura, 1952. 272p. bibliog.
One of the more complete studies of the fishing industry in Cuba, this work contains important information concerning the scope of the industry, employment data, and the economic impact of the industry.

59. Report on a Geological Reconnaissance of Cuba.
C. Willard Hoyes, T. Wayland Vaughan, and Arthur C. Spencer.
Washington, D.C.: Government Printing Office, 1901. 123p. maps.
A geological study undertaken under the auspices of the military government of Cuba, provinding a thorough survey of Cuban mines and mineral resources at the beginning of the twentieth century.

60. "Revolution for Cuba's Lobster Industry."
Richard R. Fagen and Patricia W. Fagen.
The Geographical Magazine, vol. 42, no. 12 (Sept. 1970), p. 867-75.
Considers the expansion of the fishing sector in socialist Cuba, with specific reference to lobsters, and examines new improvements in lobster fishing, methods of marketing, and the role of the maritime industries as a source of foreign exchange.

61. The Soils of Cuba.

Hugh H. Bennet and Robert V. Allison.
Washington, D.C.:   Tropical Plant Research Foundation,
1928. 410p. maps.
A detailed study of soil conditions, dealing with the
physical and chemical qualities of the principal soil types
of the island.

E. MAPS, ATLASES, and GAZETEERS

62. All the Facts You Want to Know About Cuba.
     Compiled by P.R. Yrizar and A. Tremois.
     Havana: Army Printing Press, 1928. 120p.
     A dated but still useful gazetteer covering physical
     features,   agriculture,   manufacturing,   cities,
     transportation,   mining   and   mineral   resources,
     administration, and education.

63. Anales de la isla de Cuba.
     Félix Erenchún.
     Havana: Imprenta La Antilla, 1856-61. 4 vols.
     A   comprehensive   encyclopedia   dealing   with   the
     administrative,   political,   economic,   and   statistical
     aspects of nineteenth century Cuba.

64. Atlas censo 1953.
     Cuba.   Oficina Nacional de los Censos Demográfico y
     Electoral.
     Havana: Tribunal Superior Electoral, 1958. 156p.
     This   collection   of   maps   based   on   the   1953   census,
     emphasizes   demographic   trends   and   also   includes   maps
     portraying   political   changes,   economic   development,
     location of natural resources, and geographical patterns.

65. Atlas de Cuba.
     Gerardo A. Canet Alvarez.
     Cambridge, Massachusetts: Harvard University Press, 1949.
     63p. maps. bibliog.
     A   general   atlas   of   Cuba,   richly   illustrated   with
     photographs, charts, graphs, and maps. The topics covered
     include   history,   oceanography,   geology,   climate,
     population,   social   structures,   government,   agriculture,
     industry, mining, communications, trade, and tourism. The
     text is in Spanish and English.

66. Atlas de Cuba.
     Instituto Cubano de Geodesia y Cartografía.
     Havana: Instituto Cubano de Geodesia y Cartografia, 1978.
     143p.
     The work contains a collection of 462 maps, clearly and
     colorfully produced. Maps dealing with physical features

treat separately such diverse topics as geology, minerals, soils, climate, precipitation, forests, fauna, wildlife, and atmospheric pressure. Also included are economic maps, population maps, historical maps, and political maps. The scale on the regional maps is 1:300 000.

67. Atlas nacional de Cuba, en el décimo aniversario de la revolución.
Institute of Geography of the Academy of Sciences of Cuba and Institute of Geography of the Academy of Sciences of the USSR.
Havana: Academia de Ciencias de Cuba, 1970. 132p.
A collection of detailed maps of the island, including political and physical maps.

68. Atlas de Cuba: XX aniversario del triunfo de la revolución cubana.
Instituto Cubano de Geodesia y Cartografía.
Havana: Instituto Cubano de Geodesia y Cartografía, 1978. 143p.
Perhaps the best compilation of current Cuban maps presently available. The collection includes maps of natural resources, economic maps, population maps, historic maps, political maps, and general geography.

69. "Cartografía cubana. Catálogo de mapas, 1435-1820."
Salvador Massip.
Revista Bimestre Cubana, vol. 32, no. 2 (July-Dec. 1933), p. 90-102, 256-70.
An annotated guide to maps of Cuba, compiled from books, atlases, and manuscripts.

70. Cuba: Official Standard Names Approved by the United States Board on Geographic Names.
United States Department of the Interior. Office of Geography. Washington, D.C.: Government Printing Office, 1957. 113p.
This volume contains a compilation of some 9,000 entries of places and features in Cuba.

71. Diccionario geográfico, estadístico, histórico de la Isla de Cuba.
Jacobo de la Pezuela.
Madrid: Imprenta del Establicimiento de Mellado, 1863-66. 4 vols.
Provides an indispensable guide to colonial Cuba of the mid-nineteenth century and gives a wealth of information about colonial administration. Successive chapters deal with geography, agriculture, flora and fauna, economy, colonial administration (political, ecclesiastical, military, maritime), trade and commerce, and population.

72. Exposición de cartografía, numismática y grabados antiguos
    de Cuba.
    Cuba. Archivo Nacional.
    Havana: Imprenta "El Siglo XX," 1944. 57p.
    A compilation of maps, engravings, and medals available in
    the Cuban National Archives. Includes plates.

73. A Gazetteer of Cuba.
    Henry Gannett.
    Washington, D.C.: Government Printing Office, 1902. 112p.
    maps.
    A compilation of places and natural features in Cuba.

F. TOURISM AND TRAVEL GUIDES

74. Guía geográfica y administrativa de la isla de Cuba.
    Pedro José Imbernó.
    Havana: Establecimiento Tipográfico "La Lucha," 1891.
    314p.
    This is an indispensable reference work for nineteenth
    century Cuba.   It provides information on all aspects of
    insular   geography,   natural   resources,   municipal   and
    provincial administration, church organization, currency,
    industry, and transportation.   The book also includes a
    discussion of provinces, cities, and villages as well as a
    description of natural resources, rivers, mountains, and
    lakes.

75. The Complete Travel Guide to Cuba.
    Paula DiPerna.
    New York: St. Martin's Press, 1979. 274p. maps. plates.
    The most complete and current travel guide available in
    English.   Prepared with the assistance of the Cuban
    National Tourism Institute, the guide offers useful
    information concerning travel within Cuba, with special
    reference to hotels, restaurants, transportation, and
    sightseeing for all the provinces of Cuba and most of the
    major cities. However, its usefulness concerning travel to
    Cuba, particularly for U.S. citizens, is limited and
    changes in travel regulations since the publication of the
    book have dated its sections in tourist procedures.

76. Cuba, Ideal Vacation Land. Tourist Guide, 1953-1954.
    Cuba. Instituto Cubano del Turismo.
    Havana: Instituto Cubano del Turismo, 1953.   bibliog.
    This useful tourist guide to the Cuba of the early 1950s
    provides information about sights, restaurants and hotels,
    as well as the island's history and culture.

77. Estudio estadístico del turismo en Cuba.

Cuba. Corporación Nacional del Turismo.
Havana: Corporación Nacional del Turismo, 1937.   23p.
A statistical abstract of the tourist trade in Cuba during
the 1930s, including numbers of foreign travellers, ports
of entry, and lengths of stay.

78.   Havana Mañana, a Guide to Cuba and the Cubans.
      Consuelo Hermer and Marjorie May.
      New York: Random House, 1941. 289p.
      A dated but valuable descriptive travel guide which pays
      special attention to Havana.

79.   Hildebrand's Travel Guide: Cuba.
      Heidi Rann and Peter Geide.   Trans. from the German by
      Jaqueline Baroncini.
      Frankfurt, West Germany: Karto & Grafik, 1985.   176p.
      maps.
      A versatile and well illustrated travel guide to travel to
      Cuba.   The work not only includes information on the
      obligatory sightseeing attractions, but also provides a
      wealth of background information on Cuban politics and
      history,   sports,   literature,   cuisine,   restaurants,
      architecture, and agriculture. While the book is useful to
      all   travellers   and   is   up-to-date,   the   information
      concerning travel conditions, currency exchange, and visa
      requirements is of limited value to would-be U.S. visitors.
      The manual is a translation of a travel guide designed for
      European tourists, particularly West Germans.

80.   Norton's Complete Hand-Book of Havana and Cuba.
      Albert J. Norton.
      Chicago: Rand, McNally & Company, 1900. maps. plates.
      This work is a general guide which was designed to aid
      tourists and travellers, investors and settlers in Cuba at
      the turn of the century.

81.   Standard Guide to Havana and Cuba.
      Charles B. Reynolds.
      New York: Foster and Reynolds, 1922. 188p. maps.
      A tourist guide to the island providing basic information
      necessary for travel in Cuba during the 1920s.

82.   Turismo en Cuba.
      Armando R. Maribona.
      Havana: Editorial Lex, 1959. 234p.
      An account of the tourist industry in Cuba. Emphasis is on
      the 1950s, and with specific attention given to Havana.

83.   Turismo y urbanismo.
      Reinaldo López Lima.
      Havana: n.p., 1949. 125p.

An official survey of tourism, examining the opportunities for the industry to expand.

84. Your Holiday in Cuba.
     Lyman Judson and Ellen Judson.
     New York: Harper and Row, 1952. 306p. maps.
     A description of the main tourist attractions in Havana and travel highlights in the interior provinces.

Travellers' Accounts

85. The Island of Cuba.
Alexander von Humboldt.
New York: Derby and Jackson, 1856.   trans. by J.S.
Thrasher. 397p. maps.
Humboldt travelled through Cuba early in the nineteenth
century, the critical period in which Cuban society was in
a state of transition. He was a shrewd observer of local
conditions and a serious collector of statistics and data,
providing commentary on such subjects as political-economy,
public administration, slavery, and agriculture. In this
1856 English-language edition, editor/translator J.S.
Thrasher updates many of Humboldt's statistics.

86. Letters from the Havana [sic], during the year 1820.
Robert Francis Jameson.
London: J. Miller, 1821. 135p. map.
This collection of correspondence written during travels in
Cuba is especially interesting for its observations on
slavery and the slave trade.

87. Travels in the West: Cuba, with Notices of Porto Rico
and the Slave Trade.
David Turnbull.
London: Longman, Orrime, Brown, Green. 1840. Reprinted,
New York: AMS Press, 1973. 574p.
In this richly detailed account of Cuba, the author pays
particular attention to the condition of Afro-Cubans, both
slave and free, and to economic conditions, mining, sugar,
coffee, tobacco production, and living conditions in
Havana.

88. Isla de Cuba.
José María de Andueza

Madrid: Boix, 1841. 182p.
A first-hand account of mid-nineteenth century politics, as
well as the economy, history, and geography of Cuba.

89. Viaje a La Habana.
Condesa de Merlin.
Havana: Editorial de Arte y Literatura, 1974.
This volume is a reprint of letters originally written from
Havana during the early 1840s. The correspondence serves
as one of the reflections of life in the capital during the
mid-nineteenth century. The countess was an astute
observer of public and private life in Havana, and her
commentaries deal with such diverse themes as street
scenes, family life, diet, art, theater, commerce,
religion, funerals, architecture, and social customs.

90. Notes on Cuba.
John G.F. Wurdemann
Boston: J. Munroe and Company, 1844. 359p.
This descriptive account of mid-nineteenth century Cuba by
a physician contains readable vignettes on geography,
colonial politics, social customs, and the economy.

91. The Island of Cuba.
Richard Robert Madden.
London: C. Gilpin, 1849. 252p.
A well-written account of conditions in Cuba during the
1830s which is particularly useful for its description of
the slave trade and slave conditions in Cuba.

92. Cartas desde Cuba.
Fredrika Bremer.
Havana: Editorial Arte y Literatura, 1981. 199p.
The Scandinavian novelist Fredrika Bremer who travelled
through the island in 1851 and this collection of her
letters offers thoughtful reflections about life in and
around Havana, slavery, sugar, and coffee production, and
plantation life.

93. Cuba in 1851.
Alexander Jones.
New York: Stringer and Townsend, 1851. 80p.
A travel account of population, agriculture, commerce, and
politics in mid-nineteenth century Cuba. Author was
especially attentive to the revolutionary disturbances of
the late 1840s and early 1850s.

94. History of Cuba; or, Notes of a Traveller in the Tropics.
Being a Political, Historical, and Statistical Account of
the Island, from its First Discovery to the Present Time.
Maturin Murray Ballou

New York: J.C. Derby, 1854.   Reprinted, Ann Arbor,
Michigan: University Microfilm, 1969.   230p.   plates.
An important source for mid-nineteenth century Cuba. The
author's anti-slavery attitudes make him particularly
sensitive to plantation agriculture and the slave system.

95. To Cuba and Back.
     Richard Henry Dana.
     Boston: Ticknor and Fields, 1859. Reprinted, Carbondale,
     Illinois: Southern Illinois University Press, 1966. 288p.
     In this colorful and vivid description of general
     conditions in Cuba, Dana also displays great attention to
     detail. Of particular interest are the observations made
     of Havana, life in a Matanzas sugar plantation, and the
     manners and customs of urban and rural Cuba.

96. Cuba for Invalids.
     R.W. Gibbs.
     New York: W.A. Townsend and Company, 1860. 214p.
     Provides a descriptive account of the island emphasizing
     the healthfulness of Cuba. Attention is given to health
     resorts, springs, and spas.

97. A Trip to Cuba.
     Julia Ward Howe.
     Boston: Ticknor and Fields, 1860. Reprinted, New York:
     Praeger, 1960. 251p.
     A well written account of Cuba at mid-century. Vivid
     imagery and attention to detail portray the condition of
     women, education, taxation, social customs, and politics.
     Howe's strong abolitionist sentiment made her a
     particularly astute and critical commentator of slavery in
     Cuba.

98. Isla de Cuba. Reflexiones sobre su estado social
     político y económico.
     Antonio López de Letona.
     Madrid: J.M. Ducazal, 1865. 118p.
     This study provides an informative account of Cuba in the
     mid-nineteenth century and is a perceptive memoir from a
     careful observer of social, economic, and political
     conditions in Cuba.

99. Cuba with Pen and Pencil.
     Samuel Hazard.
     Hartford, Connecticut: Hartford Publishing Company, 1871.
     584p.
     Richly detailed and elaborately illustrated, this travel
     account of the island. It provides one of the most varied
     details of life in Cuba in the middle third of the
     nineteenth century. Although half of the book is devoted

to Havana, the author also travelled into the interior and
offered interesting vignettes about rural Cuba and the
provincial capitals.

100. The Pearl of the Antilles.
     A. Gallenga.
     London: Chapman and Hall, 1873. 202p.
     An account of travel in Cuba during the Ten Years War
     (1868-1878). Of particular interest are the descriptions
     of the character of the war, the condition of the slaves,
     and the composition of the slave owners.

101. The Pearl of the Antilles.
     Walter Goodman.
     London: H.S. King and Company, 1873. 304p.
     As a thoughtful travel account of Cuba during a period of
     political disorder and economic change, the study provides
     a valuable source of reference for the period of the
     mid-nineteenth century.

102. The Mambí-Land, or, Adventures of a Herald Correspondent
     in Cuba.
     James J. O'Kelly.
     Philadelphia: Lippincott and Company, 1874. 359p.
     A war-time journal written during the Ten Years War
     (1868-1878). The author travelled across the island,
     recording detailed observations of conditions on the island
     during the conflict. Of particular interest is his account
     of life in the insurgent camps.

103. Cuban Sketches.
     James W. Steele.
     New York: G.P. Putnam & Sons, 1881. 220p.
     The book is written by a former U.S. consul in Cuba and is
     more a memoir of impressions during the years of his
     residence in Cuba. Its particular value is as a source of
     reference for the period in which the author is writing.
     An interesting commentary about various aspects of Cuba for
     the period immediately following the Ten Years War
     (1868-1878).

104. Due South; or, Cuba Past and Present.
     Maturin Murray Ballou.
     Boston: Houghton Mifflin, 1886. 2nd ed. 316p.
     Giving an unusually perceptive and detailed account of Cuba
     in the latter part of the nineteenth century, the principal
     value of the work lies in its account of socio-economic
     conditions in Cuba during a decade of depression and
     dislocation. Many poignant vignettes provide important
     insights into Cuban society.

105. Around the Corner to Cuba.
     Reau Campbell.
     New York: C.G. Crawford, 1889. 46p. maps.
     An illustrated travel account of a visit to Cuba, which is
     concerned principally with life and social customs in
     Havana.

106. Cuba por fuera.
     Tesifonte Gallego García.
     Havana: La Propaganda Literaria, 1890. 254p.
     Written by a Spaniard not especially sympathetic to Cubans,
     this travel account provides insight into prevailing and
     general Spanish views of the island during the late
     nineteenth century.

107. The Island of Cuba; a Descriptive and Historical Account
     of the "Great Antilla."
     Andrew Summers Rowan and Montrose Ramsey.
     New York: H. Holt and Company, 1896.   279p.   maps.
     bibliog.
     This historical survey and travel account of the island
     offers several interesting observations about conditions in
     Cuba on the eve of the war for independence (1895-1898).

108. Album de la trocha.
     Eva Canel.
     Havana: Imprenta "La Universal," 1897. 90p.
     A travel account of unusual historical value. The author
     visited the battle regions during the years of the war for
     independence (1895-1898), recording impressions that are
     especially useful to the study of this period.

109. Cuba: its Resources and Opportunities.
     Pulaski F. Hyatt and John T. Hyatt.
     New York: J.S. Ogilvie Publishing Company, 1898. 226p.
     This interesting book was written by two former agents of
     the United States consular service in Cuba, and is an
     important work from two perspectives. First, it provides a
     detailed account of social and economic conditions in Cuba
     immediately after the war of independence, ranging from
     agriculture, mining and forests to transportation, labor,
     trade, and climate.   Second, it offers insight into
     official United States views on Cuba, for in a very real
     sense this is an exhortatory work, seeking to encourage
     North American investment in Cuba.

110. Cuba, Past and Present.
     Richard Davey.
     London: Chapman & Hall, Ltd., 1898. 284p. map.
     A well written travel account, particularly useful for its
     description of Cuba during the war of independence

(1895-1898). The author visited most of the larger cities
and provides detailed portraits of urban life on the island
at the end of the nineteenth century.

111. The New-Born Cuba.
     Franklin Matthews.
     New York: Harper and Brothers, 1899. 388p. maps.
     Cuba at the close of the nineteenth century is presented in
     this very useful descriptive account.   It provides
     informative perceptions of conditions in Cuba after the war
     of independence and during the first year of the United
     States occupation (1899).

112. Tomorrow in Cuba.
     Charles M. Pepper.
     New York: Harper and Brothers, 1899.   316p.   maps.
     bibliog.
     A detailed account of post-war Cuba by one of the more
     perceptive war-time correspondents. The work is especially
     useful for its account of conditions in Cuba after the war
     for independence (1895-1898) and a discussion of Spanish
     and United States policy.

113. El Toro: a Motorcar Story of Interior Cuba.
     E. Ralph Estep.
     Detroit: Packard Motor Car Company, 1909. 107p.
     A colorful account of an automobile trip across the island.
     Along the way the author makes interesting and informative
     observations about living conditions in the interior.

114. A travès de Cuba.
     Charles Berchòn.
     Sceaux, France: Imprenta de Charaire, 1910. 206p. map.
     This lively and informative account was written by a
     geographer travelling across the island from end to end.
     Comments include observations on climate, agriculture,
     mining, flora and fauna, and the general economic
     conditions.

115. Un canario en Cuba.
     Francisco González Díaz.
     Havana: Imprenta "La Prueba," 1916. 347p.
     An interesting account of social, economic, political, and
     cultural conditions in Cuba told from the perspective of a
     Canary Islander.   What makes this travel memoir
     particularly useful is the running commentary concerning
     life in Cuba for immigrants, especially Spaniards and
     canarios.

116. El país de la riqueza.
     Carlos Martí.

Madrid: Renacimiento, 1918. 264p.
In this informative first-person account of conditions in
Cuba during the years of World War I, the author makes
perceptive observations about Cuban society at a time of
enormous economic expansion and general prosperity. His
travel itinerary included all the provinces and most of the
large cities, during the course of which he comments about
sugar   production,   labor,   immigration,   politics   and
government, agriculture, and railways.

117. Cuba y las costumbres cubanas.
     Frank C. Ewart.
     Boston: Ginn and Company, 1919. 157p.
     Observations by the author during a visit of several
     months, in which a large part of his time was spent in
     Havana. The focus of the work is given to the capital,
     therefore, and not all of the island.

118. Cuba, Past and Present.
     A. Hyatt Verrill.
     New York: Dodd, Mead and Company, 1920. 240p.
     A ranging description of early twentieth century Cuba.
     Author makes informative observations of all the provinces
     and the capital.

119. Sixty Years in Cuba.
     Edwin F. Atkins.
     Cambridge, Massachusetts: Riverside Press, 1926. 362p.
     One of the more important works for the study of the latter
     part of the nineteenth century. Atkins held considerable
     sugar property in central Cuba, and for the better part of
     his years in Cuba had access to high-ranking political
     leaders both in Cuba and the United States. The memoir is
     a valuable source for the insights it provides to the sugar
     system, plantation life, foreign investment and finance.
     The autobiography spans the years from 1860s to 1910s.

120. Cuba and Her People of Today.
     Charles Harcourt Ainslie Forbes-Lindsay.
     Boston: L.C. Page & Company 1928. 329p. maps. bibliog.
     A general account of conditions in Cuba that includes
     discussions of history, politics, natural resources,
     economic development, and climate information which, the
     author asserts, are "designed to aid the prospective
     investor or settler."

121. When It's Cocktail Time in Cuba.
     Basil D. Wood.
     New York: H. Liveright, 1928. 284p.
     Presents insightful observations about leisure, amusements,
     sports, and recreation in Cuba. This travel account also

provides an informative portrayal of the North American community on the island.

122. Cuban Tapestry.
Sydney A. Clark.
New York: R.M. McBride & Company, 1939. 289p.
The narrative describes conditions in Cuba during the 1930s, paying attention to the varieties of Cuban culture--people, countryside, towns, and social customs, and economy. It is one of the better accounts of this period, offering perceptive comments on social and economic conditions in Cuba in the wake of the depression and political tumult of the 1930s.

123. The Isle of a Hundred Harbors.
Olive G. Gilbson.
Boston: B. Humphries, Inc., 1940. 287p. bibliog.
A colorful account of east to west travel through Cuba in the 1930s, providing some interesting impressions of Cuba in the years following economic dislocation and political disorders. The author also offers a perceptive commentary about social conditions, cultural developments, and folklore.

124. Cuba.
Erna Fergusson.
New York: Knopf, 1946. 308p.
In this well-written and lively travelogue, the author makes astute observations on conditions in the provinces. Her historical sketches are brisk and thought-provoking.

125. "Cuban Notebook."
Mark Schleifer.
Monthly Review, vol. 13, nos. 3-4 (July-Aug. 1961), p. 72-83.
A brief but evocative essay of impressions of Cuba in January 1961, during the celebration of the second anniversary of the revolution. The author is especially good at capturing the general mood of expectation and optimism in Cuba during the early years of Fidel Castro's government.

126. 90 Miles From Home; the Face of Cuba Today.
Warren Miller.
Boston: Little, Brown, 1961. 279p.
This sympathetic account of the early days of the revolution provides an especially vivid and compelling portrait of the climate of opinion on the island during the initial period of political change.

127. The Morning After; a French Journalist's Impressions

of Cuba Under Castro.
Victor Franco.
New York: Praeger, 1963. 248p.
Presenting a vivid account of the early years of the Cuban
revolution, Franco captures the euphoria, the confusion,
and early hopes and expectations of life in Cuba during
this period.

128. The Youngest Revolution; a Personal Report on Cuba.
Elizabeth Sutherland.
New York: Dial Press, 1959. 277p.
A sympathetic account of the Cuban revolution, emphasizing
Cuban achievements in health, education, and social
programs.

129. In Granma's Wake-Girl Stella's Voyage to Cuba.
Frank Mulville.
London: Seafarer Books, 1970. 302p. map.
An account of a sailing trip around the waters of the
island.

130. Does Fidel Eat More Than Your Father? Conversations in
Cuba.
Barry Reckord.
New York: Praeger Publishers, Inc. 1971. 175p.
Presents a well-written account of Cuba during the late
1960s.   Of particular interest are the parallels and
perspectives drawn by the author, a Jamaican dramatist,
about Cuban approaches to problems affecting the Third
World.

131. Havana Journal.
Andrew Salkey.
Baltimore: Penguin, 1971. 316p.
Based on a visit to Havana in late 1967 and 1968. A
sympathetic treatment of life in the capital told in diary
form and with recorded notes of dialogues.

132. Cuba, vida cotidiana y revolución.
Enrique Raab.
Buenos Aires: Ediciones de la Flor, 1974. 84p.
A collection of journalistic vignettes of life in
revolutionary Cuba.   Among the scenes portrayed is an
account of a wedding, popular culture, cinema, the role of
the Committees for the Defense of the Revolution, and the
visit of North American volunteer workers.

133. In Cuba.
Ernesto Cardenal.
New York: New Directions Books, 1974. 340p.
Nicaraguan poet Ernesto Cardenal made two trips to Cuba

between 1970 and 1971. This account of his travels on the
island provide interesting vignettes of Cuba at a critical
point in the history of the revolution: the effort to make
the ten million ton sugar crop. Much of the book takes the
form of conversations with writers, priests, bureaucrats,
workers,   farmers,   teachers,   and   senior   government
officials, including Fidel Castro.

134. Inside Cuba.
     Joe Nicholson, Jr.
     New York: Sheed and Ward, Inc., 1974. 236p.
     A journalistic account by a reporter who travelled in Cuba
     for six weeks in 1972. The work contains informative
     observations about Cuba during the second decade of the
     revolution.

135. Cuba Today.
     Lee Chadwick.
     Westport, Connecticut: L. Hill, 1976. 212p.
     An account of socialist Cuba based on the author's travels
     through the country in 1971 and again in 1975.   Her
     comments about life in the countryside, education, arts,
     farming, and religion are both thoughtful and informative.

136. Inside Cuba Today.
     Fred Ward.
     New York: Crown Publishers, 1978. 308p.
     The author of this account of life in socialist Cuba
     travelled across the island and conducted interviews in the
     course of seven different visits.   His book, which is
     richly illustrated with photographs, examines the economy,
     politics, home life, education, public health, tourism, the
     arts, sports, mass organization, agriculture, the sugar
     industry, and Cuban foreign policy.

Flora and Fauna

137. Bibliografía botánica cubana.
Hana Samkova and Veroslav Samek.
Havana: Academia de Ciencias de Cuba, 1967. 36p.
A useful bibliography of Cuban botany.

138. The Cruise of the Thomas Barrera. The Narrative of a
Scientific Expedition to Western Cuba and the Colorado
Reefs, with Observations on the Geology, Fauna, and Flora
of the Region.
John B. Henderson.
New York: G.P. Putnam's Sons, 1916. 320p. maps.
This narrative account of an early expedition provides a
commentary on the geography, marine features, and wildlife
of western Cuba.

139. Diccionario botánico de nombres vulgares cubanos.
Juan Tomás Roig y Mesa.
Havana: Editora del Consejo Nacional de Universidades,
1965. 2 vols. bibliog.
A dictionary of the popular plant names of Cuba. Plates
area also included.

140. Diccionario botánico de los nombres vulgares cubanos y
puertorriqueños.
Compiled by Manuel Gómez de la Maza.
Havana: Imprenta "La Antilla," 1889. 115p.
A compilation of popular plant names.

141. Los equinodermos fosiles de Cuba.
Mario Sánchez Roig.
Havana: Compania Editora de Libros y Folletos, 1949.
330p.
A study of sea urchin fossils.

142. **La fauna jurásica de Viñales.**
     Mario Sánchez Roig
     Havana: Imprenta "Graphical Arts," 1920. 61p.
     A study of Jurassic paleontology in Viñales (Pinar del Río province).

143. **Flora de Cuba: datos para su estudio.**
     Manuel Gómez de la Maza and Juan Tomás Roig y Mesa.
     Havana: Imprenta Rambla, Bouza y Cía. 1914. 182p.
     Surveys of Cuban plants and botany.

144. **Flora habanera.**
     Manuel Gómez de la Maza.
     Havana: Imprenta "La Moderna Poesía," 1897. 215p.
     A study of botany in Havana province.

145. **Historia de la botánica en Cuba.**
     José Alvarez Conde.
     Havana: n.p., 1959. 353p. maps.
     Presents a history of the study of botany in Cuba from the sixteenth through the twentieth centuries. Much of the work consists of biographies of the most important botanists. The text is in English and Spanish.

146. **A Naturalist in Cuba.**
     Thomas Barbour.
     Boston: Little, Brown and Company, 1945. 317p.
     This illustrated travel memoir provides one of the most detailed and colorful accounts available of the flora and fauna of the island. Includes plates.

Prehistory and Archaeology

147. La antropología en Cuba y el conocimiento de nuestros
     indios.
     Arístides Mestre.
     Havana: Imprenta "El Siglo XX," 1925. 55p. maps.
     First presented as a lecture in 1925, this small book
     summarizes the state of research and synthesizes the then
     recent accomplishments of Cuban anthropologists. The text
     is accompanied by plates and illustrations.

148. "The Archaeology of Cuba."
     Daniel G. Brinton.
     American Archaeologist, vol. 2, no. 10 (Oct. 1898),
     p. 17-21.
     A brief review of the sites in Cuba the author believed to
     hold promising information. In the process the work
     provides a view of the state of the archaeological
     profession in 1898.

149. Arqueología indocubana.
     José Álvarez Conde.
     Havana: Junta Nacional de Arqueología y Etnología, 1956.
     329p. maps.
     A general discussion of pre-Columbian cultures in Cuba,
     with specific attention to the Ciboney, Sub-Taíno, and
     Taíno.

150. Caverna, costa y meseta. Interpretaciones de arqueología
     indocubana.
     Felipe Pichardo Moya.
     Havana: Jesús Montero, 1945. 159p. bibliog.
     This survey of pre-Columbian cultures in Cuba
     chronologically explores the varieties of Indian cultures
     on the plateaus, along the coastal areas, and in the
     mountains.

151. La cerámica taína de Cuba.
     José M. Guarch.
     Havana: Academia de Ciencias de Cuba, 1972.   78p.
     bibliog.
     A study of the pottery of the Taíno Indians based on
     archeological work undertaken in eastern Cuba.

152. The Ciboney Culture of Cayo Redondo, Cuba.
     Cornelius Osgood.
     New Haven, Connecticut: Yale University Press, 1942.   65p.
     maps.
     A study of one of the most important sites of one of the
     more important pre-Columbian cultures in Cuba.

153. Las cuatro culturas indias de Cuba.
     Fernando Ortiz Fernández.
     Havana: Orellano y Cía., 1943.   176p.
     This work includes an examination of two of the most
     important Indian cultures of Cuba, the Ciboney and Taíno.
     The author argues that sufficient differences exist between
     the   two   groups   to   warrant   further   ethnological
     distinctions.

154. Cuba before Columbus.
     Mark Raymond Harrington.
     New York: Museum of the American Indian, 1921.   2 vols.
     570p. bibliog.
     One of the most comprehensive English-language accounts of
     pre-Columbian cultures in Cuba. While some of the material
     is rather dated, it still represents one of the better
     introductory works of Cuban prehistory and archaeology.
     The text is accompanied by illustrations, plates, and maps.

155. Cuba, dibujos rupestres.
     Antonio Núñez Jiménez.
     Havana: Editorial de Ciencias Sociales, 1975.   503p.
     maps. bibliog.
     A richly-illustrated study of cave drawings and paintings
     in Cuba which examines each cave site in detail.

156. Cuba primitiva.
     Antonio Bachiller y Morales.
     Havana: M. de Villa, 1883. 2nd ed. 321p.
     An account of the Indian cultures in the Greater Antilles,
     emphasizing their origins, speech patterns, customs, and
     history.

157. Las culturas aborigines de Cuba.
     Manuel Rivero de la Calle.
     Havana: Editora Universitaria, 1866.   194p.   bibliog.

A detailed historical description of the pre-Columbian cultures of Cuba.

158. Culturas más primitivas de Cuba precolumbiana.
     Ernesto E. Tabío.
     Havana: Grupo Guama, 1951. 43p. bibliog.
     Discusses the Ciboney and Guanahatabey Indians.

159. "Desaparición de la población indígena cubana."
     Juan Pérez de la Riva.
     Universidad de La Habana, nos. 196-197 (1972), p. 61-84.
     A study of the decline of the Indian population in the aftermath of Spanish colonization and settlement.

160. La epigrafía en Cuba.
     Juan Miguel Dihigo y Mestre.
     Havana: Imprenta "El Siglo XX," 1928. 54p.
     A study of inscriptions dating largely from Spanish colonial times and found mainly in cemeteries and mausoleums.

161. Estratigrafía y fauna del jurásico de Cuba.
     C.M. Jodoley and Gustavo Furrazola-Bermúdez.
     Havana: Academia de Ciencias de Cuba, 1968. 126p. maps. bibliog.
     A paleontological study of the Jurassic age. A summary is provided in both Spanish and English.

162. "Historia de la arqueología cubana."
     Fernando Ortiz Fernández.
     Cuba Contemporánea, vol. 30, no. 117 (Sept. 1922), p. 5-35 and vol. 30, no. 118 (Oct. 1922), p. 126-64.
     These two articles provide a survey history of the developments and practice of archaeology in Cuba. The first essay discusses the findings of the principal investigators, both Cuban and non-Cuban, as well as their major published works. The latter essay deals with museums, philology, and general Antillean archaeology.

163. Historia de los indios de Cuba.
     Rafael Azcarate Rosell.
     Havana: Editorial Trópico, 1937. 254p. bibliog.
     A historical survey of Indians in Cuba--principally the Taíno--through 1810.

164. El ídolo de Bayamo.
     Ramón Dacal and Ernesto Navarro.
     Havana: Universidad de La Habana, 1972. 37p. bibliog.
     Discusses pre-Columbian culture in Cuba with specific emphasis on the eastern regions of the island.

165. Las peculiaridades de la desintegración de las comunidades primitivas cubanas.
     Estrella Rey.
     Havana: Academia de Ciencias de Cuba, 1969.   22p.
     bibliog.
     An informative anthropological account of the demise of the Indian population of Cuba early during the period of the Spanish conquest and colonization.

166. Prehistoria de Cuba.
     Ernesto E. Tabio and Estrella Rey.
     Havana: Academia de Ciencias de Cuba, 1966. 280p. maps.
     bibliog.
     An excellent summary of what was known of Cuban prehistory in the mid-1960s.   The authors organize the cultural sequence as follows: Ciboney-Guayabo Blanco, Ciboney-Cayo Redondo, Mayarí, Sub-Taíno, and Taíno.   The monograph is both a useful guide to previous research and an expression of current thinking on prehistory and history in socialist Cuba.

167. Psicografía y supervivencias de los aborígenes de Cuba.
     Fanny Azcuy Alón.
     Havana: Cárdenas y Cía., 1941. 101p. bibliog.
     Presents a general treatment of pre-Columbian cultures in Cuba, with special emphasis on the Taíno Indians. Discusses the Indian contribution to modern Cuban culture.

168. Revisión indoarqueológica de la provincia de Las Villas.
     José Alvarez Conde.
     Havana: Junta Nacional de Arqueología y Etnología, 1961.
     174p. maps. bibliog.
     A comprehensive study of the archaeology of central Cuba.

169. Revista de Arqueología y Etnología.
     Havana: Junta Nacional de Arqueología y Etnología de Cuba.
     1946-annual.
     The principal professional journal, containing articles on all aspects of research dealing with archaeology, anthropology, prehistory, ethnology, and folklore of Cuba.

History

174. The Caribbean: the Genesis of a Fragmented Nationalism.
     Franklin W. Knight.
     New York: Oxford University Press, 1978. 251p. maps.
     bibliog.
     Scholarly yet readable, this is one of the standard survey
     accounts of Caribbean history. The author presents a
     judicious balance of social, political, and economic
     developments in the region. The work adopts a thematic
     approach to the Caribbean.

175. Cuba, Haiti, and the Dominican Republic.
     John Edwin Fagg.
     Englewood Cliffs, New Jersey: Prentice-Hall, Inc., 1965.
     maps. bibliog.
     A general political history of the three larger Caribbean
     countries. Each country is treated separately in survey
     fashion.

176. The Early Spanish Main.
     Carl Ortwin Sauer.
     Berkeley: University of California Press, 1966. 306p.
     maps.
     A well-written, descriptive narrative of the early decades
     of Spanish exploration and colonization in the Caribbean
     region.

177. The European Nations in the West Indies, 1493-1688.
     A.P. Newton.
     New York: Barnes and Noble, Inc. 1967. 356p. maps.
     This reprint of 1933 edition deals with the Caribbean
     region as a focal point of imperial struggles in Europe.
     It provides a well-researched and easily readable account
     of the imperial policies and conflicts of England, France,
     Spain, and Holland.

178. From Columbus to Castro: the History of the Caribbean
     1492-1969.
     Eric Williams.
     London: Andre Deutsch Ltd., 1970. 576p.
     A survey of Caribbean history underlining the relationship
     between sugar, slavery, and capitalism and the varieties of
     European colonialism and North American imperialism.

179. The Golden Antilles.
     Timothy Severin.
     New York: Knopf, 1970. 336p. map. bibliog.
     A well-written and popular account of Caribbean history
     from the time of Columbus through the eighteenth century.

180. Main Currents in Caribbean Thought: the Historical
     Evolution of Caribbean Society in its Ideological Aspects

1492-1900.
Gordon K. Lewis.
Baltimore, Maryland: The Johns Hopkins University Press,
1983.
This represents a comprehensive and interpretative history
of ideas in the Spanish, French, and English Antilles. The
work emphasizes the unity of the Caribbean historical
experience.

181. The Restless Caribbean: Changing Patterns of Inter-
     national Relations.
     Edited by Richard Millett and W. Marvin Will.
     New York: Praeger, 1979. 295p.
     A collection of twenty essays which deals with various
     aspects of Caribbean international relations, including
     topics associated with politics, migration, tourism,
     economic development, and communism.

182. A Short History of the West Indies.
     John H. Parry and Philip M. Sherlock.
     New York: St. Martin's Press, 1971.   3rd ed.   337p.
     bibliog.
     Surveys Caribbean history from the European discovery in
     the fifteenth century up to the 1970s. A well written
     thematic approach to the region.

183. The Spanish Caribbean, from Columbus to Castro.
     Louise L. Cripps.
     Boston: G.K. Hall, 1979. 251p. bibliog.
     Presents a historical survey of the Caribbean region, the
     work pays particular attention to Cuba, the Dominican
     Republic, and Puerto Rico.

184. The Spanish Caribbean: Trade and Plunder, 1536-1630.
     Kenneth R. Andrews.
     New Haven: Yale University Press, 1978, 267p.   maps.
     bibliog.
     Studies the Caribbean region from the period of the early
     Spanish settlements to the establishment of the first
     non-Hispanic colonies in the area.

185. The Spanish Crown and the Defense of the Caribbean, 1535-
     1585.
     Paul E. Hoffman.
     Baton Rouge, Louisiana: Louisiana University Press, 1980.
     312p. maps. bibliog.
     An important study of the emergence of the northern
     European challenge to Spanish claims of colonial
     exclusivism over the Caribbean region, specifically in the
     form of pirates, buccaneers, and corsairs, and Spain's
     response to the threat.

186. West Indies.
     Philip M. Sherlock.
     New York: Walker and Company, 1966.   215p.   maps.
     bibliog.
     This general history of the Caribbean region pays
     particular attention to the English-speaking islands.

187. The West Indies and Central America to 1898.
     Bruce B. Solnick.
     New York: Alfred A. Knopf, Inc., 1970.   206p.   maps.
     bibliog.
     Surveying the circum-Caribbean region from the end of the
     sixteenth century through the end of the nineteenth, the
     volume emphasizes primarily the area's political
     developments.

B. Cuba--General

188. "Antecedents of the Cuban Revolution."
     Federico G. Gil.
     Centennial Review of Arts and Science,   vol.   6,   no.   3
     (Summer 1962), p. 373-93.
     This essay provides a general historical survey of
     twentieth century Cuba, focusing on those developments the
     author believes contributed to the making of the revolution
     of 1959.

189. Breve historia de Cuba.
     Julio LeRiverend.
     Havana: Editorial Ciencias Sociales, 1981. 198p.
     A brief survey of Cuban history, dealing principally with
     the economic and political development of the republic.

190. Contribución a la historia de la gente sin historia.
     Pedro Deschamps Chapeaux.
     Havana: Editorial de Ciencias Sociales, 1974.   282p.
     bibliog.
     A collection of historical essays by one of the foremost
     social historians in Cuba. The works deal with the history
     of the inarticulate, including African slaves, Chinese
     coolies, and the fugitive slave communities.

191. Cuba del pasado.
     Pedro Carballo Bernal.
     Santa Clara, Cuba: S.W. Jiménez, 1956. 58p.
     A brief historical study of social customs, habits, and
     local attire.

192. Cuba, economía y sociedad.
     Levi Marrero.

Madrid: Editorial Playor, 1972-1986. vols. 1-12.
This ambitious undertaking of Cuban history is scheduled to
span the history of Cuba from the pre-Columbian period to
the present. As of this writing, the work is up to volume
12, up to the period ending with the eighteenth century.
Upon completion, this massive enterprise will no doubt
stand as one of the principal reference works on Cuba.

193. Cuba: economía y sociedad.
Juan and Verena Martínez Alier.
Paris: Ruedo Ibérico, 1972. 254p. maps. bibliog.
Most of this well written survey is devoted to the
twentieth century socio-economic developments.

194. Cuba, from Columbus to Castro.
Jaime Suchlicki.
New York: Charles Scribner's Sons, 1974. 242p. bibliog.
Presents a general survey of Cuban history from
pre-Columbian times to the early 1970s. The book's
organizational format favors treatment of the twentieth
century, and particularly political developments.

195. "Cuba Painted by Cubans: the Nineteenth Century
Journalistic Essay."
Marguerite C. Suárez-Murias.
Revista Interamericana de Bibliografía, vol. 30, no. 4
(1980), p. 365-86.
The author examines the genre of the popular journalistic
essays, dealing in particular with those articles published
in local newspapers, literary journals, and periodicals
that depicted local customs and manners.

196. Cuba: the Making of a Revolution.
Ramón Eduardo Ruiz.
Amherst, Massachusetts: University of Massachusetts Press,
1968. 190p. bibliog.
This interpretive account of Cuban history covers the
latter part of the nineteenth century up to the early years
of the revolution. The work offers a view of Cuban history
from the perspective of the island's revisionist
historiography.

197. Cuba, the Pursuit of Freedom.
Hugh Thomas.
New York: Harper and Row, 1971. 1696p. maps. bibliog.
This encyclopedic tome stands as the principal
English-language reference work on Cuba between 1762 and
the 1960s. Well written and well organized, this sweep of
Cuban history is a major point of departure for all reading
on Cuba.

198. Cuba y su historia.
     Emeterio S. Santovenia and Raúl M. Shelton.
     Miami, Florida: Cuba Corporation, 1966. 2nd ed. 3 vols.
     bibliog.
     A survey of Cuban history from pre-historic times to the
     revolution.

199. "Cuban Revisionist Interpretations of Cuba's Struggle for
     Independence."
     Duvon C. Corbitt.
     Hispanic American Historical Review, vol. 43, no. 3 (Aug.
     1963), p. 395-404.
     This essay represents an important contribution to the
     general literature of Cuban historiography. It examines
     the changing interpretations in Cuba concerning the war of
     independence and the U.S. armed intervention (1895-1898),
     and documents the rise of revisionist historiography.

200. Curso de historia de Cuba.
     Elio Leiva and Edilberto Marbán.
     Havana: Casa Montero, 1943. 2 vols. bibliog.
     Surveys Cuban history from pre-Columbian times to the
     administration of President Mario G. Menocal (1913-1921).

201. Curso de introducción a la historia de Cuba.
     Edited by Emilio Roig de Leuchsenring.
     Havana: Municipio de La Habana, 1938. 463p. bibliog.
     A collection of essays covering selected aspects of Cuban
     history and written by the specialist of each area of
     study. Topics in the collection are arranged in
     chronological order and include pre-Columbian culture,
     conquest and colonization, trade and commerce, various
     periods of the colony, the wars for independence, and the
     republic. Within each section, essays deal with politics,
     art, economics, foreign relations, and culture.

202. Ensayos históricos.
     José Luciano Franco.
     Havana: Editorial   de Ciencias Sociales, 1974.   230p.
     bibliog.
     This volume brings together some of the most important
     essays written by one of Cuba's premier historians. The
     themes include discussion of early liberation movements
     between 1511 and 1868, pirates and corsairs, slavery,
     Afro-Cuban conspiracies, the Ten Years War (1868-1878) as
     seen in the U.S. press, and a brief biography of José
     Maceo.

203. Estudios de historia de Cuba.
     Fernando Portuondo.
     Havana: Instituto Cubano del Libro, 1972. 410p.

A substantial collection of essays written by one of Cuba's most prolific historians. Most of the articles were published between 1943 and 1972, although eleven have never appeared in print before. The essays are a testament to Portuondo's diversity of interest and range of his research. They deal with a variety of historical themes, including the conquest and colonization, the struggle for independence, education, José Martí, Antonio Maceo, Julio Antonio Mella, and issues of historiographical importance.

204. Historia de Cuba.
Dirección Política de las Fuerzas Armadas Revolucionarias. Havana: Instituto Cubano del Libro, 1971. 3rd ed. 624p. bibliog.
A survey of Cuban history from the pre-Columbian period to the revolution of 1933. The work offers insight into developing historiographical trends in socialist Cuba.

205. Historia de Cuba.
Juan M. Leiseca.
Havana: Montalvo, Cárdenas y Cía., 1925. 614p.
A survey of Cuban history from pre-Columbian times to the early 1920s.

206. Historia de Cuba.
Calixto C. Masó.
Miami, Florida: Ediciones Universal, 1976.   584p. bibliog.
One of the better one-volume survey narratives of Cuban history, covering the period from Spanish colonization in the sixteenth century up to the early 1960s. The larger part of the book is devoted to the nineteenth and twentieth centuries.

207. Historiografía de Cuba.
José Manuel Pérez Cabrera.
México: Instituto Panamericano de Geografía e Historia, 1962. 394p.
Discusses the principal works dealing with Cuban history published before the twentieth century. For its coverage of colonial history, hence, it is unrivalled and must be considered as the standard reference work in the field.

208. Historia de Cuba.
Fernando Portuondo.
Havana: Instituto Cubano del Libro, 1965. 6th ed. 602p. maps.
One of the most comprehensive historical surveys of Cuba. The book deals exclusively with the colonial epoch, spanning the period from conquest and colonization by Spain to the military intervention by the United States in 1898.

209. **Historia de Cuba: aspectos fundamentales.**
     Oscar Pino Santos.
     Havana: Editorial Nacional de Cuba, 1964, 2nd ed. 352p.
     bibliog.
     A historical survey of Cuba from pre-Columbian times to the
     revolution. Attention is given to social and economic
     themes, including slavery, plantation agriculture, class
     structure, and the emergence of Cuba nationality.

210. **Historia de la isla de Cuba y en especial de La Habana.**
     Antonio J. Valdés.
     Havana: Comisión Nacional Cubana de la UNESCO. 356p.
     A reprint of the original 1813 edition, the work is largely
     an historical inventory of dates, political officials,
     church authorities, and events between 1492 to 1813, paying
     with particular atention to the location of churches on the
     island and details about the English occupation of Havana
     (1762).

211. **Historia de la nación cubana.**
     Ramiro Guerra y Sánchez. (et al.)
     Havana: Editorial Historia de la Nación Cubana, S.A.,
     1952. 10 vols. bibliog.
     This multi-volume collaborative work is arguably the most
     comprehensive and detailed history of Cuba. It covers the
     period from the earliest times to 1952 and brought together
     nearly all of the most important historians in Cuba at that
     time, allowing them to write on their own areas of
     specialization. The compilation deals chronologically with
     pre-history, the colonial period, the independence
     struggles, the republic, and thematically with art,
     theater, literature, philosophy, economy, foreign policy,
     education, constitutional law, architecture, and labor.

212. **Historia de Cuba, desde Colón hasta Castro.**
     Carlos Márquez Sterling.
     New York: Las Américas Publishing Company 1963. 496p.
     bibliog.
     A well-balanced and readable survey of Cuban history, from
     pre-Columbian times to the early years of the revolution.

213. **History of Cuba.**
     Maturin Murray Ballou.
     Boston: Phillips, Sampson, 1854. 230p.
     A survey of Cuban history from the early sixteenth century
     to the mid-nineteenth century. Emphasis of work falls on
     the later period.

214. **A History of the Cuban Republic.**
     Charles E. Chapman.
     New York: The Macmillan Company, 1927. 685p. maps.

bibliog.
One of the standard history texts of early twentieth
century Cuba. The work concentrates largely on Cuban
political developments and foreign policy issues. The book
was prepared in collaboration with the State Department and
the United States embassy staff in Havana, and thus tends
to reflect the prevailing attitudes in policy circles at
the time of its publication.

215. "In the Service of the Revolution: Two Decades of Cuban
Historiography, 1959-1979."
Louis A. Pérez, Jr.
Hispanic American Historical Review, vol. 60, no. 1 (Feb.
1980), p. 79-89.
A survey of the historical literature written during the
first twenty years of the Cuban revolution.

216. La isla de Cuba en el siglo XIX vista por los extranjeros.
Juan Pérez de la Riva.
Havana: Editorial de Ciencias Sociales, 1981.   265p.
bibliog.
Presents a commentary on and collection of articles and
early impressions of Cuba from various European writers.

217. "The Long Revolution: Class Relations and Political
Conflict in Cuba, 1868-1968."
Dennis B. Wood.
Science and Society, vol. 34, no. 1 (Spring 1970), p. 1-41.
This essay examines the interplay of social formations and
political developments over a span of one hundred years.
It discusses politics, the nature of Cuban class structures,
and the evolution of the local economy in the course of the
revolutionary upheavals of the late nineteenth and early
twentieth centuries, culminating in the triumph of
socialism after 1961.

218. Las luchas campesinas en Cuba.
Antero Regalado.
Havana: Comisión de Educación Interna del Comité Central
del PCC, 1973. 204p.
Discusses peasant resistance to land expropriations and
expulsion. While there is material dealing with the
colonial period, the greater part of the work covers the
twentieth century.

219. Manual de historia de Cuba.
Ramiro Guerra y Sánchez.
Havana: Editorial de Ciencias Sociales, 1980.   6th ed.
720p.
This new edition of the original 1938 study makes the
classic work available again. Written by one of the major

historians of the twentieth century, the volume focuses on
Cuba between conquest and colonization by the Spanish in
the sixteenth century and the outbreak of the Ten Years War
in 1868. The author's discussion of economic developments,
slavery, and international relations is particularly
valuable.

220. Manual de la isla de Cuba.
     José García de Arboleya.
     Havana: Imprenta del Tiempo, 1859. 418p. maps.
     As a survey of Cuban history, from pre-Columbian times to
     the mid-nineteenth century, the book provides useful
     statistic data concerning population, agriculture, and
     commerce.   The emphasis of the work is on the nineteenth
     century.

221. Personalidades cubanas.
     Compiled by Fermín Peraza Sarausa.
     Havana: Ediciones Anuario Bibliográfico Cubano, 1957-1967.
     9 vols.
     One of the most complete biographical dictionaries
     available, the work includes Cubans of distinction from all
     spheres of activity during the colonial period and the
     republican years.

222. Resumen de la historia de Cuba.
     Isidro Pérez Martínez.
     Havana: Cultural, S.A., 1936. 188p.
     A balanced survey of Cuban history from pre-Columbian times
     to the revolutionary upheavals of the 1930s.

223. La república: dependencia y revolución.
     Julio LeRiverend.
     Havana: Editorial de Ciencias Sociales, 1973.   3rd ed.
     376p.
     A comprehensive historical survey of the Cuban republic
     from the end of the U.S. military occupation in 1902 to the
     fall of Fulgencio Batista in 1958.

224. "The Roots of Anti-Americanism in Cuba."
     Carlos Alberto Montaner.
     Caribbean Review, vol. 13, no. 2 (Spring 1984), p. 13-16,
     42-46.
     An examination of the historical origins of anti-U.S.
     sentiment in Cuba. Montaner argues that one important
     component of Cuban nationalism took the form of rejection
     of the United States, and that this sentiment was
     exacerbated by the Platt Amendment and repeated North
     American intervention. He concludes that this made Cuba
     especially susceptible to the nationalist exhortations of
     Fidel Castro.

225. "Scholarship and the State: Notes on 'A History of the Cuban Republic.'"
Louis A. Pérez, Jr.
Hispanic American Historical Review, vol. 54, no. 4 (Nov. 1974), p. 682-90.
In   1927,   Charles   Chapman   published History of the Cuban Republic, a work that quickly became the standard reference book on Cuba for more than thirty years.   This article points out that the work was commissioned by the State Department and designed as an instrument of U.S. policy.

226. "Twentieth Century Cuba Historiography."
Robert Freeman Smith.
Hispanic American Historical Review, vol. 44, no. 1 (Feb. 1964), p. 44-73.
Providing a thorough analysis of the principal historical works and trends of Cuban historiography, this essay examines the literature in the following periodization schema: colonial history to 1800, colonial period in the nineteenth century, the revolution of 1895 and the U.S. intervention, the republic, and cultural history.

227. "Toward a New Future, From a New Past: the Enterprise of History in Socialist Cuba."
Louis A. Pérez, Jr.
Cuban Studies/Estudios Cubanos,   vol. 15,   no. 1   (Winter 1985), p. 1-13.
A discussion of the development and role of history in Cuba as a means of promoting group solidarity and collective esprit.   The study of the past is not confined to scholarship, but also finds expression in the Cuban mass media and popular culture; it also engages the attention of the party, the armed forces, and workers' collectives.

228. What Happened in Cuba?
Robert Freeman Smith.
New York: Twayne Publishers, Inc., 1963. 360p. bibliog.
A collection of documentary sources for the study of Cuban history. The materials tend to favor U.S.-Cuban diplomatic history, but also included are documents dealing with the Cuban economy, politics, and military affiars.   The compilation spans the years from 1783 to 1962.

C. Provincial and Municipal

229. Baracoa, apuntes para su historia.
José Ignacio Castro.
Havana: Editorial Arte y Literatura, 1977.   132p. bibliog.

A narrative history of one of the oldest cities in Cuba,
from its pre-Columbian origins to the revolution. A large
part of the study is devoted to the nineteenth century.

230. Baracoa: cuna de historia y tradición.
G. Pelayo Yero Martínez.
Baracoa, Cuba: Imprenta La Nueva Democracia, n.d.   56p.
This informative historical survey discusses Baracoa's
social, economic, political, cultural, and religious
developments.

231. "The Beginnings of Havana."
Irene A. Wright.
Hispanic American Historical Review,   vol. 5,   no. 3
(Aug. 1922), p. 498-503.
Discusses the founding and early history of the city of
Havana between 1514 and 1550.   The author attempts to
clarify the principal points of long standing confusion
about Havana's origins by documenting the date of the
city's foundation, the name of its founder, and its
original site.

232. Camagüey (Biografía de una provincia).
Mary Cruz del Pino.
Havana: Imprenta "El Siglo XX," 1955.   261p.   bibliog.
A historical survey of Camaguey province from early Spanish
colonization in the sixteenth century to the early 1950s.
The study is well balanced and detailed, covering such
topics as politics, economics, society, culture, and
military affairs.

233. El Camagüey legendario.
Angela Pérez de la Lama.
Camagüey, Cuba: Imprenta "La Moderna," 1944.   246p.
A survey of Camagüey history and local folklore.

234. El Camagüey: Viajes pintorescos por el interior de Cuba y
por sus costas.
Antonio Perpina.
Barcelona, Spain: J.A. Bastinos, 1889.   448p.
A useful late nineteenth century account of the eastern
half of the island which provides an interesting
first-person commentary on conditions in rural Cuba.

235. Crónicas de Santiago de Cuba.
Emilio Bacardí y Moreau.
Madrid: Gráficas Breogán, 1972.   10 vols.
A detailed chronology of the major events in the history of
the city of Santiago de Cuba.   The work covers the period
from the early years of the Spanish conquest up to 1898.

236. Cuatro siglos de vida.
Eduardo Anillo Rodríguez.
Havana: Imprenta "Avisador Comercial," 1919. 184p.
This chronological history emphasizes the key developments in the city of Havana, from its founding in 1514 up to 1919. The book's format lends itself to easy reference use, emphasizing key developments in Havana on a year by year basis.

237. "De la historia provincial y local en sus relaciones con la historia general de Cuba."
Julio J. LeRiverend.
Santiago, no. 46 (June 1982), p. 121-36.
A well-argued essay underlining the relationship between Cuba's provincial and local history and its larger national history.

238. Epítome de la historia de Sancti-Spíritus.
Manuel Martínez-Moles.
Havana: Imprenta "El Siglo XX," 1936. 303p.
One of the most comprehensive histories of this important city in Las Villas province. The study covers the period from the years 1554 to 1934, and is divided into several sections, including historical chronology, biography, and documents.

239. Estudio económico social de la isla de Pinos.
Miguel A. Monzón and Eduardo Santos Ríos.
Havana: Banco de Fomento Agrícola e Industrial de Cuba, 1952. 116p. plates. maps.
A detailed study of the economy and economic potential of the Isle of Pines, examining agriculture, commerce, ranching, forestry, industry, and fishing.

240. Guantánamo.
Regino E. Boti.
Guantanamo, Cuba: Imprenta de "El Resumen," 1912, 87p.
Surveys the origins and development of the city of Guantanamo in Oriente province. The study emphasizes the city's political and administrative developments.

241. La Habana, apuntes históricos.
Emilio Roig de Leuchsenring.
Havana: Oficina del Historiador de la Ciudad, 1964. 2nd ed. 3 vols.
Provides a comprehensive historical account of the city of Havana and its suburbs from its founding in the sixteenth century to the early years of the revolution.

242. La Habana (Biografía de una provincia).
Julio J. LeRiverend.

Havana: Imprenta "El Siglo XX," 1960.   510p.   maps.
bibliog.
One of the outstanding provincial histories of Cuba. The
account provides a balanced coverage of political, social,
ecocomic, administrative, and cultural themes spanning the
years from the pre-Columbian period to the early twentieth
century.

243. "La Habana en el siglo XVI."
Calixto E. Masó.
Cuba Contemporánea, vol. 32, no. 126 (June 1923), p. 97-125
and vol. 32, no. 127 (July 1923), p. 201-25.
Discusses the emergence and development of the city of
Havana during the first critical century of its founding.
Attention is paid to public administration, the origins of
sugar production, cattle ranching, population, architecture
and public works, slavery, folklore and legends.

244. Historia de Guanabacoa.
Elpidio de la Guardia.
Guanabacoa, Cuba: Imprenta "Noticias," 1946. 272p.
One of the better histories of this large Havana suburb.
The work covers the years from 1511 to 1946, and deals
principally   with   ecclesiastical   history,   politics,
administration, the wars for independence, and the early
republic.

245. Historia de Remedios.
Manuel Martínez Escobar.
Havana: Jesús Montero, 1944. 365p.
Provides a comprehensive historical narrative of one of the
larger municipalities in Las Villas province. The study
examines a variety of aspects of the town's history,
including politics, culture, public administration, local
economy, and war. It concentrates almost entirely on the
colonial period, up to the end of the nineteenth century.

246. Historia de Santiago de Cuba.
José María Callejas.
Havana: Imprenta "La Universal," 1911. 136p.
A chronological account of the eastern-most province of the
island, covering the period from 1492 to 1823.

247. Historia de Santiago de Las Vegas.
Francisco Fina García.
Santiago de Las Vegas, Cuba: Editorial "Antena," 1954.
111p.
Surveys the history of the municipality of Santiago de Las
Vegas, an important surburb of Havana. The work treats the
period   from   the   early   sixteenth   century   to   the
establishment of the republic, with special focus on the

political and administrative aspects of the city's history.

248. Historia de Trinidad.
Francisco Marín Villafuerte.
Havana: Jesús Montero, 1945. 405p.
Surveys the history of the city of Trinidad in Las Villas province, with a concentration on the years between the seventeenth and nineteenth centuries. The themes covered include early settlement, ecclesiastic history, revolutionary struggles (1868-1898), and social and cultural developments.

249. Historial de Cuba.
Ricardo V. Rousset.
Havana: Librería "Cervantes" de Ricardo Velaso, 1918. 3 vols.
This is an excellent multi-volume history of Cuba.   What sets this work apart from the conventional historical narrative is the emphasis given to provincial and municipal history.   Each volume is devoted to two provinces.   (I. Pinar del Río and Havana; II.   Matanzas and Santa Clara; and III. Camagüey and Oriente.) The provinces are studied through the history of their municipalities (municipios).

250. In the Fist of the Revolution: Life in a Cuban Country Town.
José Yglesias.
New York: Pantheon, 1968. 307p. map.
A well-written and informative account of the impact of the revolution in the town of Mayarí in Oriente province. Yglesias lived in the town for three months in 1967, during which time he made detailed observations on the private and public lives of the residents. Much of the book is in the form of recorded dialogue.

251. Matanzas (Biografía de una provincia).
Francisco J. Ponte Domínguez.
Havana: Imprenta "El Siglo XX," 1959.   354p.   bibliog.
Outlines the development of Matanzas province from prehistoric times through the twentieth century.   The author deals with a variety of themes, including economic development, slavery, colonial administration, and the struggle for independence.

252. Matanzas en la independencia de Cuba.
Carlos M. Trelles y Govín.
Havana: Imprenta "Avisador Comercial," 1928.   193p. bibliog.
Provides a chronological account from 1868 to 1898 of the role and participation of Matanzas province in the struggle for independence.   Almost half of the volume consists of

published correspondence of leading provincial political and military figures related to the independence cause.

253. Mayarí.
Antonio Núñez Jiménez.
Havana: Sociedad Espeleológica de Cuba, 1948. 66p. maps. bibliog.
A descriptive historical survey of north central region Oriente province. Attention is also paid to geography and geology.

254. Memoria historica de Cienfuegos y su jurisdicción.
Enrique Edo.
Havana: Ucar, García y Cía., 1943. 821p.
A detailed study of the city of Cienfuegos and its suburbs in Las Villas province from the 1520s to the end of the 1880s. A large part of this work is dedicated to the nineteenth century, and for this period the book is unrivalled. The volume, which is encyclopedic in proportions, deals with almost every aspect of politics, economy, administration, church, society, culture, and education.

255. Necropolis de La Habana. Historia de los cementerios de esta ciudad.
Domingo Rosain.
Havana: Imprenta "El Trabajo," 1875. 543p.
This detailed historical account of the cemeteries of the capital deals with the special ethnic and racial burial sites of various population groups in Havana.

256. Oriente (Biografía de una provincia).
Juan Jerez Villarreal.
Havana: Imprenta "El Siglo XX," 1960. 359p. bibliog.
A historical survey of the Oriente province from pre-Columbian times to the 1930s. The emphasis of the study is on the nineteenth century, with particular attention paid to the participation of the province in the wars for independence.

257. Oriente heroico.
Rafael Gutiérrez.
Santiago de Cuba, Cuba: Tipografía "El Nuevo Mundo," 1915. 206p.
Provides a detailed account of politico-economic development in the province of Oriente from the 1880s to the early period of the war for independence (1895-1898). It was the first of a projected two-volume work, but the second volume was never completed.

258. Pinar del Río.

Emeterio S. Santovenia.
México: Fondo de Cultura Económica, 1946. 241p. bibliog.
Surveys the history of Pinar del Rio from the establishment
of Spanish rule to the 1940s. Emphasis is placed on
economic developments, and specifically to the cultivation
of tobacco, and the role the province played in the
patriotic struggles of the nineteenth century.

259. "Sugar and Social Change in Oriente, Cuba, 1898-1946."
Robert B. Hoernel.
Journal of Latin American Studies, vol. 8, no. 2 (Nov.
1976), p. 215-49.
An excellent survey of the socio-economic changes which
affected the eastern province of Oriente over a fifty-year
span. The focus of the essay is on the impact of the sugar
latifundia on local communities and culture.

D. Colonial Cuba (1512-1868)

260. Cuba colonial; ensayo histórico social de la integración de
la sociedad cubana.
Gerardo Brown Castillo.
Havana: Jesús Montero, 1952. 144p.
A thought-provoking essay examining the nineteenth-century
origins and sources of Cuban nationality (Cubanidad). The
work pays particular attention to those socio-economic
factors which played a part in the formation of national
character.

261. Cuba en la primer mitad del siglo XVII.
Isabela Macias Domínguez.
Seville, Spain: Escuela de Estudios Hispano-Americanos,
1978. 654p. maps. bibliog.
The definitive work for the history of Cuba in the
seventeenth century, focusing specifically on the social,
economic, and commercial aspects of the period.

262. Cuba, 1753-1815: Crown, Military, and Society.
Allan J. Kuethe.
Knoxville: University of Tennessee Press, 1986.   213p.
map. plates. bibliog.
This work offers thorough study of the period of the
Bourbon reforms, the English seizure of Havana (1762-1763),
and how both contributed to the emergency of creole
consciousness and Cuban nationality.

263. Cuba y la casa de Austria.
Nicasio Silverio Sainz.
Miami, Florida: Ediciones Universales, 1972.   406p.
bibliog.

A history of Cuba under the Habsburg administration
(1492-1700). The principal emphasis of the study is
institutional and policy.

264. Cuba y su evolución colonial.
     Francisco Figueras.
     Havana: Isla, S.A., 1959. 441p.
     This reprint of the 1907 edition provides a general survey
     of life in colonial Cuba. Among the themes treated are
     morality, religion, women, education, private and public
     customs, health, and demography.

265. "The Dutch and Cuba, 1609-1643."
     Irene A. Wright.
     Hispanic American Historical Review, vol. 4, no. 4 (Nov.
     1921), p. 597-634.
     A study of Dutch traders and corsairs in the Caribbean,
     with specific reference to their activities in and around
     Cuba.

266. The Early History of Cuba, 1492-1586.
     Irene A. Wright.
     New York: The Macmillan Company, 1916. 390p. map.
     One of the few English-language historical accounts for
     these early colonial years. The study remains, more than
     seventy years after its publication, one of the standard
     reference works for the period, stressing political
     developments, international affairs, and institutional and
     administrative policies.

267. "Francisco de Arango y Parreño."
     William Whatley Pierson, Jr.
     Hispanic American Historical Review, vol. 16, no. 4 (Nov.
     1936), p. 451-78.
     A study of one of the leading economists in Cuba. Arango y
     Parreno (1765-1837) lived through a period of rapid
     political and economic change, developments over which he
     exercised an enormous influence.

268. "French Colonization in Cuba, 1791-1809."
     William R. Lux.
     The Americas, vol. 29, no. 1 (July 1972), p. 57-61.
     Provides a brief assessment of the French contribution to
     Cuban agriculture, especially the production of coffee and
     sugar, in the aftermath of the rebellion in St. Domingue.

269. Historia económico-política y estadística de la isla de
     Cuba.
     Ramón de la Sagra.
     Havana: Imprenta de las Viudas de Arazoza y Soler, 1831.
     386p.

An enormously valuable work examining the economic conditions in late eighteenth and early nineteenth century Cuba. It provides considerable statistical information, the most important of which is census data for the years 1774, 1792, 1817, and 1827. The book is arranged into five sections dealing with population, agriculture, and industry, commerce, public finance, and the armed forces.

270. Historia militar de Cuba: conquista de Cuba.
Cuba. Ministerio de las Fuerzas Armadas Revolucionarias. Havana: Dirección Política de las FAR, n.d. 54p.
Discusses the military aspects of the Spanish conquest of Cuba during the sixteenth century. The study examines the role of artillery, the importance of the cavalry units, the socio-military antecedents of the conquistadores and the Indian responses to Spanish colonization efforts.

271. "'Mercedes' and 'Realengos:' a Survey of the Public Land System in Cuba."
Duvon C. Corbitt.
Hispanic American Historical Review, vol. 19, no. 3 (Aug. 1939), p. 262-85.
An important study of land grants (mercedes) and the distribution of royal lands (realengos). The ambiguity of the boundaries and the absence of surveys created confused land ownership pattern up to the twentieth century.

272. "Origins of Wealth and the Sugar Revolution in Cuba, 1750-1850."
Franklin W. Knight.
The Hispanic American Historical Review, vol. 57, no. 2 (May 1977), p. 231-53.
Examines in detail the impact of sugar production on Cuba. The articles analyze patterns of slavery, population growth, trade and commerce, land tenure changes, and the relationship between economic development and social structures.

273. Piratas y corsarios en Cuba.
Saturnino Ullivarri.
Havana: Maza, Caso y Cía. 1931. 234p.
One of the more complete studies of pirates and buccaneers operating around and against Cuba during the early centuries of the colony. It is perhaps the single best work on the subject.

274. "'Rescates': with Special Reference to Cuba, 1599-1610."
Irene A. Wright.
Hispanic American Historical Review, vol. 3, no. 3 (Aug. 1920), p. 333-61.
A study of illegitimate trade (rescates) in Cuba, paying

specific attention to the transactions between the Spanish settlers and the pirates. This essay documents government efforts to combat this practice, official attempts that in the end proved futile.

275. The Siege and Capture of Havana, 1762.
     Edited by David Syrett.
     London: Navy Records Society, 1970. 355p. maps.
     An important collection of English documents pertaining to the planning and preparation of the British assault on Havana.   The work includes correspondence, naval communiques, official orders, ledgers, and memoranda detailing the sequence of events.

276. The Siege of Havana, 1762.
     Francis Russell Hart.
     Boston: Houghton Mifflin Co., 1931. 54p. map.
     A well-written account of the British assault on Havana during the Seven Years War (1756-1763).   Provides great detail on the naval and military tactics and strategies employed by both the English attackers and the Spanish defenders.

E. Struggle for Independence and U.S. Intervention, 1868-1902

277. Los americanos en Cuba.
     Enrique Collazo.
     Havana: Editorial de Ciencias Sociales, 1972.   2nd ed. 263p.
     A reprint of the 1905 edition, this two-part work examines the political and military maneuvers practiced by Spain during the war for independence (1895-1898) and the years of the North American occupation (1899-1902).

278. "The Anarchist Challenge to the Cuban Independence Movement, 1885-1890."
     Gerald E. Poyo.
     Cuban Studies/Estudios Cubanos, vol. 15, no. 1 (Winter 1985), p. 29-42.
     An informative essay about an important aspect of separatist politics in the late nineteenth century. The rise of anarchism in the Cuban labor movement challenged the mainstream separatist leadership for control over the Cuban cigarworkers in Florida. Poyo argues that outright divisions were avoided by the skill with which José Martí united both sectors.

279. Antonio Maceo: apuntes para una historia de su vida.
     José Luciano Franco.
     Havana: Editorial de Ciencias Sociales, 1975.   3 vols.

bibliog.
This detailed life and times biography of Maceo (1845-1896)
stands among the best accounts of one of the most important
politico-military leaders in nineteenth century Cuba.

280. Antonio Maceo: the 'Bronze Titan' of Cuba's Struggle for
Independence.
Philip S. Foner.
New York: Monthly Review Press, 1977. 339p. map.
bibliog.
A biography of one of the outstanding military leaders of
the struggle for independence.

281. "Class Relations in Sugar and Political Mobilization in
Cuba, 1868-1899."
Rebecca J. Scott.
Cuban Studies/Estudios Cubanos, vol. 15, no. 1 (Winter
1985), p. 15-28.
This well documented article analyzes the relationship
between the changes in production modes on the sugar
estates in late nineteenth century Cuba and the
mobilization of opposition to Spanish colonialism. Scott
argues convincingly that the success of the separatist
movement was aided by the process of emancipation and the
transition from slavery to wage labor.

282. "El clero en la revolución cubana."
Francisco G. del Valle.
Cuba Contemporánea, vol. 18, no. 1 (Sept. 1918),
p. 140-205.
A detailed discussion of the role of the clergy in Cuba's
wars for independence between 1868 and 1898.

283. Como acabó la dominación de España en América.
Enrique José N. Piñeyro.
Paris: Garnier, 1908. 340p.
Discusses the Cuban struggle for independence through the
latter years of the nineteenth century, culminating in the
Treaty of Paris (1898) which ended Spanish sovereignty over
Cuba and Puerto Rico.

284. Cuba Between Empires, 1878-1902.
Louis A. Pérez, Jr.
Pittsburgh: University of Pittsburgh Press, 1983. 490p.
bibliog.
An examination of the political, military, diplomatic, and
social aspects of the Cuban struggle for independence and
the U.S. military occupation (1898-1902).

285. Cuba heroica.
Enrique Collazo.

Santiago de Cuba, Cuba: Editorial Oriente, 1980.   2nd ed.
465p.
The book, originally published in 1912, examines Cuba's
struggles for self-determination, beginning with abortive
seditions of the 18th century, through the revolutionary
stirrings of the early nineteenth century and culminating
in the rebellions during the period 1868-1898.

286. **The Cuban Crisis as Reflected in the New York Press, 1895-
      1898.**
      Joseph E. Wisan.
      New York: Octagon Press, 1965. 477p. bibliog.
      A reprint of the 1934 edition, this study looks at the way
      in which the Cuban struggle for independence was presented
      in New York newspapers. The account is chronological,
      concluding with the U.S. intervention in 1898.

287. **Cuba's Freedom Fighter, Antonio Maceo: 1845-1896.**
      Magdalen M. Pando.
      Gainesville, Florida: Felicity Press, 1980.   bibliog.
      144p.
      A general biography of Maceo, with the emphasis of the book
      given to the crucial period of the 1890s.

288. **Desde Yara hasta el Zanjón.**
      Enrique Collazo.
      Havana: Instituto del Libro, 1967, 2nd ed. bibliog.
      First published in 1893, this collection of essays
      discusses the leading personalities involved in the Ten
      Years War from its outbreak in 1868 in the village of Yara
      to the final peace negotiations which resulted in the Pact
      of Zanjón in 1878. The persons discussed include: Carlos
      Manuel de Céspedes, who led the armed revolt which began
      the hostilities; Salvador Cisneros Betancourt; Juan
      Bautista Spotorno; and Tomás Estrada Palma, who served as
      the provisional president of the rebel republic. The book
      also pays attention to the military aspects of the war, the
      role of the expatriate communities, and the peace
      negotiations.

289. **En el camino de la independencia.**
      Ramiro Guerra y Sánchez.
      Havana: Editorial de Ciencias Sociales, 1974.   226p.
      This study, which first appeared in 1930, examines
      U.S.-British relations in the course of the nineteenth
      century as they affected the course of the Cuban struggle
      for independence. The work ends with the North American
      intervention of 1898.

290. **Episodios de la revolución cubana.**
      Manuel de la Cruz.

Havana: Instituto del Libro, 1967. 166p.
A reprint of the 1890 edition, this work is a study of the
Ten Years War (1868-1878) based on the recollections of
veterans a decade after the end of the conflict.

291. Guerra de los diez años, 1868-1878.
Ramiro Guerra y Sánchez.
Havana: Editorial de Ciencias Sociales, 1972.   2 vols.
maps.
Considered one of the better treatments of the Ten Years
War, the work deals with the struggle from a variety of
different perspectives.   Particular attention is paid to
the politico-military developments within the insurgent
movement. The study also includes an excellent analysis of
the socio-economic antecedents of the revolution.

292. Historia de la guerra de los diez años.
Francisco J. Ponte Domínguez.
Havana: Imprenta "El Siglo XX," 1958.   481p. bibliog.
Provides a detailed politico-military account of the first
major separatist effort.   The work concentrates on issues
of political leadership, military command, constitutional
development, foreign relations, the role of the expatriate
communities, and the demise of the separatist movement.

293. "Insurrection, Intervention, and the Transformation of Land
Tenure Systems in Cuba, 1895-1902."
Louis A. Pérez, Jr.
Hispanic American Historical Review, vol. 65, no. 2 (May
1985), p. 229-254.
Examines the combined effects of the war for independence
(1895-1898) and the policy of the U.S. military occupation
on land tenure systems.

294. Leonard Wood and Cuban Independence, 1898-1902.
James H. Hitchman.
The Hague: Marinus Nijhoff, 238p. bibliog.
A sympathetic account of the U.S. military occupation of
Cuba under the administration of General Leonard Wood.

295. Liberty, the Story of Cuba.
Horatio S. Rubens.
New York: Arno Press, 1970. 447p. bibliog.
This reprint of 1932 edition provides a first-person
account of Cuba's struggle for independence during the
1880s up to the U.S. occupation government (1899-1902).
The author was the U.S. attorney to the Cuban revolutionary
junta in the United States.

296. La lucha cubana por la república, contra la anexión y la
Enmienda Platt, 1899-1902.

Emilio Roig de Leuchsenring.
Havana: Oficina del Historiador de la Ciudad, 1952. 179p.
A sympathetic account of Cuban attempts at
self-determination during the period of the U.S. military
occupation, and their efforts to prevent the imposition of
the Platt Amendment.

297. "The Martínez Campos Government of 1879:   Spain's Last
Chance in Cuba."
Earl R. Beck.
Hispanic American Historical Review, vol. 56, no. 2 (May
1976), p. 268-289.
Examines an important but often neglected phase of Spanish
colonial administration in Cuba. The article considers the
short-lived attempt to introduce reforms in the aftermath
of the Ten Years War (1868-1878), the failure of which, the
author argues convincingly, set the stage for the loss of
the colony.

298. La revolución de Yara.
Fernando Figueredo.
Havana: Instituto del Libro, 1969. 2 vols.
This reprint of the classic 1902 study of the Ten Years War
(1868-1878), provides one of the most detailed accounts of
the military and political aspects of the separatist
conflict.

299. La revolución pospuesta.
Ramón de Armas.
Havana: Editorial de Ciencias Sociales.   1975.   217p.
bibliog.
A well-written and lively account of the Cuban war for
independence (1895-1898).   The author argues that
separatist struggle sought to change fundamental political,
economic, and social relationships, and that the U.S. armed
intervention of 1898 was directed as much against Cuban
independence as it was against Spanish colonial rule.

300. Sobre la guerra de los 10 años, 1868-1878.
Edited by María Cristina Llerena.
Havana: Instituto Cubano del Libro, 1973. 425p. bibliog.
This excellent collection of more than fifty essays deals
with a variety of aspects of the first major war of Cuban
independence.   The essays cover topics which include
military strategy and tactics, international relations,
political developments, culture, slavery, labor, economy,
sugar production, and social structures.

301. The Spanish-Cuban-American War and the Birth of American
Imperialism.
Philip S. Foner.

New York: Monthly Review Press, 1972. 2 vols.
A detailed and comprehensive account of the Cuban war for
independence (1895-1898), the U.S. armed intervention in
1898, and the years of the U.S. military occupation
(1899-1902).

302. The United States in Cuba, 1898-1902.
David F. Healy.
Madison, Wisconsin: University of Wisconsin Press, 1963.
260p. bibliog.
A well-written and judicious assessment of U.S. policy in
Cuba during the years of the military occupation. Emphasis
is placed on the dynamics of policy formulation, the means
by which policy was executed, and the interaction between
U.S. officials and Cuban leaders.

303. "U.S. Control over Cuban Sugar Production, 1898-1902."
James W. Hitchman.
Journal of Inter-American Studies and World Affairs,   vol.
12, no. 1 (Jan. 1970), p. 90-106.
Presents a detailed account of U.S. investment in the sugar
industry during the military occupation. Hitchman argues
that North American penetration of the Cuban economy during
these years was not as great as is commonly believed.

304. The 'Virginius' Affair.
Richard H. Bradford.
Boulder, Colorado: Colorado Associated University Press,
1980. 180p. bibliog.
This is a readable and scholarly account of the Spanish
seizure of the 'Virginius' in 1873 and the execution of
most of its crew. Set against the backdrop of the Cuban
Ten Years War (1868-1878), the maritime incident raised
diplomatic tensions betwen the U.S. and Spain, adding
pressure for U.S. intervention.

F. The Republic (1902-1958)

305. Un análisis psicosocial del cubano: 1898-1925.
Jorge Ibarra.
Havana: Editorial de Ciencias Sociales, 1985.   344p.
This collection of nine essays deals variously with
socio-cultural issues of the early republic. The topics
include crime, literature, folklore, and visual arts.

306. Antonio Guiteras: su pensamiento revolucionario.
Olga Cabrera.
Havana: Editorial de Ciencias Sociales, 1974, 253p.
One of the few biographies of Antonio Guiteras, a leading
revolutionary in the political upheavals of the 1930s. The

study includes a representative selection of Guiteras' speeches, articles, and manifestos.

307. "The Auténtico Party and the Political Opposition in Cuba, 1952-1957."
Charles D. Ameringer.
Hispanic American Historical Review, vol. 65, no. 2 (May 1985), p. 327-351.
This account of the Cuban Revolutionary Party (Auténtico), the established political opposition to the Batista government, stresses the complexity of the revolutionary process during the 1950s. The work provides an important contribution to the study of political developments in the period.

308. Las clases olvidadas en la revolución cubana.
Marcos Winocur.
Barcelona: Editorial Crítica, S.A., 1979. 170p. bibliog.
A survey of the struggle against Fulgencio Batista during the 1950s. The principal focus of the work is on those social groups--farmers, peasants, and urban workers--who turned away from Batista to support the revolutionary opposition.

309. Como cayó el presidente Machado.
Alberto Lamar Schweyer.
Madrid: Espasa-Calpa, S.A., 1934. 221p.
A critical study of U.S. diplomacy in contributing to the ouster of Gerardo Machado (1925-1933). The author was an advisor to Machado and was thus in a position to observe and record the events of the summer of 1933.

310. La corrupción política y administrativa en Cuba, 1944-1952.
E. Vignier and G. Alonso.
Havana: n.p.., 1963. 326p.
A condemnation of the Auténtico governments of Ramón Grau San Martín (1944-1948) and Carlos Prío Socarrás (1948-1952). The book reprints news articles as a source for the study of these years.

311. The Crime of Cuba.
Carleton Beals.
Philadelphia: J.B. Lippincott Company, 1933.   441p. bibliog.
A well-written and critical study of Cuban politics, U.S. policy, and, in particular, of the Gerardo Machado regime and its support by the United States.

312. Crónica cubana, 1915-1918.
León Primelles.
Havana: Editorial Lex, 1955. 660p. bibliog.

Perhaps the most complete compilation of information and data on Cuba for the years 1915-1918. All aspects of Cuba during this period are covered, including politics, economics, communications, labor, education, literature and art, sports, religion, crime and jurisprudence, science and medicine, diplomacy, and society. The author provides an extensive bibliography after each section that includes works published in the years under study. The inclusion of a detailed index facilitates enormously the use of this work.

313. Crónica cubana, 1919-1922.
León Primelles.
Havana: Editorial Lex, 1957. 720p. bibliog.
The companion volume to Crónica cubana (q.v.), covering the years 1919-1922. The work is equally comprehensive and informative.

314. Cuba Betrayed.
Fulgencio Batista.
New York: Vantage Press, 1962. 332p.
A useful source of reference for the study of Cuba during the 1950s, written by former President Fulgencio Batista. The book is particularly valuable for the account it provides of the government perspective during the revolutionary struggle. It contains large numbers of extracts from personal correspondence and military communiques.

315. Cuba libre, 1895-1958.
Mario Riera Hernández.
Miami, Florida: Colonial Press, 1968. 224p. bibliog.
A political history of Cuba from the war of independence (1895-1898) to the collapse of the Batista government (1958).

316. Cuba, los primeros años de independencia.
Rafael Martínez Ortiz.
Paris: Imp. Artistique "Lux," 1921. 2 vols.
This is a comprehensive account of the early years of Cuba as an independent republic. The work concentrates on political affairs and foreign relations.

317. Cuba 1933: Prologue to Revolution.
Luis E. Aguilar.
Ithaca, New York: Cornell University Press, 1972. 256p bibliog.
Provides a detailed study of the revolutionary upheavals of the late 1920s and early 1930s. The role and aims of several different groups of participants--including students, workers, communists, and intellectuals--are

placed within the larger context of deteriorating economic conditions and U.S. diplomacy.

318. Cuba: primera república, segunda ocupación.
Teresita Yglesia Martínez.
Havana: Editorial de Ciencias Sociales, 1977.   435p.
bibliog.
Presents a detailed study of Cuba during the presidency of Tomás Estrada Palma (1902-1906) and the second U.S. military intervention (1906-1909).

319. Cuba: raíces y frutos de una revolución; consideración histórica de algunos aspectos socio-económicos cubanos.
Ovidio García Reguero.
Madrid: I.E.P.A.L., 1970. 371p.
A historical survey of the years immediately preceding the triumph of the Cuban revolution in 1959.

320. Cuba Under the Platt Amendment, 1902-1934.
Louis A. Pérez, Jr.
Pittsburgh: University of Pittsburgh Press, 1986. 410 p.
bibliog.
This study examines the impact of U.S. hegemony in Cuba on class formations, state structures, and political culture.

321. Facetas de la vida de Cuba republicana, 1902-1952.
Oficina del Historiador de la Ciudad.
Havana: Municipio de La Habana, 1954. 380p.
A collection of essays celebrating the fiftieth anniversary of the establishment of Cuba as an independent republic. The work deals with various aspects of the republic including local institutions, women, science, medicine, literature, the press, music, plastic arts, theater, and the national archives.

322. "Financing Castro's Revolution, 1956-1958."
Alfred Padula.
Revista/Review Interamericana, vol. 8, no. 2 (Summer 1978), p. 234-46.
Analyzes in detail the means employed to finance the cost of the armed struggle against Batista. The author argues that a large portion of the financial support was provided by local bourgeoisie, the very class the revolution would destroy.

323. Intervention, Revolution, and Politics in Cuba, 1913-1921.
Louis A. Pérez, Jr.
Pittsburgh: University of Pittsburgh Press, 1978. 198p.
bibliog.
A study of the Conservative administration of President Mario G. Menocal (1913-1921). Particular attention is paid

to the rebellion of the Liberal party in 1917, the susbsequent U.S. intervention, and the Cuban economy during the years of World War I.

324. **Las luchas estudiantiles universitarias, 1923-1934.**
Compiled by Olga Cabrera and Carmen Almododar.
Havana: Editorial de Ciencias Sociales, 1975.   441p.
A collection of documents, newspaper and magazine articles, proclamations and manifestos, and student publications chronicling the role and participation of university students in the political upheavals of this crucial decade in Cuba's history. It is an indispensable collection for all work on this period.

325. "The 'Machadato' and Cuban Nationalism, 1928-1932."
Jules R. Benjamin.
Hispanic American Historical Review,   vol. 55,   no.   1
(Feb. 1975), p. 66-91.
Examines the sources of Cuban nationalism during the regime of Gerardo Machado (1925-1933). The essay discussses the role of workers, students, intellectuals, communists, and middle class reformers in the shaping of Cuban nationalism and the impact of these new forces on the overthrow of Machado.

326. **Magoon in Cuba: a History of the Second Intervention, 1906-1909.**
David A. Lockmiller.
Chapel Hill, North Carolina: University of North Carolina Press, 1938. bibliog.
Provides an account of the second U.S. intervention in Cuba (1906-1909). The study concentrates principally on public administration, legal issues, and politics.

327. **Males y vicios de Cuba republicana. Sus causas y sus remedios.**
Emilio Roig de Leuchsenring.
Havana: Oficina del Historiador de la Ciudad, 1961. 2nd ed. 353p.
This critical study of conditions in pre-revolutionary Cuba, published originally in the early 1950s. In a wide-ranging historical survey of the first fifty years of the republic, the author advances a powerful indictment against the failures of national government. The work is a chronicle of racial discrimination, gambling and prostitution, the subversion of national institutions, graft and corruption, poverty, and landlessness.

328. **El movimiento estudiantil universitario de 1934 a 1940.**
Niurka Pérez Rojas.
Havana: Editorial de Ciencias Sociales, 1975.   361p.

bibliog.
Perhaps the best single account of student politics for
this period. The study examines the role and participation
of university students in the overall opposition to the
first Batista regime (1934-1940), a period in which the
army controlled the government through a series of puppet
presidents. The book also includes several appendices of
documents relevant to student politics during the 1950s.

329. M-26, the Biography of a Revolution.
     Robert Taber.
     New York: Lyle Stuart, 1961. 348p.
     One of the earliest accounts of the revolutionary war
     during the 1950s. Taber served as a correspondent in Cuba
     and for a time lived among the guerrillas of the 26 July
     Movement led by Fidel Castro. This sympathetic report
     remains an important source of reference for this period.

330. "The Nineteen Twenties: a Decade of Intellectual Change in
     Cuba."
     Harry Swan.
     Revista/Review Interamericana, vol 8, no. 2 (Summer 1978),
     p. 275-88.
     Discusses the cultural and artistic regeneration in Cuba
     during the 1920s and its impact on national politics. It
     provided a readable and succinct account of these critical
     years in Cuban history.

331. "Peasant Involvement in the Cuban Revolution."
     Bert Useem.
     The Journal of Peasant Studies, vol. 5, no. 1 (Oct. 1977),
     p. 99-111.
     Studies the role of the peasantry in the Cuban insurgency
     of the 1950s.   The author argues that that local
     landlord-squatter conflict soon became fused with the
     state-guerrilla conflict.

332. The Politics of Intervention: the Military Occupation of
     Cuba, 1906-1909.
     Allan Reed Millett.
     Columbus, Ohio: Ohio State University Press, 1968. 306p.
     maps. bibliog.
     This study is the standard reference work dealing with the
     U.S. occupation of Cuba between 1906 and 1909.   The
     emphasis of the work falls on the formulation of North
     American policy and its politico-military implementation.

333. A Rebel in Cuba: An American's Memoir.
     Neill Macaulay.
     Chicago: Quadrangle Books, 1970. 199p. map.
     A first person account of the Cuban revolutionary war as it

unfolded in the western province of Pinar del Río.
Macaulay served as an artillery officer in the rebel army.

334. Reminiscences of the Cuban Revolutionary War.
Ernesto Che Guevara.
New York: Monthly Review Press, 1968. 287p.
An important reference work for the study of the Cuban
revolutionary war, and especially the guerrilla movement.
The memoir provides insight into the organization,
leadership, and strategy of the rebel army betweeen 1956
and 1958.

335. La revolución del 4 de septiembre.
M. Franco Varona.
Havana: Imprenta "Marvel," 1934. 182p.
A detailed journalistic account of the tumult of the 1933
revolution, including the fall of Gerardo Machado, the
"Sergeants' Revolt" led by Fulgencio Batista, and the
provisional government of 100 days.

336. La revolución de febrero. Datos para la historia.
Bernardo Merino and F. de Ibarzabal.
Havana: Libreria "Cervantes," 1918. 2nd ed. 294p.
A detailed account of the Liberal party uprising in 1917.
The study examines the charges of fraud and corruption
surrounding the reelection of the Conservative party
President Mario G. Menocal (1913-1921) in 1916, the origins
and expansion of the Liberal conspiracy, the outbreak of
armed conflict, and the eventual government victory.

337. La revolución del 30: sus dos ultimos años.
José A. Tabares del Real.
Havana: Editorial de Ciencias Sociales, 1975, 3rd ed.
375p. bibliog.
An account of the period 1934-1935, the last two years in
the revolutionary upheavals of the decade.   The work
chronicles the defeat of the revolutionary forces and the
subsequent rise of Fulgencio Batista.

338. University Students and Revolution in Cuba, 1920-1968.
Jaime Suchlicki.
Coral Gables, Florida: University of Miami, 1969. 177p.
bibliog.
A historical survey of university students' participation
in Cuban national politics. The account emphasizes student
politics from the 1920s to the 1950s.

339. The Winds of December.
John Dorschner and Roberto Fabricio.
East Rutherford, New Jersey: Coward, McCann, and
Geoghegan, 1980. 552p. bibliog.

One of the most complete, and certainly the most multifaceted, accounts of the last month of the armed struggle against Fulgencio Batista in 1958. Based on published materials, State Department documents obtained through the Freedom of Information Act, and more than 200 interviews with eyewitnesses and participants from both sides--batistianos and fidelistas alike (including Fidel Castro himself)--the account makes for a moving chronicle of the political, diplomatic, and military aspects of the fall of Batista.

G. Socialist Cuba (1959-Present)

340. Breve historia de la revolución cubana.
     Saverio Tuttino.
     México: Ediciones Era, S.A., 1979. 233p.
     One of the better historical surveys of the Cuban revolution. The author traces the Cuban revolutionary traditions of the late nineteenth and early twentieth century to their culmination in the armed struggle of the 1950s, ending with the radicalization of the revolution during the 1960s.

341. Cuba: Tragedy in Our Hemisphere.
     Maurice Zeitlin and Robert Scheer.
     New York: Grove Press, 1963. 316p.
     A well written and largely sympathetic account of the Cuban revolution during its early years. A brief historical overview sets the developments of the early 1960s in a larger context. Much of the work deals with events between 1959 and 1962.

342. The Cuban Story.
     Herbert L. Matthews.
     New York: George Braziller, Inc., 1961. 318p.
     A narrative account of the Cuban revolution by a New York Times reporter whose coverage of the armed struggle against Batista was instrumental in gaining the guerrillas favorable attention outside of Cuba. This work concentrates on three central themes: the development of communist influence in the early months of the regime, the deterioration of relations with the U.S., and the impact of the Cuban revolution on Latin America.

343. La revolución cubana.
     Claude Julien.
     Montevideo: Ediciones Marcha, 1961. 263p.
     A historical survey of the years immediately preceding and following the triumph of the Cuban revolution. The study is particularly useful in its account of the success of the armed struggle.

Genealogy

344. Anuario de familias cubanas.
Edited by Joaquín de Posada.
Guaynabo, Puerto Rico: Art Printing Co., 1969-74. 4 vols.
A genealogical compilation of the Cuban families who sought exile after the Cuban revolution. It was originally designed to be published as an annual directory, but ceased publication after the fourth issue.

345. Historia de familias cubanas.
Francisco Xavier de Santa Cruz y Mallén.
Havana: Editorial Hercules, 1940. 2 vols.
A genealogy of socially prominent Cuban families.

346. The Jova Family of Sitges, Cuba, and the United States.
Joseph John Jova.
No place: privately published, 1970. 40p.
The genealogy of a Cuban-American family of some prominence in the sugar industry in diplomacy during the nineteenth and twentieth century.

347. Nobilario cubano, o las grandes familias isleñas.
Fernando Suárez de Tangil y de Angulo.
Madrid: F. Beltran, 1929. 2 vols.
A genealogy of the old aristocratic families of Cuba.

Population

348. Censo de la república de Cuba bajo la administración
     provisional de los Estado Unidos, 1907.
     Cuba. Oficina del Censo.
     Washington, D.C.:   United States Bureau of the Census,
     1909.   707p.   Provides the information collected by the
     1907 Census of Cuba which was published in Spanish and
     English and completed during the U.S. occupation of
     1906-1909.

349. Censo de la república de Cuba, 1919.
     Cuba: Dirección General del Censo.
     Havana: Maza, Arroyo y Caso, 1920. 977p.
     A detailed census of Cuba, published in English and
     Spanish, covering population, economic development, and
     social conditions.

350. Censo de 1943.
     Cuba: Dirección del Censo.
     Havana: P. Fernández y Cía., 1945. 1373p. maps.
     The national population census of 1943.

351. Censo de 1931.
     Cuba. Dirección General del Censo.
     Havana: Carasa y Cía., 1932. 106p.
     The population census of the island for 1931. Because of
     unsettled   political   conditions,   however,   the   census
     contains only electoral registries, a listing of eligible
     voters in all municipios. See item No. 357.

352. Censos de población, viviendas y electoral. 1953.
     Cuba.   Oficina Nacional de los Censos Demográficos y
     Electoral.   Havana: P. Fernández y Cía., 1955.   325p.
     Presents detailed statistics on population, housing, and

voting patterns.

353. "Cuba: the Demography of Revolution."
Sergio Díaz-Briquets and Lisandro Pérez.
<u>Population Bulletin</u>, vol. 36, no. 1 (April 1981), p. 1-43.
Examines the causes and consequences of the demographic
changes that accompanied the transformation of Cuban
society after the revolution in 1959. The topics studied
include life expectancy and mortality, fertility,
emigration, and the difficulties that faced the emigres who
were adjusting to life in the United States.

354. "Cuban Population Estimates, 1953-1970."
Lowry Nelson.
<u>Journal of Inter-American Studies and World Affairs</u>,   vol.
12, no. 3 (July 1970), p. 392-400.
Discusses Cuba population growth, giving emphasis to both
fertility and emigration as they affect demographic trends.

355. <u>Densidad de población y urbanización</u>.
Junta Central de Planificación. Dirección de Estadística.
Departamento de Demografía.
Havana: Instituto Cubano del Libro, 1975. 85p.
This report is based on the national population census of
1970 and places emphasis on urbanization and population
density.   Divided into two groups, the data dealing with
population contrasts urban and rural densities, compares
past censuses and projects future population growth; the
section concerned with urbanization offers historical
comparisons and gives information on growth rate and size
of urban centers, and further urban developments.

356. <u>Informe sobre el censo de Cuba en 1899</u>.
United States War Department. Cuban Census office.
Washington D.C.: Government Printing Office, 1900. 793p.
maps.   This census was taken during the United States
military occupation immediately after the war with Spain.
Published in English and Spanish. User should exercise
caution when using the 1899 census, for differences in data
and text exist between the versions in English and Spanish.

357. <u>Memorias inéditas del censo de 1931</u>.
Cuba.   Dirección de Demografía del Comité Estatal de
Estadística.
Havana: Editorial de Ciencias Sociales, 1978.   356p.
This volume is the belated publication of the 1931 census,
containing the demographic, social, and economic
information deleted in the original 1932 publication.

358. <u>La población de Cuba</u>.
Centro de Estudios Demográficos.

Havana: Editorial de Ciencias Sociales, 1976.   236p.
maps.
A comprehensive work dealing with major demographic trends,
including population growth, fertility, mortality, internal
migration   and   foreign   immigration,   labor   force
characteristics,   race,   and   population   projections.
Intended principally for the general reader, this work is
one of the most complete studies available on Cuban
demography.

359. "The Political Contexts of Cuban Population Censuses,
     1899-1981."
     Lisandro Pérez.
     Latin American Research Review, vol. 19, no. 2 (1984),
     p. 143-161.
     A detailed discussion of the political conditions in which
     the censuses of Cuba were taken. The censuses covered are
     those of 1899 and 1907, during U.S. occupations, the 1919
     census during a period of electoral crisis, the census of
     1931 at a time of political repression, those of 1943 and
     1953 during the Batista regimes, and the 1970 and 1981
     censuses under socialism.

360. "Some Problems of Enumerating the 'Peasantry' in Cuba."
     Brian Pollitt.
     The Journal of Peasant Studies, vol. 4, no. 2 (Jan. 1977),
     p. 162-80.
     An   examination   of   the   principal   censuses   of
     pre-revolutionary Cuba and the data used to classify Cubans
     as peasants. The author argues that flaws in methodology,
     presentation, reproduction, and interpretation obscure as
     much as they reveal.

361. Urgencia de los censos y estadísticas nacionales.
     Gustavo Gutiérrez y Sánchez.
     Havana: Publicaciones de la Junta Nacional de Economía,
     1949. 159p.
     Studies of the collection and use of statistical abstracts
     and census compilations in Cuba from the colonial period up
     to the 1940s. It provides a valuable guide to the range of
     statistical information produced in Cuba during these years
     by a variety of government agencies.

Immigration to Cuba

362. Los catalanes en América: Cuba.
Carlos Martí.
Barcelona: Editorial Minerva, S.A., 1920. 265p.
A study of one of the most important groups of Spaniards to emigrate to Cuba and their socio-economic role on the island.

363. "Chinese Contract Labour in Cuba, 1847-1874."
Mary Turner.
Caribbean Studies, vol. 14, no. 2 (July 1974), p. 66-81.
A detailed examination of the use of Chinese workers in the middle years of the nineteenth century. The essay concentrates on population and demographic data.

364. The Chinese and Cuban independence.
Gonzalo de Quesada.
Leipzig, Germany: Breitkopf and Hartel, 1925. 16p.
A descriptive survey of the role and contribution of the Chinese in Cuban struggles for independence. The study deals with the independence movements between 1868 and 1898.

365. Los chinos en las luchas por la liberación cubana, 1847-1930.
Juan Pastrana Jiménez.
Havana: Instituto de Historia, 1963. 164p. bibliog.
More than the title suggests, the first half of this work is a study of Chinese immigration to Cuba set in the larger context of the sugar system and slavery. The latter half of the work discusses the role of the Chinese in Cuba's struggle for independence between 1868 and 1898. The last chapter deals with Chinese immigration to Cuba during the early years of the republic.

366. La colonia española en la economía cubana.
José M. Álvarez Acevedo.
Havana: Ucar, García y Cía., 1936. 260p.
Analyzes in detail the scope and function of the economic
activities of Spaniards in Cuba between 1899 and 1933.
While much of the material is derived from the censuses of
1899, 1907, 1919 and 1931, much of the data originates from
special government reports of the period. The work is an
important reference source for all research into the
Spanish expatriate community in Cuba in the early years of
republic.

367. "Los extranjeros en Cuba."
José Sixto de Sola.
Cuba Contemporánea, vol. 8, no. 2 (June 1915), p. 105-28.
Discusses the various communities of foreigners residing in
Cuba in addition to their role and position in the society.
Included in this study are North Americans and Spaniards.

368. Idéologie et ethnicité: Les Chinois Macao a Cuba, 1847-
1886.
Denise Helly.
Montreal, Canada: Les Presses de l'Université de Montreal,
1979. 345p. bibliog.
This discussion of Chinese immigration to Cuba pays
particular attention to sugar production and slavery.

369. "Immigration in Cuba."
Duvon C. Corbitt.
Hispanic American Historical Review, vol. 22, no. 2 (May
1942), p. 280-308.
A discussion of Spanish efforts in the nineteenth century
to promote white immigration in the face of increasing
numbers of African slaves. Colonizing companies were
organized to stimulate European migration to the island.

370. La inmigración italiana y la colonización en Cuba.
Francisco Federico Falco.
Turin, Italy: Societa Tipografico Editrice Nazionale,
1912. 96p. bibliog.
A general study of Italian immigration, with specific
reference to Cuba in the nineteenth century. The work
studies the role of Italians in Cuban struggles for
independence.

371. "A Note on Haitian Migration to Cuba, 1890-1934."
Mats Lundahl.
Cuban Studies/Estudios Cubanos, vol. 12, no. 2 (July 1982),
p. 21-36.
A useful essay dealing with various aspects of Haitian
migration to Cuba. The article examines the relationship

between the economic and domestic pressures in Haiti and the patterns of the migration of Haitian workers to Cuba.

372. "Jamaican Migrants and the Cuban Sugar Industry, 1900-1934."
Franklin W. Knight.
In Between Slavery and Free Labor: the Spanish-Speaking Caribbean in the Nineteenth Century. Edited by Manuel Moreno Fraginals, Frank Moya Pons, and Stanley L. Engerman. Baltimore: The Johns Hopkins University Press, 1985, p. 84-114.
Provides a detailed account of the migration of Jamaican contract workers to Cuba during the decades of the rapid expansion of sugar production. The essay examines the sources of Jamaican migration, conditions in Cuba, and the continuing Jamaican influence in Cuba.

373. A Study of the Chinese in Cuba, 1847-1947.
Duvon C. Corbitt.
Wilmore, Kentucky: Asbury College Press, 1971. 142p. bibliog.
A survey of the Chinese in Cuba. The monograph traces the contribution of Chinese immigrants to Cuban life and culture, from the coolie labor in the nineteenth century to the successful merchants and professionals in the twentieth.

Emigration from Cuba

374. "Afro-Cubans in Exile: Tampa, Florida, 1886-1984."
Susan D. Greenbaum.
Cuban Studies/Estudios Cubanos, vol. 15, no. 1 (Winter 1985), p. 59-72.
An exploratory essay examining the condition of black Cubans in exile. The article is a case study of the "Unión Martí-Maceo" in Tampa, an Afro-Cuban club founded in the early 1900s and still flourishing. This is one of the few published works dealing with the emigration of black Cubans to the United States.

375. The Assimilation of Cuban Exiles: the Role of Community and Class.
Eleanor R. Rogg.
New York: Aberdeen Press, 1974. 241p. bibliog.
A sociological study of Cuban exiles in West New York, New Jersey as they adjust and assimilate to North American norms. Particular attention is paid to varying levels of cultural assimilation based on the experiences of 250 randomly selected heads of households in 1968, representing approximately ten percent of the total community population. The author attempts to measure the process by which Cuban immigrants were integrated into the U.S. society. Appendices include statistical tables, indices of assimilation, and copies of questionnaires in Spanish and English. Also useful is the comparison of the West New York study with others made in Miami and Indianapolis.

376. Cuban Americans: Masters of Survival.
José Llanes.
Cambridge, Massachusetts: Abt Books, 1982. 229p.
This volume offers a view of Cuban exiles based on 58 composite characters created out of extensive interviews

with 187 collaborators. The work includes material dealing
with the earliest wave of exiles during late 1950s and
early 1960s to the Mariel boat lift of 1980.   The
narratives, recounted in the exiles' own words, are linked
together by passages from the author.

377. "The Cuban Exiles: An Analytical Study."
     Lynn Darrell Bender.
     Journal of Latin American Studies, vol. 5, no. 2 (Nov.
     1973), p. 271-78.
     An examination of the various phases of Cuban emigration to
     the United States and the occupational strata represented
     by each period.   The author argues that emigration
     facilitated the government's consolidation of power in Cuba
     by permitting the political opposition to depart.

378. "Los cubanos en Tampa."
     José Rivero Muñiz.
     Revista Bimestre Cubana, vol. 74 (First Semester 1958),
     p. 5-140. bibiliog.
     Presents a detailed historical study of Cuban emigration to
     Tampa, Florida between the early 1500s and early 1950s.
     The work concerns itself largely with the nineteenth
     century and the expatriate contribution to Cuban
     independence movements. Most of the article was translated
     into English in book form by Eustasio Fernández and H.
     Beltrán under the title of The Ybor City Story, 1885-1954
     (Tampa, n.p., 1976).

379. "Cubans and Mexicans in the United States: the Function of
     Political and Economic Migration."
     Silvia Pedraza-Bailey.
     Cuban Studies/Estudios Cubanos, vol. 11, no. 2--vol. 12,
     no. 1 (July 1981-Jan. 1982), p. 79-97.
     A comparative study of Cuban and Mexican migration
     examining the reasons for migration, the role of public
     assistance, the impact of ideology and politics, and the
     class origins of emigres.

380. Cubans in Exile: Disaffection and Revolution.
     Richard R. Fagen, Richard M. Brody, and Thomas J. O'Leary.
     Stanford, California: Stanford University Press, 1968.
     161p.
     A survey of the social origins, professional training,
     racial composition, and income distribution of those Cubans
     who left the island after 1959. It provides one of the
     most thorough analyses of Cuban emigration for this period.

381. "Cubans in Tampa: From Exiles to Immigrants, 1892-1901."
     Louis A. Pérez, Jr.
     Florida Historical Quarterly, vol. 57, no. 2 (Oct. 1978),

p. 129-40.
A study of the transformation of the Cuban expatriate community in Tampa, Florida from political exile to permanent immigration. The article centers on Cuban political activity in the period immediately before and during the war of independence (1895-1898) and labor organizing after the war.

382. "Demographic and Related Determinants of Recent Cuba Emigration."
Sergio Díaz Briquets.
International Migration Review, vol. 17, no. 1 (Spring 1983), p. 59-119.
The essay highlights some of the principal demographic determinants of the 1980 Mariel sea-lift, while at the same time examining how these demographic variables interacted with other social and economic factors. The topics examined include the demography of the labor force, the demographic implications of housing policy, Cuban overseas military activity, and the social origins of the Mariel emigres.

383. "Differential Migration of Cuban Social Races."
Benigno Aguirre.
Latin American Research Review, vol 11, no. 1 (1976), p. 103-24.
An analysis of the factors that influenced the racial aspects of Cuban emigration to the United States. The essay evaluates Afro-Cuban migration from a comparative perspective, examining the factors that account for differentiation in emigration between pre-socialist and socialist Cuba.

384. La emigración cubana en los Estados Unidos, 1868-1878.
Rolando Álvarez Estévez.
Havana: Editorial de Ciencias Sociales, 1986.   168p. bibliog.
This study examines the emergence and development of the Cuban emigre community during and immediately after the Ten Years War. Attention is given to the social origins of the various Cuban communities, their contribution to the war effort, and the subsequent dispersal of emigres at the end of the war.

385. La emigración cubana y la independencia de patria.
Juan José E. Casasús.
Havana: Editorial Lex, 1953. 491p. map. bibliog.
One of the most complete histories of the nineteenth century emigration from Cuba and its role in the independence of the island. The study spans the latter half of the century and includes treatment of the

fund-raising activities, propaganda efforts, and politico-military contributions.

386. "The Exodus from Revolutionary Cuba (1959-1974): a Sociological Analysis."
Juan M. Clark.
Ph.D. Dissertation, University of Florida, 1975. 372p.
Studies of the character of Cuban emigration, the circumstances that contributed to migration, its various stages, and the conditions of exile.

387. "The Flotilla 'Entrants:' Latest and Most Controversial."
Robert L. Bach, Jennifer Bach, and Timothy Triplett.
Cuban Studies/Estudios Cubanos, vol. 11, no. 2--vol. 12, no. 1 (July 1981-January 1982), p. 29-48.
An examination of the background of Cubans who arrived in the United States during the Mariel boat lift. The factors considered include sex, marital status, employment and occupation, age, and education.

388. Heroes del destierro. La emigración. Notas históricas.
Manuel Deulofeu.
Cienfuegos, Cuba: Imprenta de M. Mestre, 1904. 211p.
A history of Cuban emigration in the late nineteenth century. The book deals largely with the exile communities in south Florida and their role in the struggles for independence.

389. "Labor Relations in the Tampa Cigar Industry, 1885-1911."
Durward Long.
Labor History, vol. 12, no. 4 (Autumn 1971), p. 551-59.
Surveys the structure of Cuban labor organizing in Tampa, Florida. The article details the emergence of trade unions, the outbreak of strikes, and manufacturers' efforts to crush the Cuban organization efforts.

390. "The New Wave: a Statistical Profile of Recent Cuban Exiles to the United States."
Alejandro Portes, Juan M. Clark, and Robert L. Bach.
Cuban Studies/Estudios Cubanos, vol. 7, no. 1 (Jan. 1977), p. 1-32.
Provides a statistical profile of a sample of Cuban emigres arriving in the United States during the mid-1970s. The emphasis of the survey is placed on the age, education, occupation, and patterns of adjustment of Cuban exiles in the U.S.

391. "The New Cuban Exodus: Political and Economic Motivations."
Robert L. Bach.
Caribbean Review, vol. XI, no. 1 (Winter 1982), p. 22-25,

58-60.
Studies the causes of the 1980 Mariel emigration. Also
examined are the reactions and reception accorded to the
new wave of emigrés in south Florida.

392. "Panamá: refugio de la rebeldía cubana en el siglo XIX."
José Luciano Franco.
Casa de las Américas, vol. 15, no. 4 (July-Aug. 1974),
p. 16-26.
An account of the Cuban expatriate community in Panama
during the last third of the nineteenth century. The
article highlights the activities of Cuban emigres on
behalf of the movements for independence between 1868 and
1898.

393. La primera emigración cubana a Yucatán.
Rodolfo Ruz Menéndez.
Mérida, Yucatán, México: Universidad de Yucatán, 1969.
33p.
A study of early Cuba emigration to the Yucatan from the
beginning of the nineteenth century to the period of the
Ten Years War (1868-1878).

394. "Reminiscences of a 'Lector': Cuban Cigarworkers in
Tampa."
Louis A. Pérez, Jr.
Florida Historical Quarterly, vol. 53, no. 4 (April 1975),
p. 443-49.
The essay examines the unique position of the reader
(lector) in the cigar factories in Tampa, Florida: the
person who read to workers the daily newspaper, novels, and
political tracts in the course of the work day. The essay
is based on an oral history of a retired reader.

395. "'La Resistencia': Tampa's Immigrant Labor Union."
Durward Long.
Labor History, vol. 6, no. 4 (Autumn 1965), p. 193-210.
A study of a Cuban cigarworker union in Tampa during the
turn of the century. It is an account of immigrant
radicalism, strikes, and violence in the early cigar
industry, tracing the rise and fall of the Cuban union
between the 1880s and 1901.

396. "Six Years Later, the Process of Incorporation of Cuban
Exiles in the United States, 1973-1979."
Alejandro Portes, Juan M. Clark, and Manuel M. López.
Cuban Studies/Estudios Cubanos, vol. 11, no. 2 (July 1981),
p. 1-24.
A longitudinal study spanning six years (1973, 1976, 1979),
based on interviews of 590 Cuban males. The essay examines
the process of assimilation, with specific references to

residential patterns, education, employment, and income, and attitudes towards self and the host society.

397. Tampa, impresiones de emigrado.
Wen Gálvez.
Tampa, Florida.: Establecimiento Tipográfico "Cuba," 1897.
239p.
A detailed account of the Cuban expatriate community in Tampa during the 1890s.

398. "Working Class Emigres from Cuba: a Study of Counter-Revolutionary Consciousness."
Geoffrey E. Fox.
Ph.D. Dissertation, Northwestern University, 1975.   194p.
An account of the personal histories and political attitudes of 47 working class and petty bourgeois Cubans interviewed in Chicago in 1969.

Slavery and Race

399. "African Cultural Dimensions in Cuba."
Lawrence Smallwood.
Journal of Black Studies, vol. 6, no. 2 (Dec. 1975), p.
191-99.
A survey of the African cultural contribution to Cuban
national life as manifested in the language, literature,
music, and the form of nineteenth and twentieth century
nationalism.

400. "The Africanization of Cuba Scare, 1853-1855."
C. Stanley Urban.
Hispanic American Historical Review, vol. 37, no. 1 (Feb.
1957), p. 27-45.
A detailed examination of the fears in the U.S. concerning
the modification and ultimate extinction of Cuban slavery,
from which developed apprehension about racial strife and
the massacre of whites. The essay offers insight into the
growing ties between Cuba and the United States during this
period.

401. "Algo acerca del problema negro en Cuba hasta 1912."
Martha Verónica Alvarez Mola and Pedro Martínez Pérez.
Universidad de La Habana, vol. 179 (May-June 1966),
p. 79-93.
Analyzes the status and situation of blacks in Cuba during
the period between the emancipation (1886) and the
organization of the Independent Party of Color (1908) and
the rebellion of Afro-Cubans in 1912. The article examines
the conditions of racial discrimination that contributed to
the black uprising of 1912.

402. "El aporte negro en las letras de Cuba en el siglo XIX."
José Fernández de Castro.

Revista Bimestre Cubana, vol. 38, no. 2 (July-Dec. 1936), p. 71-88.
Surveys the contribution of Africans and Afro-Cubans to nineteenth century Cuban literature.

403. The Autobiography of a Runaway Slave.
Esteban Montejo. Edited by Miguel Barnet.
London: The Bodley Head, Ltd., 1968. 223p.
An invaluable source for the study of Cuban socio-economic history in the latter half of the nineteenth century. The memoir offers a first-person account of conditions of slavery, life as a fugitive slave, the abolition of slavery, the war for independence, and the condition of Afro-Cubans during the early years of the republic.

404. Azúcar y abolición.
Raúl Cepero Bonilla.
Havana: Editorial de Ciencias Sociales, 1971.   278p.
A landmark study of the sugar system, slavery, and emancipation during the nineteenth century.   The work examines the class structure, the relationship between the sugar economy and slavery, abolitionist politics, and the Ten Years War (1868-1878) and its impact on abolitionism.

405. Bibliografía de temas afrocubanos.
Compiled by Tomás Fernández Robaina.
Havana: Biblioteca Nacional "José Martí," 1985.   581p.
This bibliography is currently the most comprehensive compilation of titles dealing with the Afro-Cuban experiences. Containing nearly 4,000 separate entries, the book is divided chronologically between the nineteenth and twentieth century, and organized around such topics as art and literature, women, music, poetry, politics, slavery, and folklore. A subject index facilitates its use.

406. "The Black in Post-Revolutionary Cuban Literature."
Constance S. de García Barrio.
Revista/Review Interamericana, vol. 8, no. 2 (Summer 1978), p. 263-70.
Examines the presence of Afro-Cuban themes in the literature of socialist Cuba. Among the authors discussed are Nicolás Guillén, Manuel Grandos, Miguel Barnet, Severo Sarduy, Alejo Carpentier, Edmundo Desnoes, Humberto Arenal, and Guillermo Cabrera Infante.

407. Black Man in Red Cuba.
John Clytus.
Coral Gables, Florida: University of Miami Press, 1970. 158p.
Presents a critical account of social conditions in Cuba. The author lived in Cuba for several years during the

mid-1960s and concludes that racial intolerance in socialist Cuba continues to obstruct the attainment of social justice for Afro-Cubans.

408. "The Black Man's Contribution to Cuban Culture."
Rosa Valdés-Cruz.
The Americas, vol. 34, no. 2 (Oct. 1977), p. 244-51.
The article surveys the African contribution to Cuban culture.   Examined are such diverse topics as religion, music, medicine, plastic arts, and literature.

409. Blacks in Colonial Cuba, 1774-1899.
Kenneth F. Kiple.
Gainesville, Florida: University Presses of Florida, 1976. 115p. bibliog.
A rich compilation of population census data dealing with the Afro-Cubans, both free and slaves. The data is derived from the principal population censuses completed between 1774 and 1899.

410. "The Blacks in Cuba: a Bibliography."
Rafael Fermoselle-López.
Caribbean Studies, vol. 12, no. 3 (Oct. 1972), p. 103-12.
A compilation of books and articles pertaining to Afro-Cubans.   The bibliography is organized around the following topics: general, slavery and abolition, race relations, folklore, literature, and language.

411. The Black Protagonist in the Cuban Novel.
Pedro Barreda.
Amherst, Massachusetts: University of Massachusetts Press, 1979. 179p. bibliog.
Analyzes the evolution of the Afro-Cuban as the central figure in Cuban novels, from the early abolitionist fiction of the 1800s to the avant gardist literature of the 1930s. In this examination of one of the more neglected aspects of Cuban literature the author uses fiction as an indication of changing racial attitudes in Cuba. His main emphasis is on nineteenth and twentieth century literature.

412. "The Cuban People of Color and the Independence Movement: 1879-1895."
Donna M. Wolf.
Revista/Review Interamericana, vol. 5, no. 3 (Autumn 1975), p. 403-21.
This article examines the role of Afro-Cubans in shaping the course and content of the separatist movement during the years between the two major wars for Cuban independence.

413. Cuentos y leyendas negras de Cuba.

Edited by Ramón Guirao.
Havana: Ediciones "Mirador," 1942. 126p.
A compilation of Afro-Cuban folk tales, myths, parables, and legends.

414. **Los esclavos negros.**
Fernando Ortiz Fernández.
Havana: Editorial de Ciencias Sociales, 1975.   525p.
bibliog.
This classic work, first published in 1916, is one of the most detailed studies of African slavery in Cuba. The book surveys the history of the slave trade, the demography of slavery, the conditions of slaves, the emergence of a separate Afro-Cuban culture, slave rebellions, and the abolitionist movement.

415. **Estudios sobre la isla de Cuba.**
Fermín Figuera.
Madrid: Imprenta del Colegio Sordo-Mudos y Ciegos, 1866.
132p.
A detailed account of living conditions of slaves and slave labor in mid-nineteenth century Cuba.

416. "Explaining Abolition: Contradiction, Adaptation, and Challenge in Cuban Slave Society, 1860-1886."
Rebecca J. Scott.
Comparative Studies in Society and History, vol. 26, no. 1 (Jan. 1984), p. 83-111.
Analysis expanding sugar production and the abolition of slavery. The essay examines the role of international diplomacy and domestic political presence as a source for abolition, the participation of slaves and slaveowners in abolition, and the role of technology in pre- and post-emancipation Cuba.

417. "Gradual Abolition and the Dynamics of Slave Emancipation in Cuba, 1868-1886."
Rebecca J. Scott.
Hispanic American Historical Review, vol. 63, no. 3 (Aug. 1983), p. 449-77.
This thoughtful essay examines the gradual disintegration of chattel bondage in the Cuban sugar plantation system. Emphasis is placed on both the legal context of abolition and the social consequences of emancipation.

418. "The Gradual Integration of the Black in Cuba: Under the Colony, the Republic, and the Revolution."
Marianne Masferrer and Carmelo Mesa Lago.
In Slavery and Race in Latin America.   Edited by Robert Brent Toplin.   Westport, Connecticut: Greenwood Press, 1974, p. 348-84.

Surveys conditions of Afro-Cubans from 1500 to the early 1970s. The essay compares population growth, education, slavery, and employment in the colony, life in the republic, and conditions after the revolution.

419. A History of Slavery in Cuba, 1511-1868.
Hubert H.S. Aimes.
London, England: Frank Cass and Company, Ltd., 1972. 289p.
This reprint of the 1907 edition is now somewhat dated and has been superceded by more recent scholarship. Nevertheless, it still provides useful information and a sound chronological narrative.

420. Los independientes de color. Historia del Partido Independiente de Color.
Serafín Portuondo Linares.
Havana: Ministerio de Educación, 1950.   287p.   bibliog.
One of the most detailed published accounts of racial politics in the early years of the republic.   The work provides a sympathetic assessment of the organization of the Afro-Cuban political party, the Independent Party of Color, from its inception in 1908 to its demise during the race war of 1912. It represents an important contribution to the literature of race in Cuba.

421. La liberación étnica cubana.
Elias José Entralgo.
Havana: Universidad de La Habana, 1953. 272p.
A comprehensive discussion of the role of race and the Afro-Cuban contribution to the development of Cuban nationality. The study examines the politics of abolition, the role of blacks in the patriotic movements of the nineteenth century, the racial considerations underlying nineteenth century political thought, and the process of "mulatizacion" in Cuba.

422. The Life and Poems of a Cuban Slave: Juan Francisco Manzano, 1797-1854.
Edited by Edward J. Mullen.
Hamden, Connecticut: Archon Books, 1981. 237p. bibliog.
A collection of the poetry of Juan Francisco Manzano set against a the larger context of the Afro-American slave narrative and the Afro-Hispanic literary tradition.   An excellent biographical essay provides a full picture of the life and times of the slave poet.

423. "Music and Dance in Cuba."
Odilio Urfe.
In Africa in Latin America.   Edited by Manuel Moreno Fraginals. New York: Holmes and Meier, 1977, p. 170-188.

This article studies the African contribution to music and dance, examining the impact of Africa's rhythms, instruments, and lyrics in both religious and popular Cuban music.

424. El negro en Cuba.
Alberto Arredondo.
Havana: Editorial "Alfa," 1939. 175p.
An eloquent, often moving, account of the condition of blacks and race relations in Cuba from the colonial regime to the early republic. The study examines the Afro-Cuban contribution to music, literature, and art and documents the participation of blacks in past patriotic struggles.

425. El negro en Cuba.
Pascual B. Marcos Veguer.
Havana: n.p., 1955. 30p.
This thoughtful study examines the condition of Afro-Cubans in the republic. The author contrasts the promise of social justice made to blacks in the nineteenth century with the achievements of the twentieth, and concludes that much remained undone.

426. Los negros brujos.
Fernando Ortiz Fernández.
Miami, Florida: Ediciones Universal, 1973. 2nd ed. 259p.
This reprint is a critical study of witchcraft within the Afro-Cuban population. The book examines the African sources of religious beliefs and practices, the development of witches and warlocks, and the Cubanization of African rituals and beliefs.

427. Odious Commerce: Britain, Spain and the Abolition of the Cuban Slave Trade.
David Murray.
London: Cambridge University Press, 1980. 423p. bibliog.
A detailed study of the slave trade in Cuba from 1762 to its final suppression in the 1860s. The work is meticulously documented and provides one of the most detailed accounts of the slave traffic.

428. La poesía afroantillana.
Leslie N. Wilson.
Miami, Florida: Ediciones Universal, 1979. 182p. bibliog.
A general discussion of Afro-Caribbean poetry, paying particular attention to Cuban poems and poets.

429. Política y color en Cuba. La guerrita de 1912.
Rafael Fermoselle-López.
Montevideo: Ediciones Géminis, 1974. 256p. bibliog.

An examination of the politics of race in Cuba during the early years of the republic. The study is more political and institutional than social, with emphasis given to the organization of the Independent Party of Color and its dissolution as the result of the race war of 1912.

430. "The Politics of Color: the Racial Dimension of Cuban Politics During the Early Republican Years, 1900-1912." Thomas Tondee Orum.
Ph.D. Dissertation, New York University, 1975.   310p.
A richly detailed account of condition and role of Afro-Cubans during the last years of colonial rule and in the early years of the republic.   An indispensable reference work for the study of race and republican politics.

431. "Presencia del africano en la cultura cubana." Argeliers León.
Islas, no. 41 (Jan.-April 1972), p. 155-69.
Examines the African contribution to Cuban culture. The essay surveys the acculturation process of African slaves and its attendant effects on Cuba. The specific topics examined include religion, literature, music and musical instruments, and dance.

432. "El problema negro."
Carlos de Velasco.
Cuba Contemporánea, vol. 1, no. 2 (Feb. 1913), p. 73-79.
A general discussion of the social and political conditions of Afro-Cubans, written in the aftermath of the 1912 race war.

433. "Race Relations in Cuba: a Literary Perspective." Antonio Olliz-Boyd.
Revista/Review Interamericana, vol 8, no. 2 (Summer 1978), p. 225-33.
This highly informative essay discusses Cuban authors and their definition of the Afro-Cuban social reality. The literature is taken from the nineteenth and twentieth centuries.

434. Rectificaciones. La cuestión político-social en la isla de Cuba.
Juan F. Risquet.
Havana: Tipografía "América," 1900. 209p.
This important study which examines the condition of Afro-Cubans in the nineteenth century is especially significant in its provision of vital data concerning the contribution of Cuban blacks in the struggle for independence, particularly of Afro-Cubans in exile. The work also contains biographical sketches of leading

Afro-Cuban patriots of the nineteenth century.

435. Slave Emancipation in Cuba: the Transition to Free Labor, 1860-1899.
Rebecca J. Scott.
Princeton: Princeton University Press, 1985.   319p.
plates. maps. bibliog.
This landmark study of the end of slavery in Cuba gives specific attention to the means by which slaves joined Cuban society as free men and women.   Based on Cuban archival sources, the study examines the process of emancipation as it affected individual slaves and as it occurred on individual estates.   Specific attention is given to the varieties of pressures that affected slaves and slaveowners and how they contributed to emancipation.

436. Slavery in the Americas: a Comparative Study of Cuba and Virginia.
Herbert S. Klein.
Chicago: University of Chicago Press, 1967. 270p.
A balanced comparative study of slave conditions in Cuba and Virginia. The book contrasts legal systems, education, religion, and the role of government.

437. "Slavery, Race, and Social Structure in Cuba During the Nineteenth Century."
Franklin W. Knight.
In Slavery and Race in Latin America.   Edited by Robert Brent Toplin.   Westport, Connecticut: Greenwood Press, 1974, p. 204-27.
Examines the impact of the expansion of the slave system on mid-nineteenth century Cuba. The author argues that larger numbers of slaves required greater social control, which led in turn to increased repression and greater slave resistance.

438. Social Control in Slave Plantation Societies: a Comparison of St. Domingue and Cuba.
Gwendolyn Midlo Hall.
Baltimore: The Johns Hopkins University Press, 1971.
166p. bibliog.
Presents a comparison of plantation systems in eighteenth century St. Domingue and nineteenth century Cuba.   The study examines the policies towards the slave population, including religion, education, law, and manumission. Racism is examined as an ideological instrument of social and political domination.

439. "Social Structure, Race Relations, and Political Stability Under U.S. Administration."
Erwin H. Epstein.

Revista/Review Interamericana, vol. 8, no. 2 (Summer 1978),
p. 192-203.
This treatment of U.S. military occupations of Cuba
(1899-1902 and 1906-1909) deals specifically with social
and economic policies. The article concentrates on those
policies which had their greatest effect on race relations.

440. Spain and the Abolition of Slavery in Cuba, 1817-1886.
Arthur F. Corwin.
Austin: University of Texas, 1967. 373p. map. blibliog.
This study of the abolition of slavery in Cuba emphasizes
the role of British diplomacy and creole reform gestures as
the principal elements in the emancipation process.

Folklore

441. La africanía de la música folklórica de Cuba.
Fernando Ortiz Fernández.
Havana: Ministerio de Educación, 1950. 477p. bibliog.
This comprehensive study of the African sources of Cuban
music looks specifically at form, structure, function, and
rhythms.

442. Los bailes y el teatro de los negros en el folklore de Cuba.
Fernando Ortiz Fernández.
Havana: Ministerio de Educacion, 1951. 466p. bibliog.
Provides a detailed study of Afro-Cuban dance and stage,
tracing the African origins of Cuban folkloric performing
arts.

443. Décima y folclor.
Jesús Orta Ruiz.
Havana: Ediciones Unión, 1980. 241p. bibliog.
An important contribution to the study of the décima, a
type of popular poetry and song in rural Cuba. The
composition of stanzas of ten octosyllabic lines has
enjoyed widespread popularity since the early colonial
period. In this study, the author examines surviving
décimas as a historical source, from which popular
sentiments and perceptions can be understood. The book
includes decimas dealing with anti-slavery and separatist
themes, the Ten Year War (1868-1878), the war for
independence (1895-1898), the U.S. intervention and the
early republic, and the décima after the revolution of
1959.

444. Diario abierto; temas folklóricos cubanos.
Samuel Feijóo.
Santa Clara, Cuba: Universidad Central de Las Villas,

1960. 301p.
A virtual catalogue of Cuban folklore, dealing with myth,
music and song, legends, linguistics, festivities, games,
and popular philosophy.

445. Estudio del folklore sagüero.
Edited by Ana María Arisso.
Havana: n.p., 1940. 116p.
This is a compilation of local lore and poetry from the
region around Sagua la Grande in Las Villas province.

446. Gente del pueblo.
Onelio Jorge Cardoso.
Santa Clara, Cuba: Universidad Central de Las Villas,
1962. 199p.
This series of interviews accompanied by a collection of
photographs documents the varieties of Cuban folklore. The
objective of the author's peregrinations through Cuba was
to gather information concerning work habits, dress, social
styles, customs, and recreation from the men and women
across the island.

476. "Ifá: oráculo Yoruba y Lucumí."
Julia Cuervo Hewitt.
Cuban Studies/Estudios Cubanos, vol. 13, no. 1 (Winter
1983), p. 24-40.
An examination of Afro-Cuban traditions in Cuba as seen
through the place of Ifa, a mythological figure in Yoruba
tradition.

448. Mitas y leyendas en Las Villas.
Samuel Feijóo.
Santa Clara, Cuba: Universidad Central de Las Villas,
1965. 252p.
A collection of diverse stories of local folklore and
legends originating from central Cuba. The book includes
material with origins as early as pre-Columbian period
through the colonial regime.

449. El monte.
Lydia Cabrera.
Miami, Florida: Ediciones Universal, 1975. 4th ed. 564p.
One of the more complete studies of Cuban folklore and of
Africanisms in Cuba. The book's principal themes deal with
religion, magic, and Afro-Cuban culture.

450. "Stones, Trees, and Blood: An Analysis of a Cuban Santero
Ritual."
Jorge Duany.
Cuban Studies/Estudios Cubanos, vol. 12, no. 2 (July 1982),
p. 37-53.

An analysis of an Afro-Cuban ceremony as a system of symbolic communication. The essays deal with Afro-Cuban religious beliefs and customs as a syncretic cultural response to the environment of the plantation.

451. Tradiciones cubanas.
Álvaro de la Iglesia y Santos.
Havana: Instituto del Libro, 1969. 361p.
This collection of vignettes describes aspects of Cuban customs and folklore, drawn from all parts of the island and from all classes.

Religion

452. Apuntes para la historia eclesiástica de Cuba.
Juan Martín Leiseca.
Havana: Talleres Tipográfico de Carasa y Cía., 1938.
441p.
This history of the Catholic church in Cuba, covers the period from the early missionary activities during the century of conquest and colonization up to the early twentieth century. The study includes illustrations, portraits, and plates.

453. "Christians in Cuba."
Jim Wallace.
Cuba Resource Center Newsletter, vol. 3, no. 1 (April 1973), p. 3-11.
Studies Catholic and Protestant policies as they affect church attendance, youth, and recruitment for the clergy.

454. "Church, Theology, and Revolution."
Cuba Review, vol. 5, no. 3 (Sept. 1975), p. 3-34.
A special issue devoted to the church and state relations in socialist Cuba. Among the topics examined are the impact of the revolution on theology, the condition of the Presbyterian and Methodist churches in Cuba, and the new role of the Catholic clergy in Cuba.

455. Cuba for Christ.
Una Roberts Lawrence.
Atlanta, Georgia: Board of Southern Baptist Convention, 1926. 288p.
A first person account of southern Baptist missionary activity in Cuba during the early decades of the twentieth century.

456. "Cuba: New Church in a New Country."
James Higgins.
Commonweal, vol. 96, no. 17 (July 28, 1972), p. 399-402.
Discusses church-state relations in socialist Cuba. The
article examines the make-up of the clergy, theology, and
church activities.

457. "The Cuban Church in a Revolutionary Society."
Mateo Jover.
LADOC, vol. 4, no. 47 (April 1974), p. 17-36.
The essay examines the relationship between the Catholic
church and the revolutionary government, focusing on the
interaction between church hierarchy, lay leaders, Catholic
organizations, and practicing Catholics and their
respective counterparts in the secular polity.

458. The Cuban Church in a Sugar Economy.
John Merle Davis.
New York: International Missionary Council, 1942. 144p.
A study of the evangelical church in Cuba. The book
examines the means by which missionary activities in Cuba
could better integrate themselves in the socio-economic
environment of the island. It provides much information on
the scope of Protestant missionary work in Cuba.

459. "Cuban Jews: Continuity and Change."
Donna Katzin.
Cuba Resource Center Newsletter, vol. 3, nos. 5 and 6 (Dec.
1973), p. 25-28.
An examination of the condition of the Jewish community in
Cuba and how it has fared under the revolution. The essay
examines the history of Jews in Cuba from the early
twentieth century to the early 1970s.

460. "Cuba's Catholic Church: a Glance in Passing."
Harold J. Lidin.
Revista/Review Interamericana, vol. 8, no. 2 (Summer 1978),
p. 271-74.
A brief journalistic discussion of the condition of the
Catholic church since the revolution.

461. Historia de la isla y catedral de Cuba.
Pedro Agustín Morell de Santa Cruz.
Havana: Imprenta "Cuba Intelectual," 1929.   305p.
bibliog.
This general history of Cuba underlines the role and
contribution of the Catholic Church, especially through the
perspective of Havana and the Cathedral.

462. Historia eclesiástica de Cuba.
Ismael Testé.

Burgos, Spain: Tip. de la Editorial a "El Monte Carmelo,"
1969. 4 vols.
A detailed historical account of the Catholic church in
Cuba, spanning the years between the sixteenth century
through the 1950s.   The work tends to be largely
institutional in nature, concentrating on the biographies
of hierarchy, religious orders, and formal governance and
administration.

463. Methodism's First Fifty Years in Cuba.
Sterling Augustus Neblett.
Wilmore, Kentucky: Asbury Press, 1976.   303p. bibliog.
A chronicle of Methodist activities in Cuba between 1899
and 1949, covering a comprehensive range of topics,
including the establishment of churches, missions, schools,
and clinics. This important work provides a great deal of
information about one of the most successful Protestant
denominations in twentieth century Cuba.

464. La religión afrocubana.
Mercedes Cros Sandoval.
Madrid: Editorial Playor, 1975. 287p. bibliog.
Provides a detailed account of the practice, rituals, and
symbolism of Afro-Cuban religions in Cuba.

465. Religion in Cuba Today: a New Church in a New Society.
Edited by Alice L. Hageman and Philip E. Wheaton.
New York: Association Press, 1971. 317p.
This sympathetic collection of essays deals with the place
of religion and the nature of church-state relations in
socialist Cuba. Articles by, and interviews with, leading
members of various religious organizations deal with their
views of the revolution and its impact on their
institutions, reflections on the possibilities of a
theology of revolution, historical perspectives, the
mission of the church in a socialist society, and a
re-examination of the biblical concept of work in light of
Cuban developments. One section includes documents in the
form of official statements by church authorities.

466. "Religious Penetration and Nationalism in Cuba: U.S.
Methodist Activities, 1898-1958."
Margaret E. Crahan.
Revista/Review Interamericana, vol. 8, no. 2 (Summer 1978),
p. 204-24.
The article surveys North American missionary activity in
Cuba.   The scope is larger than title suggests, for it
includes a discussion of all Protestant missions.

467. "Salvation   Through   Christ   or   Marx: Religion   in
Revolutionary Cuba."

Margaret E. Crahan.
In   Churches and Politics in Latin America.   Edited   by
Daniel H. Levine.   Beverly Hills, California: Sage
Publications, 1980. p. 238-66.
An examination of the role of religion in Cuba after the
revolution.   The author provides a useful survey of
pre-revolutionary Cuba as background, from which the author
suggests that the weakness of religion in Cuba after 1959
is due as much to the weakness of religion in Cuba before
1959 as to the revolution's discouragement of religious
practice.   The essay deals with the Catholic church,
Protestant denominations, and Afro-Cuban religions.

Social Conditions

A. General

468. Arrendamientos urbanos.
     Eduardo de Acha.
     Havana: Jesús Montero, 1959. 469p.
     This detailed discussion of urban housing and rental
     procedures. The study reviews previous efforts to regulate
     rents, culminating in the Urban Reform Law of 1959.

469. Características sociodemográficas de la familia cubana,
     1953-1970.
     Niurka Pérez Rojas.
     Havana: Editorial de Ciencias Sociales, 1979.   72p.
     bibliog.
     A general outline of the changing characteristics of Cuban
     family structures.   It is especially useful in its
     assessment of the changes that occurred in the years after
     the revolution.

470. "The Changing Family Picture."
     Cuba Review, vol. 5, no. 4 (Dec. 1975), p. 3-19.
     A comprehensive look at family structures in socialist
     Cuba.   Beginning with an examination of the Family Code,
     this issue examines maternity, divorce, homosexuality, and
     aging.

471. Condiciones económicas y sociales de la república de Cuba.
     Carlos M. Raggi Ageo.
     Havana: Editorial Lex, 1944. 214p.
     A detailed study of socio-economic conditions in Cuba.
     Published under the auspices of the Ministry of Labor, the
     work is concerned principally with the years between the
     late 1930s and early 1940s.   Among the diverse topics

examined are population and demography, employment, social services, labor, and production.

472. Un cuarto de siglo de evolución cubana.
Ramiro Guerra y Sánchez.
Havana: Librería "Cervantes," 1924. 127p.
A survey of the social and economic achievements during the first twenty-five years of Cuban independence. Particular attention is paid to population growth, employment, communications, urbanization, and education. Also examined are the persisting problems of the republic, including dependency on sugar production, international relations, and the lack of civic virtues among public officials.

473. "Cuban Food Policy and Popular Nutritional Levels."
Howard Handelman.
Cuban Studios/Estudios Cubanos, vols. 11-12, nos. 2-1 (July 1981-Jan. 1982), p. 127-46.
A study of nutrition policy and consumption patterns in Cuba after the revolution. The essay traces efforts made by the government to redistribute the available food supplies as a way of guaranteeing an adequate diet to all Cubans.

474. Delincuencia penada.
Cuba. Dirección General de Estadística.
Havana: Secretaria de Hacienda. 1935-.
Provides an annual compilation of crime statistics covering a range of categories including the varieties of offenses, sentencing, and the occurence of crime. Information is provided about convicted criminals regarding age, race, nationality, sex, marital status, education, and occupation. Material is organized by provinces. The publication appeared irregularly, and appears to have been suspended during the 1950s.

475. "El desenvolvimiento social de Cuba en los ultimos veinte años."
Miguel de Carrión.
Cuba Contemporánea, vol. 27, no. 105 (Sept. 1921), p. 5-27.
Surveys social conditions in Cuba during the course of the first two decades of the republic. Attention is given to race, family, population, class structures, and education.

476. Estudio sobre el divorcio.
Jorge Hernández, Ángel Eng, Maria T. Bermúdez, and Mariela Columbie.
Havana: Centro de Información Científica y Técnica, Universidad de La Habana, 1973. 101p.
This study by four sociologists from the University of Havana examines the reasons for the increase in divorce in

Cuba between 1958 and 1968. The authors correlate divorce to age at the time of marriage, the length of marriage, education, children, and economic activity.

477. Gays Under the Cuban Revolution.
Allen Young.
San Francisco, California: Grey Fox Press, 1982.   112p.
A study critical of the Cuban revolution for its policies toward homosexuals.   The book examines the government's harassment and intolerance of gays in official and social settings.

478. "Homosexuality, Homophobia, and Revolution: Notes Toward an Understanding of the Cuban Lesbian and Gay Male Experience."
Lourdes Arguelles and B. Ruby Rich.
Signs, vol. 9, no. 4 (Summer 1984), p. 683-99.
A thoughtful and balanced assessment of homosexuality in Cuba.   The essay examines official and popular attitudes toward homosexuality before and after the revolution.

479. Legislación sobre el divorcio en Cuba.
Compiled by Francisco Llaca y Argudén.
Havana: Imprenta de Rambla, Bouza y Cía., 1931.   197p.
The volume presents a compilation of laws and decrees regulating marriage and divorce.

480. Legislación social de Cuba.
Compiled by José R. García Pedrosa.
Havana: La Moderna Poesía, 1936.   2 vols.
A compilation of social legislation and laws, relating mainly to labor, welfare, hospital care, and immigration.

481. Living the Revolution. An Oral History of Contemporary Cuba: Four Men.
Oscar Lewis, Ruth M. Lewis, and Susan M. Rigdon.
Urbana, Illinois: University of Illinois Press, 1977. 538p.
Examines the lives of four men of different ages, occupations, races, and social origins.   The volume is based on lengthy interviews with the four subjects and shorter interviews with members of their families.   The narrative offers a compelling view of life in pre- and post-revolutionary Cuba, looking at many aspects of daily life in Cuba, including male-female relations, religion, politics, race and class antagonism, family life, work, and recreation.

482. Living the Revolution. An Oral History of Contemporary Cuba: Neighbors.
Oscar Lewis, Ruth M. Lewis, and Susan M. Rigdon.

Urbana, Illinois: University of Illinois Press, 1978.
581p. bibliog.
An oral history of dwellers in an apartment complex in
Havana. Men and women, whites and blacks, young and old,
all neighbors at the time of the interviews, provide a rich
and textured series of reminiscences. The book offers a
valuable insight into the character of pre-revolutionary
conditions and revolutionary changes in Cuba.

483. "El matrimonio en Cuba."
Dulce María Borrero de Lujan.
Cuba Contemporánea, vol. 5, no. 2 (June 1914), p. 198-211.
In this discussion of the institution of marriage, the
essay pays specific attention to the early twentieth
century debate over divorce, arguing for a relaxation of
church and state injunctions against the dissolution of
marriages.

484. "New Family Code in Cuba."
Raúl Gómez Treto.
LADOC, vol. VII, no. 71 (Nov.-Dec. 1976), p. 22-29.
A brief but sympathetic review of the Cuban Family Code by
a Cuban Roman Catholic jurist.

485. "La pena de muerte en Cuba de 1908 a 1956."
Marcos Hernández Aróstegui.
Revista Bimestre Cubana, vol. 71, no. 2 (July-Dec. 1956),
p. 69-106.
Studies the theory and application of the death penalty.
Beginning with a brief survey of capital punishment during
the colonial epoch, the author examines those specific
cases in which the death penalty was applied in the
republic.

486. The People of Buena Ventura: Relocation of Slum Dwellers
in Postrevolutionary Cuba.
Douglas Butterworth.
Urbana, Illinois: University of Illinois Press, 1980.
157p. bibliog.
A richly detailed ethnographic study of a working class
community in Havana. The work provides aspects of private
and public family life in Cuba after the revolution.

487. "Proceso de urbanización en Cuba en dos décadas de revolución."
Rita Yebra.
Revista de la Biblioteca Nacional "José Martí," vol. 21,
no. 21 (May-Aug. 1979), p. 52-88.
Surveys urban reforms in the first two decades after the
revolution.   Attention is given to demographic
developments, the distribution of economic resources, and
industrialization.

488. "Sexual Ideology in Pre-Castro Cuba: a Cultural Analysis."
     Mirta de la Torre Mulhare.
     Ph.D. Dissertation. University of Pittsburgh, 1969. 290p.
     In this examination of sex as part of the Cuban cultural
     system, data was collected through research conducted in
     pre-revolutionary Cuba and among Cuban exiles living in
     various regions of the U.S. The study focuses on the
     nature of sexual ideology, the transmission of this
     ideology, and the sources of the ideology.

489. Sociedad, democracia, trabajo: apuntes de política social.
     Carlos M. Raggi Ageo.
     Havana: La Casa Montalvo Cárdenas, 1938. 197p.
     This collection of essays deals with workers, peasants, and
     women in the Cuban economy. Many of the sections were
     written during the worst periods of the depression, and
     therefore offer informative perspectives of the economic
     crisis in Cuba.

490. 24 años de revolución en la seguridad social cubana.
     Félix M. Argüelles Valcarcel.
     Havana: Dirección de Seguridad Social. 1983. 157p.
     A survey of the social security system in socialist Cuba.

B. Social Structures

491. "Mass and Class in the Origins of the Cuban Revolution."
     Nelson Amaro Victoria.
     In Masses in Latin America.   Edited by Irving Louis
     Horowitz.   New York: Oxford University Press, 1970.
     p. 547-76.
     Examines the class structure in Cuba, both in the decades
     before the revolution and in the period following 1959.

492. "Middle-Class Politics and the Cuban Revolution."
     Hugh Thomas.
     In The Politics of Conformity in Latin America. Edited by
     Claudio Veliz. New York: Oxford University Press, 1967,
     p. 249-77.
     Analyzes the class origins of the Cuban revolution. The
     author disputes the commonly held notion that the
     revolution was primarily a middle-class phenomenon, arguing
     instead for the view that working-class participation
     played a crucial role in the early phase of the armed
     struggle.

493. "The Social Class Structure in Cuba."
     Lowry Nelson.
     In Materiales para el estudio de la clase media en América
     Latina.   Edited by Theo R. Crevenna. Washington, D.C.:
     Pan American Union, 1950-1951. 6 vols. vol. II, p. 45-72.

Provides a useful typology of class structure in pre-revolutionary Cuba. Also analyzed are ethnic groups within social structures of the island.

494. "Social Structure and Mobility in Cuba."
Wyatt MacGaffey.
Anthropological Quarterly, vol. 34, no. 1 (Jan. 1961), p. 94-109.
bibliog.
A study of Cuban class structures before the revolution.

C. Social Problems

495. "A Brief History of Mind-Altering Drug Use in Prerevolutionary Cuba."
J. Bryan Page.
Cuban Studies/Estudios Cubanos, vol. 12, no. 2 (July 1982), p. 55-71.
A study of drug use in Cuba in years before the revolution. The focus is largely on the nineteenth and twentieth centuries and deals principally with marijuana, cocaine, and pharmaceutical sedatives.

496. Criminalidad juvenial y defensa social: estudio jurídico.
Armando M. Raggi y Ageo.
Havana: Cultural, S.A. 1937. 2 vols.
A detailed study of juvenile delinquency. Also treated in depth is the system of juvenile courts and child law.

497. "Juvenile Delinquency in Postrevolutionary Cuba: Characteristics and Cuban Explanations."
Luis P. Salas.
Cuban Studies/Estudios Cubanos, vol. 9, no. 1 (Jan. 1979), p. 43-61.
The article examines the conditions that contributed to the rise of juvenile delinquency in post-1959 Cuba. Also analyzed in the official Cuban explanation for the persistence of delinquency among some of the island's youth. The author concludes that the character of juvenile delinquency in Cuba is similar to that of other societies, involving urban lower-class males without much formal education.

498. La policía y sus misterios en Cuba.
Rafael Roche Monteagudo.
Havana: La Moderna Poesía, 1925. 3rd ed. 1,000p.
Written by a former police officer, this work is a vast compendium of law enforcement procedures and policies of several law-enforcement agencies in Cuba, including the judicial police, the national police, and local police. Of

equal value, the work provides a virtual catalogue of criminal behavior and the nature of police work in the early decades of the republic.

499. El problema de los seguros sociales in Cuba.
Gustavo Gutiérrez y Sánchez.
Havana: Consejo Nacional de Economía, 1955.   2 vols.
A detailed examination of social problems in Cuba, particularly those relating to the poverty of social security projects.

500. Social Control and Deviance in Cuba.
Luis P. Salas.
New York: Praeger, 1979. 398p.
This well-researched study examines various aspects of criminality and deviant behavior in Cuba.   Using Cuban standards of deviant behavior, the author examines juvenile delinquency, homosexuality, and suicide.   The book also assesses the court system, the police and the Committees for the Defense of the Revolution as agents of social control.

Women

501. "Avellaneda, Nineteenth-Century Feminist."
Beth K. Miller.
Revista/Review Interamericana, vol. 4 no. 2 (Summer 1974),
p. 177-83.
Examines of the feminist aspects of the works of Gertrudis
Gómez de Avellaneda as expressed in her themes, plots,
characters, and her autobiographical works.

502. "A Bibliography of Cuban Periodicals Related to Women."
Nelson P. Valdés.
Cuban Studies/Estudios Cubanos, vol. 12, no. 2 (July 1982),
p. 73-80.
An inventory of fifty-six different periodicals and
magazines, published in Cuba between the 1880s and 1980s,
dealing specifically with women. The bibliography
indicates the location of the collection and the run of
each title.

503. "Confluences in Social Change: Cuban Women and Health
Care."
Virginia Olesen.
Journal of Interamerican Studies and World Affairs, vol.
17, no. 4 (Nov. 1975), p. 398-411.
This article examines the relationship between the changing
roles of women and the attendant transformation of the
health care system. The emphasis of the work is on the
delivery of health care, the formal health structures, and
the principal health issues in socialist Cuba. The essay
pays attention to the changing participation of women in
economic activities and in society in general, putting
particular emphasis on the manner in which developments in
the health care system have facilitated these changes.

504. Cuban Women Now.
     Margaret Randall.
     Toronto, Canada: The Women's Press/Dumont Press Graphix,
     1974. 375p. bibliog.
     A vivid account of the revolution from the perspective of
     Cuban women.   Based on twenty-five interviews the author
     provides a detailed look at a representative cross-section
     of women in socialist Cuba.   While all the interviews
     stress basic common themes, each is an account of a unique
     personal experience.   The volume is indispensable for the
     study of Cuban revolutionary society generally, and of
     women in particular.   The interviews provide important
     insights into the changing attitudes and status of women in
     Cuba.

505. El derecho de la mujer casada.
     Eduardo Le Riverend.
     Havana: Jesús Montero, 1945. 333p.
     A detailed exposition of the legal rights of women as
     defined in the 1940 constitution.

506. "El empleo femenino en Cuba."
     Ramiro Pavón.
     Santiago, no. 22 (Dec. 1975), p. 97-137.
     Analyzes in detail the role and impact of women on the
     labor force during the period from 1953 to 1970. The essay
     includes data on age, marital status, occupation, health,
     and education.

507. "Employment Without Liberation--Cuban Women in the United
     States."
     Myra Max Ferree.
     Social Science Quarterly, vol. 60, no. 1 (June 1979),
     p. 35-50.
     Discusses the employment of emigre Cuban women in the
     United States.   The emphasis is placed on the changing
     economic situation and the effect of these new conditions
     on attitudes towards women's participation in the paid
     labor force.

508. Florilegio de escritoras cubanas.
     Edited by Antonio González Curquejo.
     Havana: Libreria Imprenta "La Moderna Poesía," 1910.
     3 vols.
     A collection of the major lyric poems, essays, and
     principal works of fiction by women writers in nineteenth
     century Cuba.

509. "Honor, Shame, and Women's Liberation in Cuba: Views of
     Working Class Emigré Men."
     Geoffrey E. Fox.

In Female and Male in Latin America.   Edited by Ann
Pescatello. Pittsburgh: University of Pittsburgh Press,
1973. p. 273-90.
This essay examines the response of Cuban men to the
changing status and condition of women after the
revolution. These new circumstances required men to adjust
behavior and attitudes, a requirement that many resisted.
The result was strong reactions, often expressed in terms
of hostility and opposition to the revolutionary government
which was held responsible for the changes.

510. "Images and Exile: the Cuban Woman and Her Poetry."
Polly F. Harrison.
Revista/Review Interamericana, vol. 4, no. 2 (Summer 1974),
p. 184-219.
An examination of the principal works of women poets in
Cuba. The essay skillfully evaluates the conflicts and
tensions resulting from the place of women as poets in
Cuban society, and their perception of that social reality
and the development of key symbols, themes and values as
they change from the colonial period to the revolution and
exile.

511. Living the Revolution. An Oral History of Contemporary
Cuba: Four Women.
Oscar Lewis, Ruth M. Lewis, and Susan M. Rigdon.
Urbana, Illinois: University of Illinois Press, 1977.
443p. bibliog.
This is a collection of lengthy oral histories from four
very different Cuban women, including an educated married
woman and member of the Communist Party; a single woman
living with her parents, formerly active in
counter-revolutionary activities; a young former
prostitute; and a middle-aged housewife formerly a domestic
servant. The histories provide an informative personal
look at the condition of women in Cuba before and after the
revolution.

512. Marriage, Class and Colour in Nineteenth Century Cuba: a
Study of Racial Attitudes and Sexual Values in a Slave
Society.
Verena Martínez-Alier.
London: Cambridge University Press, 1974. 202p. bibliog.
A landmark study of the interplay of racial attitudes,
marriage norms, and control of women in the late colonial
period.

513. "Modernizing Women for a Modern Society: the Cuban Case."
Susan Kaufman Purcell.
In Female and Male in Latin America.   Edited by Ann
Pescatello. Pittsburgh: University of Pittsburgh Press,

1973. p. 257-71.
Analyzes the Cuban transition from a traditional to modern
polity and the accompanying changes in the status and role
of women. In examining the modernization of Cuban women,
the study emphasizes their behavioral changes.

514. La mujer en Cuba socialista.
Havana: Editorial ORBE, 1977. 392p.
A collection of documents, statutes, proclamations, and
legal codes pertaining to women in Cuba after 1959.

515. La mujer en el 68,.
Armando O. Caballero.
Havana: Editorial Gente Nueva, 1978.   79p.   bibliog.
Presents a general account of the participation of women in
the Ten Years War (1868-1878).   Much of the book is
organized around chapters containing individual biographies
of the most prominent women.

516. "La mujer en la revolución de Cuba."
Francisco J. Ponte Domínguez.
Revista Bimestre Cubana, vol. 33, no. 1 (Jan.-June 1933),
p. 276-300.
Outlines the role of women in the struggle for independence
during the nineteenth century.   Particular attention is
paid to the Ten Years War (1868-1878).

517. Mujeres.
Havana: Monthly. 1960-.
This magazine of general interest to women, published by
the Federation of Cuban Women (FMC), deals with such
diverse issues as the participation of women in the
revolution, national news of women's activities, politics,
culture, fashion, and household affairs.

518. Mujeres ejemplares.
Havana: Editorial ORBE, 1977. 345p.
A collection of thirty-three biographical essays dealing
with women prominent in revolutionary struggle. While some
of essays deal with the role of women outside Cuba, most
concentrate on their experience in Cuba from the middle of
the nineteenth century to the years of the revolution.

519. Mujeres en la revolución.
Margaret Randall.
México: Siglo Veintiuno, 1975. 2nd ed. 375p.
A series of lengthy interviews and articles describing the
condition of women across the island, from all walks of
life, and engaged in a variety of occupations.

520. "On Cuban Women."

Chris Camarano.
Science and Society, vol. 25, no. 2 (Spring, 1971),
p. 48-57.
A general discussion of the status and condition of women
in socialist Cuba.

521. La prostitución en Cuba, y especialmente en La Habana.
Cuba. Comisión de Higiene Especial.
Havana: P. Fernández y Cía., 1903.   2 vols.   maps.
bibliog.
A detailed discussion of prostitution in Cuba during the
latter half of the nineteenth century and the early years
of the twentieth. Organized into several sections dealing
with historical antecedents, medical aspects, and social
backgrounds, the work also contains useful statistical data
dealing with age, race, nationality, and demography.

522. La 'reeducación' de la mujer cubana en la colonia.
Rolando Alvarez Estévez.
Havana: Editorial de Ciencias Sociales, 1976.   116p.
bibliog.
A detailed discussion of the establishment in 1746 of the
women's house of correction in Havana. The study examines
the 150 year history of the institution as it served to
disseminate   and   impose   the   prevailing   patriarchal
ideologies of the colonial social order.

523. Sobre maternidad obrera.
Edited by Eugenio Flamand Montero.
Havana, Cuba: Imprenta "El Lápiz Rojo," 1937. 36p.
A compilation of laws and statutes affecting maternity
insurance and the employment of women.

524. "Speculation on Women's Liberation in Cuba."
Linda Gordon.
Women: A Journal of Liberation, vol. 1, no. 4 (Summer
1970), p. 14-15.
Provides a general sympathetic account of the improvement
of the condition of women in Cuba. The essay is not
oblivious of those areas of Cuban life where the
achievements of women have fallen far short of the promise.
The emphasis is on attitudes and consciousness.

525. "La vida civil de la mujer cubana en su relación con la
historia de Cuba."
Medardo Vitier.
Cuba Contemporánea, vol. 14, no. 4 (Aug. 1914), p. 323-40.
The general discussion of the legal status of women pays
attention to their role and participation in all aspects of
national development, and shows how that involvement has
affected the juridical status.

526. Women and the Cuban Revolution.
     Edited by Elizabeth Stone.
     New York: Pathfinder Press, 1981. 156p.
     This volume presents a collection of translated documents
     and speeches dealing with women in Cuba after the
     revolution, including several speeches made by Fidel Castro
     and Vilma Espin, the president of the Federation of Cuban
     Women (FMC). The documents consist of the Communist Party
     thesis on the full exercise of women's equality (1975), the
     maternity law for working women, and the Family Code.

527. "Women in Cuba."
     Joan Berman.
     Women: A Journal of Liberation, vol. 1, no. 4, (Summer
     1970), p. 10-14.
     Analyzes the changing status and condition of women in Cuba
     since the revolution. Based on personal travel experience
     in Cuba, the article is generally sympathetic with the
     advances registered in the decade after 1959.

528. "Women in Cuba: the Revolution Within the Revolution."
     Johnetta B. Cole.
     In Comparative Perspectives of Third World Women.   Edited
     by Beverly Lindsay. New York: Praeger, 1980. p. 162-178.
     bibliog.
     The essay provides a comparative analysis of the condition
     and status of women before and after the revolution. The
     essay focuses on health, education, housing, work, and
     culture.

529. Women in Cuba: Twenty Years Later.
     Margaret Randall.
     Brooklyn, New York: Smyrna Press, 1981. 168p. bibliog.
     A two-decade assessment of the changes in the status and
     condition of women in socialist Cuba. Among the central
     topics discussed are the lives of peasant women, women's
     reproductive role, women and the family, the participation
     of women in the arts, and the activities of the Federation
     of Cuban Women (FMC).

530. Women of Cuba.
     Inger Holt-Seeland.
     New York: Lawrence Hill and Company, Inc., 1982. 109p.
     Providing a generally sympathetic account of the condition
     of women in Cuba after the revolution. The work includes a
     series of interviews with women of different social
     origins, occupational positions, and educational
     backgrounds--specifically, a farm worker, brigade leader,
     student, homemaker, and factory worker.

Social Service, Health and Welfare

531. Apuntes históricos relativos a la farmacia en Cuba.
Manuel García Hernández and Susana Martínez Fortún y Foyo.
Havana: Ministerio de Salud Pública, 1967. 73p.
A historical survey of pharmacy in Cuba from the colonial
period to the 1950s. The study examines the education of
pharmacists, professional pharmaceutical organizations, and
the practice of the profession.

532. "Apuntes para una cronología y un poco más de los
hospitales cubanos, 1523 a 1899."
Mario del Pino y de la Vega.
Revista Bimestre Cubana, vol. 72, no. 1 (Jan.-June 1957),
p. 60-104.
This essay surveys the hospitals in Cuba during the
colonial period and also provides a good overview of the
history of medicine on the island. The account of the
hospitals is organized around the number and names of all
the institutions in each province.

533. "La atención médica in Cuba hasta 1958."
Roberto E. Hernández.
Journal of Inter-American Affairs, vol. 11, no. 4 (Oct.
1969), p. 533-57.
Surveys in detail the health care system in Cuba before the
revolution. The author argues that the pre-revolutionary
medical system while deficient in some areas, was basically
able to provide adequate health attention to the Cuban
people. The emphasis is on hospital care, infant
mortality, the number and distribution of physicians, and
the training of medical personnel.

534. Biografía de la Federación Médica de Cuba, 1925-1944.
Augusto Fernández Conde.

Havana: Colegio Médico de La Habana, 1946. 158p.
A historical account of Cuba's principal medical
association.

535. Cronolgía médica cubana. Contribución al estudio de la
historia de la medicina en Cuba.
José A. Martínez-Fortún y Foyo.
Havana: Eudaldo Valdés e Hijos, 1947-1951. 3 vols.
A chronological compilation of significant dates and
events, covering the years from 1492 to 1839.

536. "The Cuban Health System: a Trial of a Comprehensive
Service in a Poor Country."
Z. Stein and M. Susser.
International Journal of Health Services, vol. 2, no. 4
(Fall 1972), p. 551-66.
This is a generally favorable review of Cuban health
programs based on six goals adopted by the government after
1959.   The goals examined include: 1) the effort to
provide universal and comprehensive health care; 2) the
training of health personnel in numbers adequate to meet
comprehensive service; 3) the coordination of all health
programs; 4) the necessity to keep health services aware of
human needs; 5) to improve and maintain health of the
nation as a whole as well as meeting the needs of
individual patients; and 6) to maintain constant evaluation
of health programs.

537. "The Cuban Hospital System."
Willy de Geyndt.
World Hospitals (London), vol. 8, no. 3 (July 1972),
p. 279-84.
This analysis of Cuban hospitals examines the organization
of the hospital system with the model of concentric
circles: increasing specialization and sophistication at
each successive higher level.   Most hospitals serve as
community health centers, which act as the level at which
people enter the health care system.   Other aspects
discussed include hospital management, rural hospitals, and
maternal and child health care.

538. Cuban Medicine.
Ross Danielson.
New Brunswick, New Jersey: Transaction Books, 1979. 247p.
bibliog.
Provides a detailed account of Cuban health services. The
early part of the book offers an historical survey of
medicine in Cuba.   The focus is largely on the
transformation of the practice of Cuban medicine since the
revolution,   with   concomitant   emphasis   on   the
socio-political   formation   of   health   workers,   the

organization of rural and primary medical care, and economic trade-offs necessitated by Cuban medicine.

539. "Cuba's Revolutionary Medicine."
Willis P. Butler.
Ramparts, vol. 7, no. 12 (May 1969), p. 6, 10-14.
A sympathetic assessment of medicine in socialist Cuba by a U.S. physician. First-hand information based on travels to Cuba and interviews with Cuban doctors, administrators, and patients. While lauding most areas of Cuban health care systems, the author is critical of deficiencies in nursing, dentistry, and research.

540. "Determinants of Mortality Transition in Developing Countries Before and After the Second World War: Some Evidence From Cuba."
Sergio Díaz-Briquets.
Population Studies, vol. 35, no. 3 (1981), p. 399-411.
Studies declining mortality rates in Cuba, with particular emphasis on Havana, and the factors responsible for the decline. The essay sets the question of mortality against the larger social, economic, medical, and public health context of Cuba.

541. La donación de sangre en Cuba.
Mario del Pino y de la Vega.
Havana: Ministerio de Salud Pública, 1969. 74p. bibliog.
This study of the history of blood banks, transfusions, and blood donation in Cuba. Contains a statistical appendix of blood donation in Havana between 1945 and 1968.

542. Epidemiología, síntesis cronológica.
José A. Martínez-Fortún y Foyo.
Havana: Ministerio de Salubridad y Asistencia Pública, 1952. 51p.
A chronological listing of major epidemics in Cuba.

543. "Health and Revolution in Cuba."
Nelson P. Valdés.
Science and Society, vol. 35, no. 3 (Autumn 1971), p. 311-31.
An examination of the health care and health delivery system in Cuba, comparing developments in socialist Cuba with pre-revolutionary conditions. The topics examined include nutrition, housing, the training of health personnel, general and infant mortality, and the prevention and treatment of disease.

544. "Health, Health Planning, and Health Services in Cuba."
Vincente Navarro.
International Journal of Health Services, vol. 2, no. 3

(Summer 1972), p. 397-432.
Socio-economic changes, most notably agrarian and urban reforms, have equalized the distribution of resources between regions and social class. This essay is a study of the manner in which an equal distribution of health resources has affected mortality and morbidity patterns. The emphasis of the work is on the education and training resources and decision-making and planning methods.

545. The Health Revolution in Cuba.
Sergio Díaz-Briquets.
Austin, Texas: University of Texas Press, 1983.   227p.
A study of health conditions in twentieth century Cuba, paying particular attention to an examination of the decline of mortality rates in Cuba since its independence. The work includes a brief discussion of the achievements of the health system since the revolution.

546. "Health Services in Cuba: An Initial Approach."
Vicente Navarro.
The New England Journal of Medicine, vol. 298 (Nov. 9, 1972), p. 954-59.
Describes Cuban efforts after 1959 to minimize inequalities in the availability and consumption of health resources. The essays outline the means used to reach these objectives, including the centralization of in-patient services, a decentralization of ambulatory services, and an increase in the use and training of paramedical and auxiliary personnel within the health services.

547. "High-Tech Medicine in the Caribbean: 25 Years of Cuban Health Care."
Robert N. Ubell.
The New England Journal of Medicine, vol. 309 (Dec. 8, 1983), p. 1468-72.
A survey of health conditions and health delivery systems in socialist Cuba.   The focus of the essay is on polyclinics, hospitals, medical education, and clinical research.

548. Historia de la medicina en Cuba.
José A. Martínez-Fortún y Foyo.
Havana: n.p., 1956. 45p.
This brief survey of Cuban medical history during the seventeenth century provides information concerning epidemics, the hospitals, the distribution of physicians, and the general state of medicine in Cuba at that time.

549. La medicina en La Habana.
Havana: Consejo Científico del Ministerio de Salud, 1970. 318p.

A survey of medical history and medical practices in Cuba, with specific emphasis in Havana.

550. **Médicos en la Sierra Maestra, apuntes históricos.**
Julio Martínez Páez.
Havana: Ministerio de Salubridad y Asistencia Social, 1959. 72p.
A study of the number and role of those physicians who participated in the revolutionary struggle against Fulgencio Batista in the Sierra Maestra mountains.

551. **Médicos y medicinas en Cuba: historia, biografía, costumbrismo.**
Emilio Roig de Leuchsenring.
Havana: Academia de Ciencias de Cuba, 1965.   269p. bibliog.
This collection of essays examines the history of Cuban medicine and medical practices.   The work includes biographical sketches on some of Cuba's most prominent physicians, including Tomás Romay, Juan Guiteras, and Carlos Finlay. Attention is also paid to the practice of folk medicine.

552. "The Nutriture of Cubans: Historical Perspective and Nutritional Analysis."
Antonio M. Gordon, Jr.
Cuban Studies/Estudios Cubanos, vol. 13, no. 2 (Summer 1983), p. 1-34.
A comparison of nutrition in Cuba with that in other Third World countries. This analysis includes a discussion of food production, the efficiency of local food industries, and the character of imports and exports of foodstuffs.

553. "A Promise Kept: Health Care in Cuba."
Cuba Review, vol. 8, no. 1 (Mar. 1978), p. 3-38.
A special issue devoted to a variety of aspects of the health delivery system in socialist Cuba. Among the topics covered are mental health, occupational illness, hospitals, polyclinics, dental clinics, and government health policies.

554. "Public Health Care in Cuba."
Roy John, David Kimmelman, Joanna Haas, and Peter Orris.
Cuba Resource Center Newsletter, vol. 2, no. 3 (May 1972), p. 4-9.
This article provides an examination of the organization of public health in Cuba after the revolution.

555. Regla: su aporte a la medicina cubana en el siglo XIX.
Eduardo Gómez Luaces.
Havana: Ministerio de Salud Pública, 1973. 169p.

bibliog.
This study of medicine in the city of Regla in Havana province provides more than local history, for it is, in fact, a detailed examination of public health, the education of physicians and the practice of medicine.

556. "La sanidad en Cuba: sus progresos."
Jorge LeRoy.
Cuba Contemporánea, vol. 3, no. 1 (Sept. 1915), p. 43-63.
Presents a survey of health and mortality conditions from the early nineteenth century to the 1910s.

557. "The Undergraduate Education of Physicians in Cuba."
Willis P. Butler.
Journal of Medical Education, vol. 48, no. 10 (Sept. 1973), p. 846-57.
Examines the ideological goals of undergraduate medical education in socialist Cuba, including such issues as the teaching of medicine in a larger social framework, the dissemination of health care, and the reduction of professional elitism. The author indicates that Cuban education stresses the development of collectivist and cooperative attitudes over individualist and competitive approaches, with a heavy emphasis on practical clinical teaching in small groups.

Human Rights

558. Cuba and the Rule of Law.
International Commission of Jurists.
Geneva, Switzerland: H. Studer, S.A., 1962. 267p.
A critical study of conditions in Cuba three years after
the triumph of the revolution condemning "the establishment
of a totalitarian regime." The subjects examined include
constitutional law, criminal legislation, infringements of
the freedom of the press, freedom of travel, religious
freedom, and offences against property.

559. Human Rights and United States Policy Toward Latin America.
Lars Schoultz.
Princeton, New Jersey: Princeton University Press, 1981.
421p. bibliog.
Provides a general appraisal of the impact of U.S. foreign
policy on human rights in Latin America. The discussion of
Cuba is within the larger Hemispheric context, and deals
with pre- and post-revolutionary conditions.

560. Human Rights in Cuba.
U.S. Congress. House of Representatives. Committee on
Foreign Affairs. Subcommittee on Human Rights and
International Organizations.
Washington, D.C.: Government Printing Office. 1984.
Ninety-Eighth Congress, 2nd Session. 123p.
The transcription of hearings held in June 1984 discussing
human rights conditions in Cuba. This generally critical
testimony was provided by representatives of the State
Department, Cuban exiles, a representative of Amnesty
International, and a spokesperson for the Americas Watch.

561. Report on the Situation of Political Prisoners and Their
Relatives in Cuba.

Inter-American Commission on Human Rights.
Washington, D.C.: Pan American Union, 1963. 64p.
An indictment of the Cuban revolutionary government for
violation of civil liberties.   The central focus of the
report is on the condition of political prisoners and the
situation of women in political prisons.

562. The Situation of Human Rights in Cuba.
General   Secretariat.   Organization   of American States.
Washington, D.C.: Organization of American States, 1983.
183p.
Presents a general overview of human rights conditions in
Cuba   with   particular   attention   to   political   rights,
personal security, right to life, religious freedom, the
right of residence and movement, the right to work, food,
health and social security, and the right to an education.
In almost all these areas, the OAS report is generally
critical   of   Cuba's   performance,   although   the   report
comments favorably on the socio-economic achievements of
the revolution.

Politics

A. General

563. Cuba: Order and Revolution.
Jorge I. Domínguez.
Cambridge, Massachusetts: Harvard University Press, 1978.
682p. maps. bibliog.
A sweeping panorama of Cuban politics during the twentieth
century. The work is particularly strong in its discussion
of developments in Cuba after 1959, which constitutes
three-quarters of the book. An indispensable reference
work for the study of socialist Cuba.

564. "The Cuban Communists in the Early Stage of the Cuban
Revolution: Revolutionaries or Reformists?"
Samuel Farber.
Latin American Research Review, vol. 18, no. 1 (1983),
p. 59-84.
Discusses communist party (PSP) policy toward the end of
the Fulgencio Batista regime and in the early years of the
revolution. Farber argues that the PSP was overtaken by
the radicalism of the revolutionary leadership, and that it
was the bold direction of Fidel Castro, rather than the
strategic and tactic conservativism of one PSP, that
accounts for the success of communism in Cuba.

565. Cuba política, 1899-1955.
Mario Riera Hernández.
Havana: Impreso Modelo, S.A., 1955. 628p. bibliog.
This vast compendium of republican politics contains an
account of every election held in Cuba--national,
provincial, and municipal--between 1898 and 1955 with all
the names of the candidates, victors and losers, for all
elective offices, including presidency, senate, house of

representatives, governors, mayors, and municipal aldermen. The book also examines the elections for constituent assemblies in 1901, 1928, and 1940, political party histories, and military coups in 1933 and 1952.

566. Cuba republicana, 1899-1958.
Mario Riera Hernández.
Miami, Florida: Editorial AIP, 1974. 248p.
Provides an annotated registry of all elected officials for the full period between 1899 and the Cuban revolution. This useful reference work includes the names of all the participants of constituent assemblies (1902, 1928, 1940), the cabinet members of every presidential administration, and the names of senators, congressmen, governors, and mayors from all the provinces and municipalities.

567. Directory of Officials of the Republic of Cuba.
Central Intelligence Agency.   National Foreign Center.
Washington, D.C.:   National Technical Information Service, 1979.
A compilation of the names of all Cuban officials, from the head of state to the local municipal functionaries. The information was compiled during mid-1979.

568. The Early Fidel: Roots of Castro's Communism.
Lionel Martin.
Secaucus, New Jersey: Lyle Stuart, 1978. 272p.
A political biography of Fidel Castro from his student days up to the triumph of the insurrection.

569. Funerales y responso.
Vicente Pardo Suárez.
Havana: Imprenta de Rambla, Bouza y Cía., 1926.   382p.
A sweeping indictment of the maladies and maladministration in the early republic.

570. "Las ideas políticas en Cuba durante el siglo XIX."
Eliseo Giberga.
Cuba Contemporánea, vol. 10, no. 4 (April 1916), p. 347-81.
Discusses in detail the principal trends of political thought during the nineteenth century. Starting with the influence of the Spanish liberal constitution of 1812, the essay explores the successive development of liberalism, reformism, annexationism, autonomy, conservatism, and separatism.

571. Listen, Yankee: the Revolution in Cuba.
C. Wright Mills.
New York: McGraw-Hill, 1960. 192p. bibliog.
A polemical, and in places strident, defense of the Cuban revolution. It is, nevertheless, an important contribution

to the early political literature about the revolution, for
Mills effectively renders into English and captures the
tenor of the early arguments on behalf of radical change.

572. El nuevo pensamiento político de Cuba.
Diego de Pereda.
Havana: Editorial Lex, 1943. 829p.
Presents a collection of political speeches, proclamations,
and policy statements made by nearly 100 important Cuban
political leaders during the 1930s and 1940s.

573. Pensamiento revolucionario cubano.
Edited by Departamento de Filosofía.
Havana: Editorial de Ciencias Sociales, 1971.   476p.
This anthology of Cuban political thought includes the
works of Cuban revolutionary leaders in three distinct
periods: the nineteenth century struggle for independence,
the early republic, and the revolution of the 1930s.

574. Revolution and Reaction in Cuba, 1933-1960.
Samuel Farber.
Middletown, Connecticut: Wesleyan University Press, 1976.
283p. bibliog.
An important contribution to the study of Cuba,
particularly for the years between 1933 and 1959. The
author examines the evolution of the important political
groups as they developed out the revolutionary upheavals of
the 1930s and against the larger setting of Cuban class
structures.   The case is made that both Fulgencio Batista
and Fidel Castro represent Bonapartist responses to
different periods of profound social crisis.

575. The Unsuspected Revolution: the Birth and Rise of
Castroism.
Mario Llerena.
Ithaca, New York: Cornell University Press, 1978. 323p.
A political memoir of the armed struggle against Fulgencio
Batista during the 1950s by an early supporter--and later
an early opponent--of Fidel Castro. It is an important
source of reference for the study of these years.

B. Political Parties

576. Historia del partido comunista de Cuba.
Jorge Montes and Antonio Alonso Avila.
Miami, Florida: Ediciones Universal, 563p.   bibliog.
A detailed historical account of the communist party in the
decades before the triumph of the revolution in 1959. The
larger part of this work deals with the period between 1930
and 1958, paying only cursory attention to the early

history of the communist party.

577. Partidos políticos: organización y reorganización.
     Edited by Enrique Menéndez Jiménez.
     Sancti-Spíritus, Cuba: Tipografía Venus, 1949.   160p.
     A compilation of laws relating to the organization and
     legal status of political parties in Cuba.

578. Political Parties of the Americas.
     Edited by Robert J. Alexander.
     Westport, Connecticut: Greenwood Press, 1982.   2 vols.
     bibliog.
     This work offers a useful chapter on Cuban politics in
     volume one.

579. El primer partido socialista cubano.
     José Rivero Muñiz.
     Santa Clara, Cuba: Universidad Central de Las Villas,
     1962.   123p.
     A history of the founding of the Cuban Socialist Party
     (PSC) in 1899.   The study provides a biographical profile
     of its founder, Diego Vicente Tejera, and follows the PSC
     from its organization to its demise.

580. Los primeros partidos políticos.
     Mario Averhoff Purón.
     Havana: Instituto Cubano del Libro, 1971.   115p.   bibliog.
     Discusses the origins and organization of Cuban political
     parties.   The study focuses on the period of the U.S.
     military occupation (1899-1902) and the early years of the
     republic.

C.   Cuban Revolution

581. Castroism: Theory and Practice.
     Theodore Draper.
     New York: Praeger, 1965.   263p.
     This three-part study provides an interpretative analysis
     of fidelismo set against a larger context of
     Marxism-Leninism, a discussion of the class origins of the
     revolution, and a description of the evolution of its
     economic policies.

582. Castro's Cuba, Cuba's Fidel.
     Lee Lockwood.
     New York: Vintage Books, 1969.   364p.
     Richly illustrated with black and white photographs, the
     greater part of this book consists of an extensive
     interview with Fidel Castro.   Lockwood is an excellent
     interviewer, directing the discussion to cover a wide range

of subjects, including relations with the U.S. and the
U.S.S.R., land reform, industrialization, education,
censorship, art, communism, the armed struggle against
Fulgencio Batista, exiles, sports, and human rights.

583. "Castro's Revolution, Cuban Communist Appeals, and the
Soviet Response."
Edward González.
World Politics, vol. 21, no. 1 (Oct. 1968), p. 39-68.
Studies the early period of the seizure of power by the
revolutionary forces, with emphasis on the shifting
coalitions between the Cuban communist party (PSP) and the
26 July Movement. The essay details the radicalization
phase and the part played by Soviet policy.

584. Castro's Revolution: Myths and Realities.
Theodore Draper.
New York: Praeger, 1962. 211p.
Presents a collection of three lengthy essays. One essay
seeks to locate the ideological sources of fidelismo by
examining the nature of the armed struggle during the late
1950s.   The second section examines the Bay of Pigs
invasion in 1961. The last part discusses the implications
of Castro's public embrace of Marxism-Leninism.

585. "The Consolidation of the Cuban Political System."
J. David Edwards.
World Affairs, vol. 139, no. 1 (Summer 1976), p. 10-16.
An examination of the institutionalization of the
revolution, specifically the change of emphasis from
revolutionary zeal, ideology and charismatic leadership to
legitimacy, consistency and administrative stability.
Attention is given to the new socialist constitution, the
communist party, the armed forces, and people's power.

586. "Continuity and Change in the Cuban Political Elite."
William M. LeoGrande.
Cuban Studies/Estudios Cubanos, vol. 8, no. 2 (July 1978),
p. 1-31.
Studies the political elites in Cuba during the 1960s and
1970s, and examines the membership of the Central
Committee of the Cuban Communist Party. The essay outlines
the shifting patterns of institutional relationships in the
political system.

587. Cuba, Anatomy of a Revolution.
Leo Huberman and Paul M. Sweezy.
New York: Monthly Review Press, 1960. 176p. map.
A sympathetic account of the first year of the Cuban
revolution.

588. "Cuba and Communism."
J. P. Morray.
Monthly Review, vol. 13, nos. 3-4   (July-Aug. 1961),
p. 3-55.
Presents a detailed and sympathetic account of the early
period of the Cuban revolution. The essay examines the
early reform measures, the development of mass
organizations, Cuban foreign policy, and the role of the
communist party.

589. Cuba: Castroism and Communism, 1959-1966.
Andrés Suárez.
Cambridge, Massachusetts: M.I.T. Press, 1967.   266p.
Analyzes in detail the radicalization of the revolution and
the Cuban transition to socialism. The study examines
these developments as a function of larger domestic
political consideration and as responses to foreign policy
needs.

590. Cuba, Dilemmas of a Revolution.
Juan M. del Aguila.
Boulder, Colorado: Westview Press, 1984. 193p.
Discusses the Cuban pre-revolutionary past as a source for
the populist authoritarian tendencies that characterized
the revolution. The study examines the accomplishments and
failures of socialism in Cuba, placing emphasis on economic
development, and political culture.

591. Cuba in the 1970s: Pragmaticism and Institutionalization.
Carmelo Mesa-Lago.
Albuquerque, New Mexico: University of New Mexico Press,
1974. 200p. bibliog.
A thorough study of the social and economic policies of the
revolution during the early 1970s. Detailed attention is
paid to such inter-related topics as capital efficiency,
labor   productivity,   the   introduction   of   material
incentives, and economic diversification. The work also
examines Cuban efforts to separate government functions,
the democratization of labor organization, and the
establishment of popular power.

592. Cuba: the Measure of a Revolution.
Lowry Nelson.
Minneapolis, Minnesota: University of Minnesota Press,
1972. 241p. bibliog.
The   study   examines   the   social   conditions   in
pre-revolutionary Cuba as a background to the socialist
period. The principal focus is on the impact that the
revolution had on a variety of aspects of Cuban life,
including agriculture, economic diversification, labor,
education, family, religion, press, class, and social

services.

593. Cuba Under Castro: the Limits of Charisma.
Edward González.
New York: Houghton Mifflin Company, 1974. 241p.
A concise and clearly-written description of the
development of the Cuban revolution, starting with
developments in the nineteenth century through 1970. The
work also examines the origins and function of the
charismatic personality of Fidel Castro, arguing that it
was not adequate to meet the challenges of adequate
economic development.

594. The Cuban Insurrection, 1952-1959.
Ramón L. Bonachea and Marta San Martín.
New Brunswick, New Jersey: Transaction Books, 1973. 450p.
maps. bibliog.
This comprehensive account of the Cuban revolutionary war
is based on published and unpublished field reports and
battle accounts. The authors deal with the different
revolutionary organizations, the variety of revolutionary
strategies, and different revolutionary leaders. They
argue that the revolutionary victory over the Batista
dictatorship was as much the result of the effort of the
urban underground as the rural guerrillas.

595. "The Cuban Revolution: the Road to Power."
Andrés Suárez.
Latin American Research Review, vol. 7, no. 3 (Autumn
1972), p. 5-29.
Analyzes the varieties of interpretations concerning the
triumph of the 26 July Movement. Among the topics covered
are the attack on the Moncada barracks (1953), the landing
of "Granma" (1956), the origins of the guerrilla movement,
the April 1958 general strike, the role of the vommunist
party, and the impact of Fidel Castro.

596. Fidel, a Biography of Fidel Castro.
Peter G. Bourne.
New York: Dodd, Mead & Company, 1986.   332p. plates.
bibliog.
A generally sympathetic biography of Fidel Castro, with
attention given to youth and the years of armed struggle.
The author's training as a psychiatrist gives this
biography its unique attribute, for the volume adopts a
psycho-analytic approach to Fidel's political development.

597. Fidel: A Critical Portrait.
Tad Szulc.
New York: Morrow, 1986.   685p.   map.   plates.
bibliog.

This most recent biography of Fidel Castro is among the most comprehensive.   Particular attention is given to the years subsequent to the triumph of the revolution.

598. Fidel Castro.
Herbert L. Matthews.
New York: Simon and Schuster, 1969.   382p.   bibliog.
A sympathetic political biography of Fidel Castro.   Set against the larger context of national politics, Matthews chronicles the emergence of Castro from an aspiring political office seeker in the early 1950s to his success as a revolutionary leader of the 1960s.

599. Fidel Castro's Political Programs from Reformism to 'Marxism-Leninism.'
Loree Wilkerson.
Gainesville, Florida: University of Florida Press, 100p. bibliog.
Studies the ideological transformation of the Cuban revolution, examining three key aspects: the early personal experiences that influenced Fidel Castro's political thinking, the speeches and programs of Castro during the years of his political activism and revolutionary struggles, and the programs of the first three years of the revolutionary government.

600. Guerrillas in Power.   The Course of the Cuban Revolution.
K.S. Karol.
New York: Hill & Wang, 1970.   624p.
A detailed political history of the Cuban revolution.   It is especially useful in its discussion of the antecedents of the revolution during the 1930s, and in particular the role of the communist party.   It is richly detailed for the years of the late 1950s and 1960s.

601. "Ideology, Socialist Development, and Power in Cuba."
Arthur MacEwan.
Politics and Society, vol. 5, no. 1 (Aug. 1975), p. 67-81.
Analyzes the emergence in Cuba of a theory of socialist development, placing emphasis on the role of ideology and social development.

602. "The 'Institucionalización' of Cuba's Revolution."
Max Azicri.
Revista/Review Interamericana, vol. 8, no. 2 (Summer 1978), p. 247-262.
Discusses the process by which the Cuban revolution entered into the institutionalization phase.   Emphasis is given to mobilization strategies of the 1970s.

603. "Integrating International Revolution and Detente.   The

Cuban Case."
José A. Moreno and Nicholas O. Lardas.
Latin American Perspectives, vol. 6, no. 2 (Spring 1979),
p. 36-61.
An analysis of Cuba within the context of the international
conditions in which it emerged, the conflicts and
confrontations it engendered, and the adaptations and
accommodations it experienced between 1959 and 1975.
Within this setting, the authors proceed to analyze both
the national and international shifts of the revolution.

604. The Origins of Cuban Socialism.
James O'Connor.
Ithaca, New York: Cornell University Press, 1970.   338p.
bibliog.
A general survey of a decade of Cuban economic planning
under the revolution, with emphasis on agrarian reform,
industrial planning, and labor. The work provides one of
the better analyses of economic conditions in the
pre-revolutionary period. Two appendices provide data on
labor, rural economic development, and employment between
1957 and 1967.

605. Realidad y perspectivas de la revolución cubana.
Luis Emiro Valencia.
Havana: Casa de las Américas, 1961. 407p.
Beginning with the late nineteenth century, the author
surveys Cuba's political, social, and economic developments
as a background to the revolution. The latter third of the
book studies the triumph of the revolution and the
subsequent social economic programs implemented.   An
appendix includes the text of important revolutionary laws.

606. La revolución cubana; su significación histórica.
Silvio Frondizi.
Montevideo: Editorial Ciencias Políticas, 1960.   178p.
This lengthy essay examines the final years of the
Fulgencio Batista government during the late 1950s and the
first year of the revolution.

607. The Rise and Decline of Fidel Castro. An Essay in
Contemporary History.
Maurice Halperin.
Berkeley, California: University of California Press,
1972. 380p. bibliog.
An account of the consolidation of the revolution between
1959 and 1964. The emphasis falls on foreign relations,
and particularly on the debate within the Cuban government
over the ideological trajectory Cuba was to pursue in its
relations with socialist bloc nations.

608. "Revolution and Institutionalization in Cuba."
Nelson P. Valdés.
Cuban Studies/Estudios Cubanos, vol. 6, no. 1 (Jan. 1976),
p. 1-37.
Examines the process by which Cuban revolutionary
leadership seized political power, consolidated that
control, and institutionalized revolutionary change between
1959 and the early 1970s.

609. Revolutionary Struggle, 1947-1958. Selected Works of Fidel
Castro.
Edited by Rolando E. Bonachea and Nelson P. Valdés.
Cambridge, Massachusetts: The MIT Press, 1972.   471p.
bibliog.
An invaluable collection of the translated speeches,
essays, and political statements made by Fidel Castro from
his early days at the University of Havana to the triumph
of the revolutionary war against Fulgencio Batista.
Further material is taken from speeches, manifestos,
newspaper and magazine articles, letters, messages, and
interviews. The introductory essay provides an excellent
context within which to study the collection.

610. The Second Revolution in Cuba.
J.P. Morray.
New York: Monthly Review Press, 1962. 175p.
By "second revolution" Morray means the radicalization
process in the period immediately following the triumph of
the armed struggle. The focus of the book is on the period
1959-1962. The work is especially effective in setting the
internal politics of the early years of the revolution in a
larger international context.

611. Socialism in Cuba.
Leo Huberman and Paul M. Sweezy.
New York: Monthly Review Press, 1969. 221p.
A general and sympathetic assessment of conditions in Cuba
after 1959.   Among the topics examined include health,
education, strategies for economic development,
diversification, and technology.

612. The Theory of Moral Incentives in Cuba.
Robert M. Bernardo.
University, Alabama: University of Alabama Press, 1971.
759p. bibliog.
Provides an account of the Cuban experiment with the use of
moral incentives as a source of economic development during
the 1960s. The work presents a detailed examination of the
debate within Cuban policy circles as well as a treatment
of the implementation and effect of moral incentives.

613. The Transformation of Political Culture in Cuba.
Richard R. Fagen.
Stanford, California: Stanford University Press, 1969.
271p.
This is an important contribution to the literature
examining the early years of Cuba's transition to
socialism.   The focus of the study is on the literacy
campaign of 1961, the schools of revolutionary instruction,
and the establishment of the Committees for the Defense of
the Revolution (CDR).

614. With Fidel: a Portrait of Castro and Cuba.
Frank Mankiewicz and Kirby Jones.
New York: Playboy Press, 1975. 269p.
This book is the result of some thirteen hours of interview
with Fidel Castro made in the course of three visits to
Cuba by the authors between 1974 and 1975. The work is
particularly useful since it provides an insight into the
personality and politics of the Cuban leadership.   It
presents a wide-ranging discussion, covering such topics as
relations with the U.S., the missile crisis, Cuban foreign
policy towards Latin America, and the role of the State,
the party, and the military.

D. Armed Forces

615. Army Politics in Cuba, 1898-1958.
Louis A. Pérez, Jr.
Pittsburgh: University of Pittsburgh Press, 1976.   240p.
bibliog.
Traces the development of the Cuban army from its inception
under the auspices of two successive U.S. occupations
(1898-1902 and 1906-1909) to its emergence as one of the
most potent political forces on the island and finally to
its collapse and ultimate defeat during the revolutionary
war of 1956-1958.

616. "Army Politics in Socialist Cuba."
Louis A. Pérez, Jr.
Journal of Latin American Studies, vol. 8, no. 2 (Nov.
1976), p. 251-71.
A study of the origins and development of the Rebel Army
and its emergence as a political force in the first decade
of the revolution.

617. "A Bureaucratic Approach to Civil-Military Relations in
Communist Political Systems: the Case of Cuba."
William M. LeoGrande.
In Comparative Communist Civil-Military Relations.   Edited
by Dale R. Herspring and Ivan Vogyes. Boulder, Colorado:

Westview Press, 1978. p. 201-18.
A study of the political-civil relations with the armed
forces. Of particular interest is the discussion of the
relationship between the communist party and the army.

618. "Civil-Military Relations in Cuba: Party Control and
     Political Socialization."
     William M. LeoGrande.
     Studies in Comparative Communism, vol. 11, no. 3 (Autumn
     1978), p. 278-91.
     Examines the relations between the Revolutionary Armed
     Forces (FAR) and the various civil political organizations,
     culminating in the organization of the Cuban Communist
     Party (PCC). The essay assesses the role of revolutionary
     instructors in the army and the development of the
     communist party in the armed forces.

619. Cuba and the Revolutionary Myth: the Political Education
     of the Cuban Rebel Army, 1953-63.
     C. Fred Judson.
     Boulder, Colorado: Westview Press, 1984. 295p. bibliog.
     An examination of the historico-social sources of
     revolutionary elan in the rebel army during the armed
     struggle of the 1950s. At the same time, the author
     assesses how the successes and victories of the rebel army
     during the 1950s themselves became part of the
     revolutionary myth that served for the political education
     of the new armed forces after 1959.

620. "The Cuban Rebel Army: a Numerical Survey."
     Neill Macaulay.
     Hispanic American Historical Review, vol. 58, no. 2 (May
     1978), p. 284-95.
     A detailed analysis of the size and composition of the
     guerrilla rebel army during the revolutionary war against
     Fulgencio Batista. Macaulay argues convincingly that the
     insurgent force was larger than generally supposed and made
     up of more peasants than previously believed.

621. "The Development of the Cuban Army."
     Emilio T. González.
     Military Review, vol. 61, no. 4 (April 1981), p. 56-64.
     A general overview of the development of the Cuban armed
     forces, from the early days of the guerrilla columns to the
     organization of the Revolutionary Armed Forces (FAR).
     Particular treatment is given to the performance of Cuban
     armed forces in Angola and Ethiopa.

622. "The Development of the Cuban Military as a Socio-Political
     Elite, 1763-83."
     Allan J. Kuethe.

Hispanic American Historical Review, vol. 61, no. 4 (Nov. 1981), p. 695-704.
A study of military reforms during the Bourbon period.

623. El ejército nacional de la república neocolonial, 1899-1933.
Federico Chang.
Havana: Editorial Ciencias Sociales, 1981. 288p.
One of the most thorough studies of the Cuban armed forces during the early republic. The emphasis of the work falls on the institutional character of the military and its role in national politics.

624. "El ejército oligárquico en la política neocolonial cubana, 1925-1952."
Maricela Mateo.
Santiago, no. 22 (June 1976), p. 87-120.
Surveys the role of the army in Cuban politics from the decisive Machado years up to the Batista coup of 1952. Its focus is on the relations between the army and the Autentico governments of 1933-1934 and 1944-1952.

625. "Institutionalization and Civil-Military Relations in Cuba."
Jorge I. Domínguez.
Cuban Studies/Estudios Cubanos, vol. 6, no. 1 (Jan. 1976), p. 39-65.
A detailed and thoughtful analysis of the role of the armed forces and the institutionalization of the revolution. The essay examines the changes in the socio-economic and political missions of the military in this process and the nature of the civil-military relationship in socialist Cuba.

626. Militarismo, anti-militarismo, seudo-militarismo.
Cuba.   Consejo Corporativo de Educación, Sanidad y Beneficencia.
Havana: Instituto Cívico-Militar, 1939. 127p.
A collection of speeches and published correspondence by Generals Fulgencio Batista and Arístides Sosa de Quesada during the late 1930s. The material is a defense of military values and exaltation of martial virtues during years when army authority over all of Cuba was rapidly expanding.

627. El militarismo in Cuba.
Jorge Mañach.
Havana: Seoane, Fernández y Cía., 1939. 18p.
This collection of essays is generally critical of the expanding role of the Cuban army in national life during the late 1930s.

628. "The Military and the Dynamics of the Cuban Revolutionary Process."
M.L. Vellinga.
Comparative Politics, vol. 8, no. 2 (Jan. 1976), p. 245-71.
A critical study of the rise of the military as an instrument of mobilization and the tendency towards adopting military organizational models for other sectors of the society. The essay looks at the development of the new military, professionalism, and the relationship between the armed forces and the state.

629. "Military Origins of the Cuban Revolution."
Irving L. Horowitz.
Armed Forces and Society, vol. 1, no. 4 (Summer 1975), p. 402-418.
Examines various ideological models adopted in Cuba after 1959. The author suggests that the importance of the armed forces in Cuba after 1959 originated with the guerrilla war, and that as difficulties mounted, it was a natural response of the leadership to rely on military structures.

630. "Racial and Ethnic Relations in the Cuban Armed Forces: A Non-Topic."
Jorge I. Domínguez.
Armed Forces and Society, vol. 2, no. 2 (Feb. 1976), p. 273-90.
Provides an attempt to examine an important subject from meager and often incomplete research materials. The author contends that the subject is a "non-topic" due to the paucity of information. Among the tentative conclusions advanced are that the military has no formal racial policy and that the assumption that equality of opportunity will lead to equality in achievements has not been disregarded.

631. "The Rise and Fall of the Cuban Rural Guard, 1898-1912."
Allan R. Millett.
The Americas, vol. 29, no. 2 (Oct. 1972), p. 191-213.
Surveys the development by the U.S. of the Cuban rural guard in the course of the first and second interventions (1895-1902 and 1906-1909). The essay also documents the emergence of the rural guard as a political factor in the Liberal administration of José Miguel Gómez (1909-1912).

Foreign Relations

A. General

632. "Cuba and the Third World: the Sixth Nonaligned Nations
     Conference."
     H. Michael Erisman.
     Caribbean Review, vol. 9, no. 1 (Winter 1980), p. 21-25.
     Analyzes the Cuban role in the 1979 meeting of the
     Nonaligned Nations Conference in Havana.

633. "Cuban Foreign Policy."
     Jorge I. Domínguez.
     Foreign Affairs, vol. 57, no. 1 (Autumn 1978), p. 83-108.
     A general survey of Cuban foreign policy during the 1960s
     and 1970s. The essay traces the shifts in the Cuba's
     international position as expressed principally in its
     relations with the Soviet Union, Africa, and Latin America.

634. Cuba in the World.
     Edited by Cole Blasier and Carmelo Mesa-Lago.
     Pittsburgh: University of Pittsburgh Press, 1979.
     343p. bibliog.
     This collection of essays deals with various aspects of
     Cuban foreign policy, including relations with the U.S.,
     the Soviet Union, Latin America, and theoretical
     considerations.

635. The Cuban Threat.
     Carla Anne Robbins.
     New York: McGraw Hill Book Company, 1983. 351p.
     Cuban foreign policy generally, and the U.S. response to
     Cuban policy specifically, serve as the principal points of
     discussion in this work. Using an historical approach, the
     author examines the development of Cuban policies from the

early Eisenhower-Kennedy years up to the Reagan period.
She argues that North American authorities have
misunderstood and over-reacted to the Cuban foreign policy
initiatives.

636. Cuba's International Relations: the Anatomy of a
     Nationalistic Foreign Policy.
     H. Michael Erisman.
     Boulder, Colorado: Westview Press, 1985. 203p.
     The study stresses the nationalist sources of Cuban foreign
     policy after 1959. The author argues that the nationalist
     aspects of Cuban globalism have been obscured by charges
     that Havana functions as a surrogate of the Soviet Union.

637. "Cuba's Israel Policy: the Shift to the Soviet Line."
     Yoram Shapiro and Edy Kaufman.
     Cuba Studies/Estudios Cubanos, vol. 8, no. 1 (Jan. 1978),
     p. 22-23.
     Surveys Cuban-Israeli relations from 1959 to the mid-1970s.
     The authors trace developments within both the context of
     Third World politics and Soviet policies.

638. Polftica internacional de la revolución cubana.
     Havana: Editora Política, 1966. 2 vols. maps.
     A compilation of the major foreign policy speeches, essays,
     and lectures from the principal leaders of the Cuban
     revolution.

639. Proyección internacional de la revolución cubana.
     Compiled by Juan J. Soto Valdespino.
     Havana: Editorial de Ciencias Sociales, 1975.   432p.
     A collection of the principal foreign policy statements of
     the Cuban revolution.

B. Latin America

640. "Castro: Economic Effects on Latin America."
     Alfonso González.
     Journal of Inter-American Studies, vol. 11, no. 2 (April
     1969), p. 286-309.
     An assessment of the positive and negative aspects of the
     Cuban revolution in Latin America. Among the adverse
     consequences suggested by the author are increased military
     spending in Latin America, and instability and the threat
     of nationalization. The positive aspects include increased
     U.S. foreign aid, the adoption of reform programs, and the
     expansion of the U.S. market for Latin American exports.

641. Castroism and Communism in Latin America, 1959-1976.
     William E. Ratliff.

Stanford,   California: Hoover   Institution   on   War,
Revolution, and Peace, 1976. 240p.
An account of Cuban policy in Latin America. The study
analyzes the inter-action of Soviet and Chinese communism
as it affects the approaches of the Cuban revolution.
Special attention is paid to Havana's role in supporting
guerrilla movements in Latin America.

642. "Cuba and the Commonwealth Caribbean."
Anthony P. Maingot.
Caribbean Review, vol. 9, no. 1 (Winter 1980), p. 7-10,
44-49.
This thoughtful essay details the history of diplomatic
relations between Cuba and the English-speaking West
Indies, with particular emphasis on Jamaica, Grenada, and
Trinidad.

643. "Cuba and the Crisis in Central America."
Juan Valdés Paz.
Contemporary Marxism, no. 10 (1985), p. 38-67.
Discusses Cuban policy towards Central America vis-a vis
U.S. policy. The essay is representative of Cuban thinking
on Central American political tensions, written by the head
of the Latin American section of the Center for the Study
of America in Havana.

644. "Cuba and Nicaragua: From the Somozas to the Sandinistas."
William M. LeoGrande.
Caribbean Review, vol. 9, no. 1 (Winter 1980), p. 11-14.
A survey of relations between Havana and Managua between
1959 and 1979. The essay deals with Somoza's opposition to
the Cuban revolution, Cuban support of the anti-Somoza
opposition,   and   the   collaboration   between   the   new
Sandinista government and Cuba.

645. "Cuba and Panama."
Steve C. Rapp.
Caribbean Review, vol. 9, no. 1 (Winter 1980), p. 15-20.
Provides a brief history of the relations between Cuba and
Panama since 1959. The emphasis of the article is on the
period of the Torrijos regime in Panama.

646. Cuban Foreign Policy and Chilean Politics.
Miles D. Wolpin.
Lexington, Massachusetts: D.C. Heath and Company, 1972.
414p. bibliog.
A valuable study of the impact of both the Cuban revolution
and the United States policy on Chile for the period
between 1959 and 1970. The author documents his contention
that external forces exercised a great influence on the
course of Chilean domestic policies.

647. "Cuba's Relations with Caribbean and Central American Countries."
Jorge I. Domínguez.
Cuban Studies/Estudios Cubanos, vol. 13, no. 2 (Summer 1983), p. 79-112.
A thorough analysis of Cuban foreign relations with states in the Caribbean region between 1979 and 1981. The key topics of discussion include the objectives, characteristics, and phases of Cuban policy.

648. The Cuban Revolution and Latin America.
Boris Goldenberg.
New York: Praeger, 1965. 376p. bibliog.
In this two part study of Cuba, the first section deals with the general history of twentieth century Cuba through the revolution. The second section examines the development of the early years of the revolution and its impact, real and potential, on Latin America.

649. México y la revolución cubana.
Olga Pellicer de Brody.
México: El Colegio de México, 1972, 131p. bibliog.
A study of Mexico's foreign policy toward the Cuban revolution. The volume is not confined to an examination of Cuba-Mexico relations but deals with the larger consideration of how Mexico's policy towards Cuba affected its relations with other countries, particularly the U.S.

650. Misión en La Habana.
Gerardo Falconí R.
Quito: Casa de la Cultura Ecuatoriana, 1968. 217p.
An examination of Cuba-Ecuador relations told in the first person by Ecuador's ambassador to Cuba.

651. The New Cuban Presence in the Caribbean.
Edited by Barry Levine.
Boulder, Colorado: Westview Press, 1983. 247p.
The essays deal with geo-political and cultural competition in the Caribbean and Cuban relations with the U.S., the Commonwealth Caribbean, Nicaragua, Panama, Mexico, and Venezuela. Other themes include Cuba and the Latin American Communist Parties, Cuba and Africa, Cuba and the Third World, Cuba and the Soviet Union.

652. "On the Limits of the New Cuban Presence in the Caribbean."
Gordon K. Lewis.
Caribbean Review, vol. 9, no. 1 (Winter 1980), p. 33-35.
The author argues that strong traditions of multi-party democracy, free speech, and the legal system in the English-speaking Caribbean impose severe limits on the attraction of Cuba as a model for socio-economic change.

C. Africa

653. "Cuba and Africa: the Politics of the Liberation
     Struggle."
     Gordon Adams and Michael Locker.
     Cuba Review, vol. 8, nos. 3-4 (Oct. 1978), p. 3-9.
     Examines Cuba's policy towards Africa against the wider
     setting of African developments and U.S.-Africa policy.

654. "Cuban Foreign Policy in the Horn of Africa."
     Nelson P. Valdés.
     Cuban Studies/Estudios Cubanos, vol. 10, no. 1 (Jan. 1980),
     p. 49-80.
     A survey of Cuban relations with Somalia and Ethiopia, with
     particular reference to Eritrea.

655. "The Cuban Military in Africa and the Middle East: From
     Algeria to Angola."
     William J. Durch.
     Studies in Comparative Communism,   vol.   1,   nos. 1-2
     (Spring/Summer 1978), p. 34-74.
     Examines the Cuban military presence in Africa, Syria, and
     Iraq between 1959 and 1970. The essay assesses Cuba's
     African policy within a larger context of Cuban-Soviet
     relations. It offers a concise and detailed chronology of
     the deployment of Cuban military forces in the region.

656. "The Cuban Operation in Angola: Costs and Benefits for the
     Armed Forces."
     Jorge I. Domínguez.
     Cuban Studies/Estudios Cubanos, vol. 8, no. 1 (Jan. 1978),
     p. 10-20.
     Analyzes the effects of Cuban participation in the Angolan
     civil war.   The essay examines the institutional
     consequences of overseas operations and concludes that
     Cuban versatility was enhanced, but at a cost of consensus
     at the policy levels of government.

657. "Cubans in Africa."
     Aaron Segal.
     Caribbean Review, vol. 7, no. 3 (Summer 1978), p. 4-10.
     A survey of Cuban activity in Angola and Ethiopia. The
     essay examines the impact of the Cuban military presence,
     both in Africa and at home.

658. "Economic Aspects of Cuban Involvement in Africa."
     Sergio Roca.
     Cuban Studies/Estudios Cubanos, vol. 10, no. 2 (July 1980),
     p. 55-90.
     A detailed economic cost-benefit analysis of Cuban
     involvement in Africa, particularly in Angola and Ethiopia,

during the 1970s.   The essay examines the potential
benefits and liabilities attending Cuba's African policies.

659. "Political and Military Limitations and Consequences of
     Cuban Policies in Africa."
     Jorge I. Domínguez.
     Cuban Studies/Estudios Cubanos, vol. 10, no. 2 (July 1980),
     p. 1-35.
     This article provides an analysis of the political and
     economic costs of Cuban military involvement in Africa.
     The essay also examines the Cuban role as a source of
     stability and restraint in the internal affairs of its
     African allies.

660. "The Soviet-Cuban Intervention in Angola, 1975."
     Jiri Valenta.
     Studies in Comparative Communism, vol. 11, nos. 1-2
     (Spring/Summer 1978), p. 3-33.
     Analyzes in detail the role of the Cuban military presence
     in Angola.   The essay sets Cuban activities within a larger
     context of Soviet policy on the one hand and U.S., Chinese,
     and South African activities on the other.

D.   Soviet Union

661. Castro, the Kremlin, and Communism in Latin America.
     D. Bruce Jackson.
     Baltimore: The Johns Hopkins University Press, 1969.
     163p.
     A specialized study of Cuban-Soviet relations within the
     larger context of the socialist bloc.   The focus of the
     book is on the period between 1964 and 1967, a time
     international crisis and rising tension among socialist
     countries.

662. "Cuban-Soviet Relations and Cuban Policy in Africa."
     William M. LeoGrande.
     Cuban Studies/Estudios Cubanos, vol. 10, no. 1 (Jan. 1980),
     p. 1-37.
     A study of Cuban policy in Africa between 1959 and 1979
     within the larger framework of Cuban-Soviet relations.
     Particular attention is paid to the Cuban presence in
     Angola and Ethiopia.

663. "The Cuban-U.S.-Soviet Triangle, Changing Angles."
     Cole Blasier.
     Cuban Studies/Estudios Cubanos, vol. 8, no. 1 (Jan. 1978),
     p. 1-9.
     A survey of the inter-action of the U.S.S.R., the U.S., and
     Cuba during the 1960s and 1970s.   The focus is on relations

between Cuba and the United States during the Carter
administration.

664. Las relaciones cubano-soviéticos, 1959-1968.
     Blanca Torres Ramírez.
     México: Colegio de México, 1971. 142p. bibliog.
     This chronological study of Cuban-Soviet relations deals
     successively in four chapters with the early period
     (1959-1960), the integration of Cuba into the socialist
     bloc (1960-1962), the period of early conflict (1963-1965),
     and the years of increasing tension (1966-1968).

665. "Soviet Submarine Visits to Cuba."
     Barry M. Blechman and Stephanie E. Levison.
     United States Naval Institute Proceedings, vol. 101, no. 9
     (Sept. 1975), p. 30-39.
     Examines the construction of a submarine facility in
     Cienfuegos.   The authors assess the politico-military
     implications of the Soviet naval presence in Caribbean
     waters.

666. The Soviet Union and Cuba: Interests and Influence.
     W. Raymond Duncan.
     New York: Praeger, 1985. 220p. bibliog.
     This comprehensive analysis of Cuban-Soviet relations
     examines chronologically the development of diplomatic
     relations and policy options from the early phases of the
     Cuban revolution to the 1970s.

667. The USSR and the Cuban Revolution: Soviet Ideological and
     Strategical Perspectives, 1959-1977.
     Jacques Levesque. Translated from the French by Deanna
     Drendel Leboeuf.
     New York: Praeger, 1978. 215p. bibliog.
     A systematic analysis of Cuban-Soviet relations, from the
     triumph of the revolution.   This study emphasizes the
     Soviet view of its relations with Cuba, specifically the
     Soviet Union's ideological and strategic perception of the
     Cuban revolution.

E. United States

668. "Análisis y consecuencias de la intervención norteamericana
     en los asuntos interiores de Cuba."
     Emilio Roig de Leuchsenring.
     Cuba Contemporánea, vol. 32,   no.   126   (June   1923),
     p. 138-53.
     A critical study of U.S. intervention in Cuba under the
     Platt Amendment.   Author argues that the basis of U.S.
     intervention in Cuban internal affairs was based not on law

but force.   Examined also are the destabilizing
consequences which were attributed to North American
intermeddling in Cuban political affairs.

669. The Bay of Pigs.
Haynes B. Johnson.
New York: Dell Publishing Co., 1964.   352p.   bibliog.
A journalistic account of the abortive 1961 invasion based
on published materials, interviews, and accounts provided by
the Cuban members of the U.S.-organized brigade.

670. Bay of Pigs: the Untold Story.
Peter Wyden.
New York: Simon and Schuster, 1979.   352p.
Provides a well-written account of the abortive invasion of
Cuba in 1961.   The work is based in part on interviews with
some key participants both in Cuba and the United States
and on new documentary materials obtained through the
Freedom of Information Act.

671. Cuba and the United States: Long Range Perspectives.
Edited by John Plank.
Washington, D.C.:   The Brookings Institution, 1967.   265p.
bibliog.
Ten essays exploring various aspects of Cuba-U.S.
relations.   Among the themes discussed are historical
antecedents, economic factors, U.S. response to the Cuban
revolution, bilateral relations in the Hemispheric context,
the Cold War, and military-strategic considerations.

672. Cuba and the United States, 1900-1935.
Russell H. Fitzgibbon.
New York: Russell and Russell, 1964.   311p.   map.
bibliog.
This reprint of the 1935 edition provides a historical
survey of relations between Cuba and the United States.
The study also surveys Cuban domestic political
developments during the first third of the century.

673. "Cuba and the U.S.:   On the Possibilities of
Rapproachment."
Max Azicri.
Caribbean Review, vol. 9, no. 1 (Winter 1980), p. 26-29,
50-52.
This thoughtful article was written at a time when the
United States, under the Carter administration, had made
gestures of reconciliation toward Cuba.

674. Cuba and the U.S.:   the Tangled Relationship.
Robert D. Crassweller.
New York: Foreign Policy Association, 1976.   63p.

bibliog.
Surveys U.S.-Cuban relations from the early days of the
Cuban revolution to the late 1960s. The study sets Cuba's
relations with the U.S. in a larger international context,
exploring the impact of socialist-bloc powers on
Hemispheric developments.

675. Cuba, Castro, and the United States.
Philip W. Bonsal.
Pittsburgh: University of Pittsburgh Press, 1971. 318p.
A three-part account of the deterioration, and eventually
the break, in U.S.-Cuban relations between 1958 and 1961 by
the last U.S. ambassador to Cuba. The first part examines
the details of relations between both countries up to the
end of diplomatic ties in January 1961. Part two discusses
the years 1958-1961 against a larger historical background
in an effort to trace the origins of the revolution. The
last section places U.S.-Cuba relations in a Hemispheric
setting and discusses the influence of Cuba in Latin
America.

676. Cuba y los Estados Unidos, 1805-1898.
Emilio Roig de Leuchsenring.
Havana: Sociedad Cubana de Estudios Históricos e
Internacionales, 1949. 279p. bibliog.
A critical survey of United States policy in the nineteenth
century, culminating in the North American intervention of
1898. The study is a synthesis of nearly thirty years of
research and writing by one of Cuba's most eminent
revisionist historians.

677. "Cuban-American Relations Concerning the Isle of Pines."
Janet Delavan Frost.
Hispanic American Historical Review, vol. 11, no. 3 (Aug.
1931), p. 336-50.
A study of U.S.-Cuban negotiation over the final status of
the Isle of Pines. Cuban authorities insisted that the
island properly belonged under Cuban jurisdiction; the
United States argued that the Isle of Pines was simply
another island in the Caribbean. The Cuban view prevailed
in the Hay-Quesada Treaty of 1925.

678. The Cuban Missile Crisis: International Crises and the
Role of Law.
Abram Chayes.
New York: Oxford University Press, 1974. 154p.
This study by a noted international lawyer examines the
1962 Cuban missile crisis from a legal viewpoint. The
author argues persuasively that U.S. policy was shaped
largely by considerations of law, both as a constraint on
North American action and as a source of legitimacy for

policy.

679. The Cuban Policy of the United States.
Lester P. Langley.
New York: John Wiley and Sons, 1968. 203p. bibliog.
Surveys United States policy toward Cuba from the early
nineteenth century to the early years of the revolution.
The emphasis is on the study of U.S. policy formulation.

680. Dagger in the Heart. American Policy Failures in Cuba.
Mario Lazo.
New York: Twin Circle Publishing Company, 1968. 447p.
An acrimonious attack against U.S. policy and policy
officials by a U.S.-born and Cuba-raised attorney. The
author's principal contention is that the United States
misjudged Castro and once aware of his politics failed to
act decisively to overthrow him.

681. "The Embargo of Cuba: An Economic Appraisal."
Donald Losman.
Caribbean Studies, vol. 14, no. 3 (Oct. 1974), p. 95-119.
A detailed examination of the economic dislocation and
adjustments Cuba experienced as a result of the United
States trade embargo.

682. La enmienda Platt.
Luís Machado y Ortega.
Havana: Imprenta "El Siglo XX," 1922. 132p.
A critical analysis of the origins, interpretation, and
application of the Platt Amendment.

683. Essence of Decision. Exploring the Cuban Missile Crisis.
Graham T. Allison.
Boston: Little, Brown, and Company, 1971. 338p.
An attempt to apply bureaucratic and political theory to
developments surrounding the missile crisis of 1962. The
author uses three analytical models--rational factor,
organizational process, and government politics--as a means
by which to assess the factors that affected the
assumptions and categories of decision-making.

684. The Fish Is Red: the Story of the Secret War Against Castro.
Warren Hinckle and William W. Turner.
New York: Harper and Row, 1981. bibliog.
An account of U.S. covert operations against Cuba during
the 1960s and 1970s. The study details U.S. efforts to
sabotage Cuban industry, cripple its agricultural
production, and assassinate the principal leaders of the
revolution, including Fidel Castro.

685. The Fourth Floor; an Account of the Castro Communist
Revolution.

Earl E. T. Smith.
New York: Random House, 1962. 242p.
A personal memoir of the U.S.-Cuban relations during the
tumultuous years between 1957 and 1959 by the former U.S.
ambassador in Havana. The author is critical of the State
Department, arguing that Washington was responsible for the
triumph of the revolution.

686. "Geographic Factors in the Relations of the United States
     and Cuba."
     D.S. Whittlesey.
     The Geographical Review, vol. 12, no. 2 (April 1922), p.
     241-56.
     Examines the role of geography as a determining factor in
     U.S.-Cuban political relations.

687. Give Us This Day.
     Howard Hunt.
     New Rochelle, New York: Arlington House, 1973. 235p.
     A first-person account by one of the key CIA organizers of
     the preparation and performance of the ill-fated Bay of
     Pigs invasion.

688. Historia de Cuba en sus relaciones con los Estados Unidos
     y España.
     Herminio Portell Vilá.
     Havana: Jesús Montero, 1938-1941. 4 vols. bibliog.
     Perhaps the most comprehensive analysis of U.S.-Cuban
     relations by one of the premier revisionist historians of
     Cuba. The study spans the years between the eighteenth
     century and the early 1900s. Based on prodigious research,
     both in Cuba and the United States, the work is
     representative of the best of Cuban scholarship. It is one
     of the standard studies and a necessary reference work to
     consult for reading and research on U.S.-Cuban relations.

689. Historia de la enmienda Platt.
     Emilio Roig de Leuchsenring.
     Havana: Oficina del Historiador de la Ciudad, 1961. 2nd
     ed. 2 vols.
     A critical and detailed examination of United States-Cuba
     relations under the aegis of the Platt Amendment. The
     study analyzes the origins, evolution, and application of
     various interpretations of the amendment up to its
     abrogation in 1934.

690. A History of Cuba and its Relations With the United States.
     Philip S. Foner.
     New York: International Publishers, 2 vols. 1962-1965.
     Together both volumes cover the period between 1492 and
     1868. The first volume (1492-1845) tends to concentrate

more on Cuban internal developments, while the second
volume (1845-1868) discusses Cuban relations with the U.S.

691. On Negotiating with Cuba.
     Roger W. Fontaine.
     Washington, D.C.: American Enterprise Institute for Public
     Policy Research, 1975. 99p. bibliog.
     On the assumption that at some future date the United
     States and Cuba will begin to negotiate a normalization of
     diplomatic relations, this work attempts to set in relief
     the principal issues before both countries. The study
     examines the history of U.S.-Cuban relations, the problems
     inherent in big-power small-power relationships, and the
     advantages to the U.S. of normal relations with Cuba.

692. The Politics of Hostility: Castro's Revolution and U.S.
     Policy.
     Lynn Darrell Bender.
     Hato Rey, Puerto Rico: Inter-American University Press,
     1975. 168p. bibliog.
     Surveys relations between the United States and
     revolutionary Cuba. Particular attention is paid to U.S.
     policy between 1959 and 1974 and the effect of Cuban-Soviet
     relations on U.S. policy.

693. El presidente Polk y Cuba.
     Emeterio S. Santovenia.
     Havana: Imprenta "El Siglo XX," 1936. 182p.
     Presents a detailed account of U.S.-Cuban policy under the
     Polk administration, paying particular attention to North
     American efforts to acquire the island in 1848.

694. "Las relaciones económicas entre Cuba y los Estados
     Unidos."
     Luis Marino Pérez.
     Cuba Contemporánea, vol. 28, no. 112 (April 1922),
     p. 264-70.
     Discusses the economic determinants of U.S.-Cuban
     relations. The essay examines U.S. investments, loans to
     the government, commerce, and North American industries.

695. Response to Revolution. The United States and the Cuban
     Revolution, 1959-1961.
     Richard E. Welch, Jr.
     Chapel Hill, North Carolina: University of North Carolina
     Press, 1985. 243p. bibliog.
     A four-part discussion of U.S.-Cuban relations during the
     first two critical years of the revolution. The first part
     treats the background to revolution in Cuba. Part two
     examines Eisenhower-Kennedy diplomacy. Part three explores
     North American public opinion and part four examines

U.S.-Cuban relations in the larger context of the Cold War.

696. Roosevelt and Batista: Good Neighbor Diplomacy in Cuba, 1933-1945.
Irwin F. Gellman.
Albuquerque, New Mexico: University of New Mexico Press, 1973. 303p. bibliog.
An account of U.S.-Cuban relations during the period of the "good neighbor" policy. The work examines the ways in which U.S. policy took form during these years, concluding that the exercise of North American hegemony, although modified, remained unaffected by U.S. policy changes.

697. "The Sanctity of Property.   American Responses to Cuban Expropriations, 1959-19843."
Susan Fernández.
Cuban Studies/Estudios Cubanos, vol. 14, no. 2 (Summer 1984), p. 21-34.
Outlines the response of the United States to the expropriation of North American property in Cuba after 1959.   The article examines the way in which tax legislation provided relief to expropriated property owners. Attention is also given to the variety of means through which the United States has sought to settle the compensation claims.

698. The United States and Cuba.
Harry F. Guggenheim.
Freeport, New York: Books for Libraries Press, 1969. 268p. bibliog.
This reprint of the 1934 edition provides both a historical narrative and a personal memoir of U.S.-Cuban relations by a former ambassador to Cuba.   Guggenheim was in Havana during the troubled early 1930s and concluded that the Platt Amendment had contributed to creating Cuban difficulties.   The book is an appeal for a new policy approach to Cuba.

699. The United States and Cuba: Business and Diplomacy, 1917-1960.
Robert Freeman Smith.
New Haven, Connecticut: College and University Press, 1960. 256p. bibliog.
A well-researched and clearly-written chronicle of U.S.-Cuban relations as determined by the North American economic stake on the island. Some of the sections have been surpassed by more recent monographic studies, but overall it stands as one of the better discussions of relations between Cuba and the United States.

700. The United States and Cuba: Hegemony and Dependent Development, 1880-1934.

Jules Robert Benjamin.
Pittsburgh: University of Pittsburgh Press, 1977. 266p.
bibliog.
This detailed examination of the sources of United States
hegemony in Cuba present a balanced discussion of politics,
diplomacy, and economic development.

701. "U.S. Business Interests in Cuba and the Rise of Castro."
Leland L. Johnson.
World Politics, vol. 17, no. 3 (April 1965), p. 440-59.
Examines the relationship between the massive U.S.
investment in Cuba and the course of political relations
between Havana and Washington during the early 1960s,
particularly its part in contributing to the radicalization
of the revolution.

702. The United States, Cuba, and Castro.
William Appleman Williams.
New York: Monthly Review Press, 1962. 179p.
A historical survey of U.S.-Cuban relations leading up to
the diplomatic rupture in 1961. This sympathetic account
of Cuban efforts at self-determination advances a critique
of U.S. policy in its relations with Cuba generally and
towards the revolution in particular.

703. "U.S. Cuban Policy under the Nixon Administration: Subtle
Modifications."
Lynn Darrell Bender.
Revista/Review Interamericana, vol. 2, no. 3 (Autumn 1972),
p. 330-41.
Analyzes U.S. policy during the late 1960s and early 1970s
in which the author argues that Washington adapted a
"semi-conciliatory posture" toward Cuba.

704. "The U.S. Imperial State in Cuba, 1952-1958: Policymaking
and Capitalist Interests."
Morris H. Morley.
Journal of Latin America Studies, vol. 14, no. 1 (May
1982), p. 143-70.
A detailed analysis of U.S. hegemony in Cuba during the
last Fulgencio Batista period. The essay examines the
relationship between North American capital and the Batista
government and the principal instruments of U.S. policy,
specifically the defense department and the executive
branch.

705. The War that Never Was: An Insider's Account of CIA Covert
Operations Against Cuba.
Bradley Earl Ayers.
Indianapolis, Indiana: Bobbs-Merrill, 1976. 235p.

A first-person account of U.S., covert operations against Cuba in the aftermath of the Bay of Pigs.

Constitution, Law, and Judicial Systems

706. Comentarios a la constitución socialista.
Fernando Alvarez Tabío.
Havana: Editorial de Ciencias Sociales, 1981. 434p.
This analysis of socialist constitutionality in Cuba
establishes the central assumption that the island's
transition to Marxist-Leninist legality was consistent with
Cuba's historico-cultural traditions.

707. Como se hizo la constitución de Cuba.
Antonio Bravo y Correoso.
Havana: Imprenta de Rambla, Bouza y Cía., 1928. 113p.
An informative first-person account by a member of the
Constituent Assembly that drafted the 1901 constitution.
The work provides important insights into the discussions
and debates preliminary to the ratification of the first
republican constitution.

708. Compilación ordenada y completa de la legislación cubana.
Edited by Milo Andrián Borges and M. Sánchez Roca.
Havana: Editorial Lex, 1952-1960. 4 vols.
Presents a compilation of legislation from the late
nineteenth century through the end of 1958. The volumes
are organized in the following order: I: 1889-1936; II:
1937-1950; III: Index; IV: 1951-1958.

709. La constitución a la luz de la doctrina magistral y de la
jurisprudencia.
Juan José Exposito Casasús.
Havana: Cultural, S.A., 1946. 929p. bibliog.
This comprehensive study of the constitution of 1940
contains an extensive commentary on the debates of the
constituent assembly, assesses the juridical antecedents of
key portions of the constitution, and provides commentary

outlining the impact of the new law of the land.

710. Constitución cubana.
Nicanor Trelles.
Regla, Cuba: Imprenta M. Gómez, 1900. 121p.
Discusses the United States constitution and its potential relevance to the conditions in Cuba. The volume also contains texts of the constitutions of the insurgent provisional governments of 1869, 1895, and 1897.

711. Constitución de Cuba.
Andrés M. Lazcano y Mazón.
Havana: Cultural, S.A., 1941. 3 vols.
Provides a compilation of the transcripts of the key debates and discussions of the constituent assembly framing the 1940 constitution. It is an indispensable work for an understanding of the juridical, philosophical, and ideological currents of the constituent assembly.

712. Constitución de la república de Cuba.
José Clemente Vivanco.
Havana: n.p., 1902. 160p.
A detailed commentary on the constitution of 1901 by a leading Cuban jurist.

713. Constituciones cubanas, desde 1812 hasta nuestros días.
Compiled by Leonel Antonio de la Cuesta.
New York: Ediciones Exilio, 1974. 539p. bibliog.
This valuable compilation of Cuban constitutions starts with the Spanish constitution of 1812 and ends with the fundamental laws of the Cuban revolution. The volume also includes texts of the provisional constitutions of the insurgent republics during the course of the nineteenth century struggles for independence. Included, too, are the amendments and legislative revisions made for the constitutions of 1901 and 1940. In addition, the volume contains an extensive annotated bibliography of Cuban constitutional law.

714. Las constituciones de Cuba.
Edited by Andrés M. Lazcano y Mazon.
Madrid: Ediciones Cultura Hispanica, 1952.   1066p. bibliog.
A compilation of all the constitutions of Cuba accompanied by extensive commentary dealing with constitutional law and history.

715. "The Cuban Socialist Constitution: Its Originality and Role in Institutionalization."
Leonel Antonio de la Cuesta.
Cuban Studies/Estudios Cubanos, vol. 6, no. 2 (July 1976),

p. 15-30.
Discusses the 1975 socialist constitution. The essay examines the origins of the document and the role of the new constitution in the larger process of institutionalization.

716. Derecho constitucional.
Julio Fernández Bulte, Gilberto Muñoz, Miguel A. D'Estefano, and Mercedes Rodríguez.
Havana: Universidad de La Habana, n.d. 684p.
Written by four faculty members of the University of Havana Law School, this work reviews the sources and origins of socialist constitutionality, beginning with the 1812 constitution and continuing through the constitutions of the provisional governments of the nineteenth century and the republic in the twentieth century.

717. Derecho constitucional.
Edited by Juan Clemente Zamora y Lopez.
Havana: Imprenta "El Siglo XX," 1925. 311p.
A collection of select documents for the study of the constitutional history of Cuba.

718. Derecho de familia.
Daniel A. Peral Collado.
Havana: Ministerio de Educación Superior, 1980. 237p.
Presents a thorough analysis of the Cuban family code--the new law governing family relations. The study analyzes the principal difference between the old bourgeois family and the new Cuban family, centering on socio-economic issues. Topics of analysis include the evolution of family structures in Cuba, changes in matrimonial relations, differentiation of spouse obligations, parental responsibilities for children, and procedures for adoption and child support.

719. Los fundamentos históricos y filosóficos de la constitución de 1901.
Enrique Hernández Corujo.
Havana: Editorial Lex, 1953. 31p.
A brief discussion of the juridical antecedents and the philosophical inspiration of the 1901 constitution.

720. Historia constitucional de Cuba.
Enrique Hernández Corujo.
Havana: Compania Editoria de Libros y Folletos, 1960. 2 vols. bibliog.
This balanced and detailed survey of the constitutional history of Cuba. Covers the nineteenth and twentieth centuries, providing lucid interpretations and complete data.

721. Historia constitucional de Cuba.
Ramón Infiesta.
Havana: Editorial Selecta, 1942. 383p. bibliog.
This well-balanced constitutional history was designed
principally as an introduction to Cuban law for first-year
law students.

722. Historia del estado y el derecho en Cuba.
Julio A. Carreras.
Havana: Ministerio de Educación Superior, 1981.   559p.
An excellent study of the development of the state in Cuba
from the colonial regime to the revolution. The emphasis
of the work falls on the twentieth century and is divided
between pre- and post-revolutionary developments.

723. Jurisprudencia constitucional, 1903-1944.
Gustavo Ramírez Olivella.
Havana: Jesús Montero, 1944. 671p.
Analyzes in detail the cases and judicial reviews
determining the constitutionality of laws, statutes, and
presidential decrees.   The work deals with those cases
settled by the Cuban supreme court (Tribuno Supremo).

724. Jurisprudencia cubana.
Angel C. Betancourt y Miranda.
Havana: Imprenta de Rambla, Bouza y Cía., 1912-1929.   2
vols.
Presents a comprehensive discussion of the theory and
practice of jurisprudence in Cuba.   The topics examined
include criminal law, civil law, the administration of
justice, and the organization of the legal system.

725. Jurisprudencia electoral cubana.
Antonio Leal y González.
Havana: Editorial Selecta, 1941. 324p. bibliog.
Discusses the origins and scope of decrees and statutes
affecting Cuban electoral law between 1935 and 1940.

726. "Justice and Law in Latin America: a Cuban Example."
Francisco José Moreno.
Journal of Inter-American Studies and World Affairs,   vol.
12, no. 3 (July 1970), p. 367-78.
A   specialist   on   Cuban   jurisprudence   examines   the
revolutionary trials that occurred immediately after the
overthrow of Batista in 1959, and concludes that, in
keeping up with the Latin American traditions, the demand
for justice prevailed over the dictates of law.

727. La legalidad socialista, firme baluarte de los intereses
del pueblo.
Francisco Ordóñez Martínez.

Havana: Editorial de Ciencias Sociales, 1982.   218p.
A comprehensive introductory study of the socialist legal
system.

728. Leyes complementarias de la constitución.
Edited by Juan B. Moré y Benítez
Havana: Cultural, S.A., 1941. 191p.
A compilation of the articles of the constitution requiring
additional legislation in the form of by-laws.

729. "New Laws for a New Society."
Robert Cantor.
Cuba Resource Center Newsletter, vol. 3, Nos. 5-6 (Dec.
1973), p. 3-20.
Studies the development of the socialist legal system,
specifically the establishment of new laws and legal
institutions   with   particular   emphasis   on   criminal
jurisprudence.

730. Nociones sobre la constitución de 1940.
Marco Ortega y Díaz.
Havana: Editorial Lex, 1947. 422p.
A juridical treatise on the constitution of 1940.

731. Nuestro problema constitucional.
Enrique Gay Calbó.
Havana: Librería Nueva, 1936. 130p.
This review of changing conditions in Cuba during the
1930s, emphasizes those politico-juridical issues that
contributed to rendering the 1901 constitution obsolete.

732. La nueva constitución cubana y jurisprudencia, 1940-1944.
Edited by Emilio Menéndez Menéndez.
Havana: Jesús Montero, 1945. 286p.
This work includes the full text of the 1940 constitution as
well as the acts and judgments passed under its auspices
during the first four years of its promulgation.

733. Obligaciones y contratos civiles.
Daniel A. Peral Collado.
Havana: Ministerio de Educación Superior, n.d. 466p.
A detailed compendium examining the contractual obligations
and civil liabilities among state enterprises and private
individuals in socialist Cuba.

734. Servicio civil.
Edited by Máximo Alvarez Mena.
Havana: Seoane, Fernández y Cía., 1942. 5 vols.
A compilation of the laws, statutes, decrees, and
resolutions affecting civil service.

735. <u>Teoría general de la constitución cubana.</u>
Fernando Álvarez Tabío.
Havana: Jesús Montero, 1946. 357p. bibliog.
A well-written and well-conceived study of the theory of
constitutional law in Cuba. It is essential to any work
dealing with Cuban jurisprudence and constitutional
history.

736. <u>Textos de las constituciones de Cuba, 1812-1940.</u>
Compiled by Antonio Barreras y Martínez.
Havana: Editorial Minerva, 1940. 622p.
A compilation of the texts of all Cuban constitutions
between 1812 and 1940.

737. "The   Transformation   of   Justice   Under   Socialism:
Contrasting Experiences of China and Cuba."
James Brady.
<u>Insurgent Sociolgist</u>, vol. 11, no. 1 (Summer-Autumn 1982),
p. 5-24.
A comparative examination of radical criminology. The
essay addresses the issue of justice in socialism,
emphasizing the definitions of crime, social conflict, and
the development of institutions of justice. The work also
assesses the historical evolution of the crime and justice
policies against the larger transformation of politics,
economics, and the community.

Administration
and Local Government

738. Clave numérica de la división política del territorio
     nacional.
     Cuba. Ministerio de Hacienda. Dirección General de
     Estadística.
     Havana: Imprenta P. Fernández, 1950. 129p.
     The numerical codification of Cuban provinces,
     municipalities, and neighborhoods; providing the specific
     code assigned to each unit of administration.

739. Curso de historia de las instituciones locales de Cuba.
     Andrés Angulo y Pérez.
     Havana: Cultural, S.A., 1943. 178p.
     An historical survey tracing the origins of Cuban municipal
     administration to Rome and medieval Spain.

740. El gobierno municipal en nuestra constitución.
     Francisco Gómez Hernández.
     Havana: n.p., 1941. 52p.
     A legal treatise discussing the constitutional sanctions
     defining and protecting the authority of municipal
     government.

741. Historia de la división política-administrativa de la isla
     de Cuba, 1607-1976.
     Alfredo Mateo Domingo.
     Havana: Editorial Arte y Literatura, 1977. 135p. maps.
     bibliog.
     A historical survey of the development of the provincial
     and municipal administrative units of Cuba. Attention is
     given to the origins, development, and funding of local
     institutions. About half the volume is devoted to the
     territorial reorganization of the island enacted during the
     1970s.

742. Introducción a la historia de las instituciones locales de Cuba.
F. Carrera y Justiz.
Havana: Imprenta "La Moderna Poesía," 1905.   2 vols.
Outlines the development of local governmental and administrative units with particular emphasis on municipal structures. The author traces the origins of the Cuban municipalities to Rome and Spain examining the ways local traditions and needs modified the European forms.

743. Legislacion municipal de la república de Cuba.
Edited by Mariano Sánchez Roca.
Havana: Editorial Lex, 1947. 684p.
A compilation of all legislative measures, constitutional clauses, laws, and legal dispositions affecting the government and administration of municipalities.

744. Los municipios cubanos a través de la jurisprudencia.
Edited by Augusto Venegas Muiña.
Havana: Jesús Montero, 1941. 2 vols.
A compilation of laws, decrees, and statutes affecting the governance of the municipalities in Cuba.

745. El régimen provincial.
Edited and compiled by Nicolás Duarte Cajides.
Havana: Impresora Mundial, S.A., 1959.   843p.
A compilation of all relevant laws, charters, constitutional clauses, and legislation affecting provincial government and administration.

746. Temas municipales.
Andrés Angulo y Pérez.
Havana: Imprenta Cuba Intelectual, 1936. 148p.
A collection of essays dealing with a variety of urban themes, including municipal administration, municipal law, urban reform, and the development of urban services.

Statistics

747. Anuario estadístico de la república de Cuba.
Cuba. Secretaría of Hacienda. Sección de Estadística.
Havana, 1914-1961.
An annual compilation of general statistics produced by the
Cuban government based on data provided by executive
departments. This series was suspended early in the
revolution.

748. "Availability and Reliability of Statistics in Socialist
Cuba."
Carmelo Mesa-Lago.
Latin American Research Review, vol. 4, no. 2 (Spring
1969), p. 53-91 and vol. 4, no. 3 (Summer 1969), p. 47-81.
Examines in detail the use and misuse of statistical data
in Cuba after the revolution.

749. Cuadro estadístico de la siempre fiel isla de Cuba.
Correspondiente el año de 1846.
Cuba. Comisión de Estadística.
Havana: Imprenta del Gobierno y Capitanía General, 1847.
44p.
Presents a detailed statistical survey of the island in the
mid-nineteenth century, dealing principally with the
economic aspects of the colony, including agriculture,
commerce, and industry in each of the island's six
provinces, thereby providing important information on local
developments.

750. Cuba: a Handbook of Historical Statistics.
Compiled by Susan Schroeder.
Boston: G.K. Hall and Company, 1982. 589p.
Easily the most comprehensive statistical compilation
available in English. The material spans the early

colonial period up to the revolution, and includes data on
the climate, population, slavery, education, labor,
agriculture, finance, mining, and energy, industry, foreign
trade, culture, sports, tourism, politics, and armed
forces.

751. Cuba 1968.
Edited by C. Paul Roberts and Mukhtar Hamour.
Los Angeles, California: Latin America Center, University
of California, 1970. 213p. maps.
This supplement to the annual UCLA publication
Statistical Abstract of Latin America provides statistical
information on a wide variety of areas. Among the subjects
included are spatial characteristics, demography,
education, health, transportation, communication,
agriculture, industry, foreign trade, domestic commerce,
wages, and employment.

752. Estadística de divorcios, 1918 a 1925.
Cuba.   Comisión de Estadística y Reformas Económicas.
Havana: Imprenta y Papelería de Rambla, Bouza y Cía.,
1927. 26p.
A compilation of divorce statistics for period immediately
following the liberalization of the Cuban divorce law.

753. Noticias estadísticas de la isla de Cuba, en 1862.
Cuba. Centro de Estadística.
Havana: Imprenta del Gobierno, 1864. 210p.
This general compilation of vital statistics from
mid-nineteenth century Cuba. Deals principally with
economic data, and in particular trade, industry, and
agriculture.

754. Statistical Yearbook.
United Nations Department of Economic and Social Affairs.
Statistical Office.
New York: United Nations, 1948--annual.
A comprehensive statistical abstract dealing with a wide
variety of subjects, including population, labor,
agriculture, forestry, fishing, industry, mining,
manufacturing, trade, energy, transportation,
communication, balance of payment, finance, health,
housing, education, and culture.

755. Yearbook of International Trade Statistics.
United Nations Department of International Economic and
Social Affairs. Statistical Office.
New York: United Nations, 1951--annual.
Two annual publications: one providing data on trade by
country, the other on trade by commodity.

Economy

756. Aspectos económicos de las revolución cubana.
Juan F. Noyola.
Havana: Comisión Nacional Cubana de la UNESCO, 1961. 24p.
Analyzes the socio-economic conditions in Cuba during the
years immediately before and after the triumph of the
revolution.

757. Características fundamentales de la economía cubana.
Julián Alienes y Urosa.
Havana: Banco Nacional de Cuba, 1950. 406p. bibliog.
One of the most useful works examining the Cuban economy,
focusing principally on the 1930s and 1940s. The volume
provides a detailed study of the principal elements of
economic growth. Particular attention is given to sugar,
productivity, population and demography, natural resources,
capital accumulation, the import-export sector, and the
industrial infrastructure.

758. Commercial Cuba.
William J. Clark.
New York: Charles Scribner's Sons, 1898. 514p. maps.
A veritable encyclopedia of economic conditions and
investment opportunities in Cuba at the close of the war of
independence (1895-1898). Also discussed are such diverse
themes as geography, population, climate, legal and
administrative systems, flora and fauna, commerce, and
resources.

759. Cuba: capitalismo dependiente y subdesarrollo, 1510-1959.
Francisco López Segrera.
Havana: Editorial de Ciencias Sociales, 1981. 288p.
bibliog.
Surveys Cuban economic history, emphasizing the role and

place of the island in the international system. The work establishes seven distinct phases through which the Cuban economy passed: the encomienda (1510-1550), the hacienda (1550-1700), the rupture of autonomous development (1700-1762), the plantation (1762-1880), from colonialism to neocolonialism (1880-1902), imperialism (1902-1934), and dependent capitalism (1934-1959).

760. Cuba: datos sobre una economía en ruinas, 1902-1963.
José M. Illán González.
Miami, Florida: n.p. 1964, 2nd ed. 160p.
A critical study of the performance of the Cuban economy in the first five years of the revolution. The greater the portion of the pre-1959 material is confined to a discussion of the Cuban economy in the 1950s. The post-1959 section is an indictment of mismanagement, poor planning, and production errors.

761. "Cuba: Dependence, Plantation Economy, and Social Classes."
Francisco López Segrera.
In   Between Slavery and Free Labor: the Spanish-Speaking Caribbean in the Nineteenth Century.   Edited by Manuel Moreno Fraginals, Frank Moya Pons, and Stanley L. Engerman. Baltimore: The Johns Hopkins University Press, 1985. p. 77-93.
Surveys Cuban economic development from the British seizure of Havana (1762) to the establishment of the republic (1902). Of particular interest is the attention given to the regional socio-economic inequities between the east and west.

762. Cuba, From Primitive Accumulation of Capital to Socialism.
Jorge Gilbert.
Toronto: Two Thirds Editions, 1981.   203p.   bibliog. Presents a history of capitalism in Cuba, from the establishment of Spanish colonial rule in the sixteenth century to the triumph of the revolution. The last chapter discusses the transition to socialism.

763. Cuba, the Economic and Social Revolution.
Dudley Seers, Andres Bianchi, Richard Jolly, and Max Nolff. Chapel Hill, North Carolina: University of North Carolina Press, 1964. 432p.
A collection of four lengthy essays, dealing with the economic and social background of the revolution, education, agriculture, and industry.

764. Cuba: tierra indefensa.
Alberto Arredondo.
Havana: Editorial Lex, 1945. 490p. bibliog.

This economic history survey covers the years between the pre-Columbian epoch and the revolutionary tumult of the 1930s.   It examines in historical perspective all key sectors of the economy, including sugar, tobacco, livestock, coffee, banking and monetary policy, and finance.

765.   "Cuban Dependency: a Comparison of Pre-Revolutionary and Post-Revolutionary International Economic Relations." William M. LeoGrande.
Cuban Studies/Estudios Cubanos, vol. 9, no. 2 (July 1979), p. 1-28.
Provides a thoughtful essay examining the patterns of dependency in capitalist (pre-revolutionary) Cuba and socialist (post-revolutionary) Cuba.   The article utilizes a number of indicators to measure levels of dependency, including export data, trading partner patterns, capital dependency, and external debt.

766.   Cuban Economic Policy and Ideology: the Ten Million Ton Sugar Harvest.
Sergio Roca.
Beverly Hills, California: Sage Publications, 1976, 70p. A concise discussion of the one of the more significant periods of the revolution.   The attempt to harvest the ten million ton crop is is examined from the point of view of planning and consequences.   The study provides a rich source of economic statistics.

767.   "The Cuban Revolution: Economic Organization and Bureaucracy."
Nelson P. Valdés.
Latin American Perspectives, vol. 6, no. 1 (Winter 1979), p. 13-37.
A detailed and thorough analysis of the various stages of economic organization through which the Cuban revolution passed between 1959 and 1979, including the model of moral incentives, the decentralized budgetary system, and institutionalization.

768.   El desarrollo económico de Cuba.
Gustavo Gutiérrez y Sánchez.
Havana: Publicación de la Junta Nacional de Economía, 1952.   259p.
This study of Cuban economic development over a fifty year period deals with all sectors of production, including agriculture, mining, industry, banking, finance, and commerce.

769.   "The Develoment of Capitalism in Cuban Sugar Production, 1860-1900."

Fe Iglesias.
In   Between Slavery and Free Labor: the Spanish-Speaking
Caribbean in the Nineteenth century.   Edited   by   Manuel
Moreno Fraginals, Frank Moya Pons, and Stanley L. Engerman.
Baltimore: The Johns Hopkins University Press, 1985.
p. 54-75.
A reflective and detailed discussion of the evolution of
sugar production in Cuba. The essay examines the role of
technology   and   capital,   the   changes   in   the   labor
requirements, and transformation of land tenure systems.

770. Economía de post-guerra y desempleo.
      Julián Alienes y Urosa.
      Havana: Cámara de Comercio, 1946. 101p.
      Surveys the economy of Cuba between the years 1918 and
      1945, with particular emphasis on years during World War
      II. This work is official in character, in that it was
      commissioned by the Cuban Chamber of Commerce to anticipate
      and prepare for post-war economic adjustments. It provides
      one of the most detailed examinations of Cuban economic
      conditions during the war.

771. La economía cubana entre las dos Isabelas, 1492-1832.
      Roland T. Ely.
      Bogotá: Adita Editores, 1962. 143p. bibliog.
      A comprehensive economic history of Cuba, paying particular
      attention to the development and expansion of sugar
      production.

772. The Economic Development of Revolutionary Cuba: Strategy
      and Performance.
      Archibald R.M. Ritter.
      New York: Praeger, 1974. 373p. bibliog.
      Provides a comprehensive analysis of Cuban developmental
      strategy and the performance of the economy between 1959 to
      1972. The four dimensions of economic performance examined
      inlude income distribution, employment, economic growth,
      and the reduction of economic dependence.

773. Economic History of Cuba.
      Julio LeRiverend.
      Havana: Book Institute, 1967. 277p. bibliog.
      A translated and revised version of the original 1956
      edition in Spanish. The book arranges Cuban economic history
      into six parts: pre-Columbian and Iberian economic
      organizations, conquest and colonization, the early
      colonial economy (1510-1659), the development and demise of
      the slave economy (1659-1886), the imperialist phase
      (1886-1958), and the revolution. Each part contains a
      separate bibliographic section.

774. The Economic Transformation of Cuba.
Edward Boorstein.
New York: Monthly Review Press, 1968. 302p.
A first-person account of the transition to socialism
during the early 1960s. Boorstein worked for a number of
important Cuban agencies, including the National Bank, the
Bank of Foreign Commerce, and the Ministry of Foreign
Commerce. He participated in the planning and execution of
a wide range of decisions affecting varous sectors of the
economy. The work serves as an important source for the
study of these years.

775. The Economy of Socialist Cuba: a Two-Decade Appraisal.
Carmelo Mesa-Lago.
Albuquerque, New Mexico: University of New Mexico Press,
1981. 235p.
This comprehensive overview of economic performance in
revolutionary Cuba. The study examines economic growth,
diversification efforts, Cuban efforts at economic
independence, employment patterns, distribution of income,
and social services.

776. El empleo en Cuba.
Raúl Lorenzo.
Havana: Seonne, Fernández y Cía., 1955. 143p.
Offers a general assessment of the conditions of
employment, unemployment, and underemployment in a
monoculture economy. The author deals extensively with
such diverse issues as foreign trade, public finances, and
monetary policies especially as they affect employment.
The work is particularly useful in providing a view of key
aspects of the Cuban economy in the years immediately
before the revolution.

777. Filosofía de la producción cubana, agrícola e industrial.
Ramiro Guerra y Sánchez.
Havana: Cultural, S.A., 1944, 214p.
This work attempts to develop a philosophical construct
around the peculiarities of the Cuban economic system. The
author argues that Cuban production system should be
organized around the reality of available resources and
within specific limits of potential economic growth.

778. Historia económica de Cuba.
H.E. Freidlaender.
Havana: Jesús Montero, 1944. 598p. bibliog.
A comprehensive economic history of Cuba. The economy is
examined within a chronological context and by sector,
looking at sugar, tobacco, coffee, commerce, banking, and
finance. Also examined are the shifting ideological and
philosophical currents as they affect economic development.

779. Historia económica de Cuba.
     Levi Marrero.
     Havana: Instituto Superior de Estudios e Investigaciones
     Económicas, Universidad de La Habana 1956.   352p.   maps.
     bilbiog.
     Provides a readable and well-balanced survey of the
     economic history of Cuba from the pre-Columbian era to the
     seventeenth century.

780. "Ideological Radicalization and Economic Policy in Cuba."
     Carmelo Mesa-Lago.
     Studies in Comparative International Development, vol. 5,
     no. 10 (1969-1970), p. 203-16.
     Discusses the reorganization of economic policies during
     the late 1960s as they affected capital accumulation and
     economic development. The essay emphasizes both economic
     and ideological sources for their adoption.

781. "Measuring   Income   Distribution   in   Pre-   and
     Post-Revolutionary Cuba."
     Claes Brundenius.
     Cuban Studies/Estudios Cubanos, vol. 9, no. 2 (July 1979),
     p. 29-44.
     Assesses the qualitative changes in the standards of living
     in Cuba. The study examines income distribution during the
     years immediately before the revolution and the first
     fifteen years thereafter.

782. Our Cuban Colony.
     Leland Hamilton Jenks.
     New York: Vanguard Press, 1928. 341p.
     An early critical study of the exercise of U.S. hegemony in
     Cuba. The work focuses largely on North American economic
     penetration of Cuba during the latter part of the
     nineteenth century and the early decades of the twentieth.
     The work offers a wealth of data and information concerning
     U.S. investments in sugar, transportation, utilities,
     banking, and mining.

783. Presente y futuro de la economía cubana.
     Gustavo Gutiérrez y Sánchez.
     Havana: Publicaciones de la Junta Nacional de Economía,
     1950. 84p.
     Discusses the general condition of the Cuban economy,
     particularly for the years between 1944 and 1950. It is a
     useful work dealing with the principal period of the
     Autentico governments.

784. Report on Cuba.
     Francis Adams Truslow (et al.).
     Washington, D.C.:   International Bank for Reconstruction

and Development, 1951. 1053p. maps.
An encyclopedic study of economic conditions in Cuba. The
volume is arranged into ten "books," each dealing with
policy recommendations, the general economy, production,
aids to production, human problems, administration,
finance, international economic relations, economic
development, and technical problems and possibilities.

785. Revolutionary Cuba: the Challenge of Economic Growth with
Equity.
Claes Brundenius.
Boulder, Colorado: Westview Press, 1983. 224p. bibliog.
Presents a general analysis of socio-economic aspects of
the Cuban revolution. The study focuses on economic
growth, employment, income distribution, and the meeting of
basic needs. Comparisons are made with Brazil and Peru for
approximately the same period.

786. La riqueza de Cuba.
Fernando Berenguer.
Havana: Imprenta "El Arte," 1917, 240p.
This detailed account of the condition of the Cuban
political-economy. The study examines banking and finance,
investment, agriculture, and industry as well as the
problems associated with cost and standards of living,
poverty, and immigration.

787. A Study on Cuba.
Cuban Economic Research Project.
Coral Gables, Florida: University of Miami Press, 1965.
774p.
A comprehensive reference work dealing with the major
aspects of the Cuban economy from the colonial period
through the early years of the revolution.   The work
provides a wide range of statistical information on
population, public administration, finance, banking, sugar,
agriculture, international trade, labor, mining, fisheries,
industry, commerce, transportation, communication, and
social security.

Investment, Finance, Banking, and Currency

788. Cuba, the Pearl of the Antilles.
Ramón Bustamante.
St. Louis, Missouri: Foreign Publishing Company, 1916.
267p. map.
A descriptive guide to Cuba for early twentieth century
businessmen and investors. The book provides information
about currency, weights and measures, cable and mail rules,
existing transportation systems to and in Cuba, tariff
regulations, and credit sources.

789. Investment in Cuba.
United States Department of Commerce. Bureau of Foreign
Commerce.
Washington, D.C.: Government Printing Office, 1956. 200p.
maps.
A comprehensive study of economic conditions prepared by
the Commerce Department as "basic information for United
States businessmen." The volume was of a series designed
to provide North American investors with data about
business law, labor law, the investment climate, and
general information about the land and people. Also
included is a vast array of statistical information in the
form of tables and graphs concerning virtually every aspect
of the Cuban economy.

790. Monetary Problems of an Export Economy; the Cuban
Experience, 1917-1947.
Henry Christopher Wallich.
Cambridge, Massachusetts: Harvard University Press, 1950.
357p. bibliog.
One of the most detailed studies of Cuban economic
conditions, specifically focusing on monetary issues and
currency problems.

Trade and Commerce

791. Commercial Cuba. A Book for the Businessmen.
William J. Clark.
New York: Charles Scribner's Sons, 1898. 514p. maps.
This very useful survey of Cuba was written immediately
after the conclusion of the war of independence. The work
provides a wealth of information on all aspects of late
nineteenth century Cuba, including data on population,
climate, geography, and social customs. It is particularly
useful for matters dealing with the economy such as
banking, finance, currency, agriculture, and
transportation. It provides a detailed discussion of
conditions in Cuba province by province.

792. Commercial Cuba in 1905.
United States Department of Commerce. Bureau of
Statistics.
In Monthly Summary of Commerce and Finance of the United
States, May 1905, No. 11, Series 1904-1905. United States
Congress, House of Representatives, 58th Congress, Document
No. 15.
Washington, D.C.: Government Printing Office, 1905.
p. 3897-4095. map.
An extremely useful publication dealing with a wide variety
of topics, including commerce, manufacture, agriculture,
mining, and trade. It offers a rich collection of
statistical data, and is particularly important for its
treatment of U.S.-Cuba trade under the reciprocity treaty
of 1903.

793. Comerciantes cubanos del siglo XIX.
Roland T. Ely.
Havana: Editorial Librería Martí, 1960. 210p. bibliog.
Examines some of the more important merchants and

commercial houses in nineteenth century Cuba.

794. Comercio exterior: exportaciones.
Junta Central de Planificación.   Dirección General de
Estadísticas.
Havana: 1960-annual.
This multi-volume series details Cuban exports by sector,
value, and country of destination.

795. Comercio exterior: importaciones.
Junta Central de Planificación.   Dirección General de
Estadísticas.
Havana: 1960-annual.
An annual multi-volume series providing statistical data on
Cuban imports of different goods by sector, value and
country of origin.

796. Comercio exterior, 1930-1939.
Cuba. Dirección General de Estadística.
Havana: n.p. 195p.
Provides a statistical compilation of Cuban foreign trade
statistics, including imports-exports, custom collections,
and the distribution of foreign trade by country and
sector.

797. Cuba y el mercado internacional azucarero.
Arnaldo Silva León.
Havana: Editorial de Ciencias Sociales.   1975.   186p.
Presents a history of the relationship of Cuban sugar
production and world market forces. The book examines four
distinct periods: World War I, the Machado years and the
depression (1925-1933), World War II, and sugar production
after the triumph of the revolution.

Industry and Mining

798. Derecho minero cubano.
Edited by José Isaac del Corral.
Havana: Sociedad Editorial Cuba Contemporánea, 1920-1923.
2 vols.
A compilation of all laws, decrees, and legislation
affecting mines and mining in the early twentieth century.

799. Estado de la minería en Cuba al finalizar el año 1939.
Antonio Calvache.
Havana: Compañía Editora de Libros y Folletos, 1940. 42p.
Discusses of the condition of mining in Cuba and the
availability of the island's mineral resources. The work
also includes a survey of mining laws.

800. Filosofía de la producción cubana: agrícola e industria.
Ramiro Guerra y Sánchez.
Havana: Cultural, S.A., 1944. 214p.
An attempt to formulate theoretical constructs through
which to analyze Cuba production systems.

801. Historia y desarrollo de la minería en Cuba.
Antonio Calvache.
Havana: Editorial Neptuno, 1944. 170p. maps. bibliog.
Provides a valuable study of mining in Cuba from
prehistoric times to the mid-twentieth century. The work
covers a variety of mining enterprises in Cuba, including
iron, manganese, gold, copper, and nickel. Attention is
also given to efforts to regulate and supervise mining by
legislation.

802. Industrial Cuba. Being a Study of Present Commercial and
Industrial Conditions, with Suggestions as to the
Opportunities Presented in the Island for American Capital,

Enterprise, and Labour.
Robert P. Porter.
New York: Arno Press, 1976. 428p. maps.
This reprint of the 1899 edition provides a detailed
analysis of conditions in Cuba in the period immediately
following the war of independence (1895-1898). Among the
topics examined are banking and currency, tariff, commerce,
agriculture, forestry, mining, transportation, and
navigation.

803. "The International Political Economy of Cuban Nickel
Development."
Theodore H. Moran.
Cuban Studies/Estudios Cubanos, vol. 7, no. 2 (July 1977),
p. 145-65.
Analyzes the Cuban nickel industry in relation to the
international nickel trade. Emphasis is placed on Cuban
nickel development within the context of the evolution of
United States-Cuban relations.

804. "Iron Mining and Socio-Demographic Change in Eastern Cuba,
1884-1940."
Lisandro Pérez.
Journal of Latin American Studies, vol. 14, no. 2 (Nov.
1982), p. 381-405.
This informative article details a wide range of mining
activities in Oriente province, the site of some of the
richest mines on the island. The essay examines the
development of mining in a larger social context,
evaluating the relationship between the mines and
demography and population growth.

805. "La minería cubana."
L.V. de Abad.
Revista Bimestre Cubana, vol. 46, no. 1 (Jan.-June 1941),
p. 131-40.
Surveys mining conditions during the first third of the
twentieth century with particular emphasis on the iron
mines of eastern Cuba.

806. Mining and Manufacturing Industries in Cuba.
United States Tariff Commission.
Washington, D.C.: Government Printing Office, 1947, 47p.
A brief but detailed compendium on the state of two key
industries in Cuba. The work provides important statistics
on the condition of mining and manufacturing.

807. Report on the Mineral Resources of Cuba in 1901.
Harriet Connor Brown.
Baltimore: Press of Guggenheimer, Weil, and Company, 1903.
121p.

A survey of mines and mineral resources made under the
auspices of the United States military occupation
(1899-1902).   The principal purpose of the study was to
disseminate information concerning the investment potential
of mining in Cuba.

Forestry

808. Derecho forestal cubana.
     José Isaac del Corral.
     Havana: Imprenta F. Fernández y Cía., 1936.   2 vols.
     A study dealing with forestry law and legislation,
     including a compilation of appropriate statutes and decrees
     affecting forestry in the early twentieth century.

809. The Forests of Cuba.
     Earl Emmett Smith.
     Cambridge, Massachusetts: Harvard University Press, 1954.
     98p.
     A descriptive survey of Cuba's principal forests.

810. Manual de selvicultura.
     Alberto J. Fors.
     Havana: Ministerio de Agricultura, 1947. 323p. bibliog.
     Presents a study of forests and forestry in Cuba which was
     undertaken under the auspices of the Ministry of
     Agriculture.   The work advocates greater conservation for
     the preservation and more efficient utilization of national
     forests.

811. "El problema forestal en Cuba."
     José Isaac del Corral.
     Cuba Contemporánea, vol. 32, no. 125 (May 1925), p. 5-30.
     A discussion lamenting the rapidly disappearing forests of
     Cuba and the long-term consequences of these developments,
     including flooding, droughts, and the deterioration of the
     condition of the soil.

812. Selvicultura.
     Alberto J. Fors.
     Havana: Cía. Tipográfica, S.A. 1937.   244p.   bibliog.

Discusses forests and forestry in Cuba, with particular
emphasis on ecology and environmental issues.
Conservationist in tenor.

Agriculture

813. "Agrarian Reform in Cuba, 1959-1963."
James O'Connor.
Science and Society, vol. 32, no. 2 (Spring 1968),
p. 169-217.
Examines the early agrarian reform measures adopted by the
revolutionary government. The discussion of the National
Institute of Agrarian Reform (INRA) serves as the central
element of the essay. Also examined are policies related
to ranching, expropriation of cane lands, small and medium
size farms, and the establishment of farm cooperatives.

814. La agricultura cubana, 1934-1966.
Oscar A. Echevarría Salvat.
Miami, Florida: Ediciones Universal, 1971. 116p.
Surveys Cuban agriculture from 1934 to 1966. The emphasis
of the book is on workers' standard of living, principally
income, health, nutrition, housing, employment, and living
conditions. Attention is also placed on the Agrarian
Reform Law of 1959 and its impact on agriculture and
agricultural workers.

815. El café.
Fernando Agete y Piñeiro.
Havana: Cultural, S.A., 1937. 118p.
This study of coffee cultivation includes statistical
information concerning previous production levels as well
as an examination of the condition of coffee agriculture on
the island.

816. El café. Historia de su cultivo y explotación en Cuba.
Francisco Pérez de la Riva.
Havana: Jesús Montero, 1944. 383p. bibliog.
The single most comprehensive study of the origins and

growth of coffee production in Cuba.

817. La caña de azúcar en Cuba.
     Fernando Agete y Piñeiro.
     Havana: Ministerio de Agricultura, 1946.   2 vols.
     bibliog.
     A technical study of sugar cane, examining the varieties of
     cane species, the origins of the species, and the state of
     cane cultivation and experimentation.

818. Cuando reinaba su majestad el azúcar.
     Roland T. Ely.
     Buenos Aires: Editorial Sudamericana, 1963.   875p.   map.
     bibliog.
     A detailed and richly illustrated discussion of the golden
     age of Cuban sugar production during the early nineteenth
     century. The work pays attention to the development of a
     monoculture economy and the accompanying social and
     political consequences.

819. Cuba, Agriculture and Planning.
     Cuban Economic Research Project.
     Coral Gables, Florida: University of Miami Press, 1965.
     325p.
     A critical survey of agricultural development and state
     planning during the early years of the revolution.
     Particular attention is given to sugar production, the
     agrarian reform, livestock, and the relationship between
     rationing and production.

820. Cuba: Socialism and Development.
     René Dumont.
     New York: Grove Press, 1970.   240p.   bibliog.
     An indictment of Cuban agricultural planning during the
     early 1960s by an agricultural economist who served as an
     advisor to the Cuban government between 1960 and 1963.

821. "Cuban Agricultural Productivity: a Comparison of State
     and Private Farm Sectors."
     Nancy Forster.
     Cuban Studies/Estudios Cubanos, vols. 11-12, nos. 2-1 (July
     1981-Jan. 1982), pp. 106-25.
     Analyzes in detail the comparative agricultural outputs of
     the state and private farms in socialist Cuba.   The
     inventory is made on a crop by crop basis.

822. Cuban Counterpoint: Tobacco and Sugar.
     Fernando Ortiz Fernández.
     New York: Knopf, 1947.   Trans. Harriet de Onis.   312p.
     One of the more important treatises about the two principal
     sectors of the agrarian economy of Cuba.   The work deals

with more than economic history, however, for it
skillfully blends elements of the economy with folklore,
social custom, and popular culture. An indispensable
study.

823. Cuban Sugar Policy from 1963 to 1970.
Heinrich Brunner.
Pittsburgh: University of Pittsburgh Press, 1977,
163p. bibliog.
A detailed analysis of the planning policies and the
development strategies employed in socialist Cuba. The
study examines the origins of the theoretical guidelines,
the application of the theory, and the specific relevance
to sugar production. It provides an important contribution
to an understanding of the events that led to the debacle
of ten million ton sugar crop in 1970.

824. "Geographical Relations in the Development of Cuban
Agriculture."
R.H. Whitbeck.
The Geographical Review, vol. 12, no. 2 (April 1911),
p. 222-40.
A detailed but dated analysis of Cuban topography, harbors,
soil, and climate as they affect agricultural production
and marketing, and especially sugar and tobacco.

825. La industria azucarera de Cuba. Su importancia, su
organización, sus mercados, su situación actual.
Ramiro Guerra y Sánchez.
Havana: Cultural, S.A., 1940. 304p.
One of the best overviews of sugar production in Cuba.
While the study is set in a larger historical context, it
is concerned largely with twentieth century issues. Among
the various facets of the sugar system assessed in detail
are cultivation, labor, and wage structures, manufacture,
trade, tariff, and commerce and the role of government.

826. El ingenio: complejo económico-social cubano del azúcar.
Manuel Moreno Fraginals.
Havana: Editorial de Ciencias Sociales, 1978. 3 vols.
bibliog.
One of the outstanding historical works of the last
twenty-five years. It is a meticulous study of sugar
production, richly documented, and engagingly written. The
material deals with slavery, the character of the producing
classes, production and manufacturing, economics
development, and trade. The first two volumes contain the
text; the third volume provides an appendix containing
historical statistics, a glossary, and an extensive
annotated bibliography. This is a standard reference text
for late eighteenth and nineteenth century economic

history.

827. El latifundismo en la economía cubana.
Raúl Maestri.
Havana: Editorial "Hermes," 1929. 78p.
This critical study of the pernicious effects of land
concentration in Cuba emphasized the role of the large
sugar estates and the degree to which they have obstructed
diversified agricultural production.

828. Las malas hierbas y su control químico en Cuba.
G. Pérez Navarro and S. Rodríguez García.
Havana: Editorial Pueblo y Educación, 1981. 242p.
A detailed study examining Cuban use of pesticides in
agriculture.

829. "Mechanization of Sugar Cane Harvesting in Cuba."
Charles Edquist.
Cuban Studies/Estudios Cubanos, vol. 13, no. 2 (Summer
1983), p. 4164.
Analyzes Cuban efforts to mechanize the harvesting of sugar
from the late 1950s to the early 1980s.

830. Memoria del censo agrícola nacional, 1946.
Cuba.   Ministerio de Agricultura.   Comisión del Censo
Agrícola Nacional.
Havana: P. Fernandez, 1951. 1253p.
A thorough study of Cuban agriculture.   The book is
indispensable for all research during the 1940s.   It is
wide-ranging, and includes an assessment of all sectors of
agriculture, all types of land tenure and ownership.   The
volume is encyclopedic in proportion and presents a rich
source of statistical data.

Transportation
and Communications

831. Memoria sobre los ferrocarriles de la isla de Cuba en los
     años económicos de 1882-1883 hasta 1901.
     Cuba. Inspección General de Ferrocarriles.
     Havana: Imprenta "La Universal," 1902. 419p.
     A comprehensive report of the development and condition of
     railways in Cuba. The book treats in detail railway
     construction in all provinces. Unquestionably one of the
     most important works on the subject of rail systems on the
     island for this period.

832. "Las perspectivas económico-sociales del primer ferrocarril
     de Cuba."
     Fernando Ortiz Fernández.
     Revista Bimestre Cubana, vol. 40, no. 2 (July-Dec. 1937),
     p. 161-76.
     A thoughtful historical analysis of the impact of the first
     railroad in Cuba. The essay covers the founding and
     operation of the railroad and assesses its economic
     consequences.

833. "En el primer centenario de los ferrocarriles cubanos
     (1837-1937)."
     L.V. de Abad.
     Revista Bimestre Cubana, vol. 40, no. 2 (July-Dec. 1937),
     p. 177-95.
     A historical survey of railroad construction in Cuba over
     the course of one hundred years.

Labor

834. Azúcar y lucha de clases: 1917.
John Dumoulin.
Havana: Editorial de Ciencias Sociales, 1980. 284p.
This is important contribution to Cuban labor history. The study examines the rapid expansion of sugar production in Cuba during World War I and the concurrent movement by sugar workers to organize unions. The volume contains several documentary appendices.

835. Contratos y convenios del trabajo.
Carlos M. Raggi y Ageo.
Havana: Cultural, S.A., 1940. 625p.
A juridical study of labor contracts, labor laws and legislation, collective bargaining, and arbitration. The volume includes a compilation of the most important statutes relating to labor which were enacted up to 1940.

836. "Cuban Labor and the Communist Party, 1937-1958: An Interpretation."
Harold D. Sims.
Cuban Studies/Estudios Cubanos, vol. 15, no. 1 (Winter 1985), p. 43-58.
Analyzes relations between the Cuban communist party and the organized labor movement during the years of Batista government. The essay also examines party relations with the different regimes of the period and the emerging 26 July Movement.

837. "The Cuban Working Class Movement From 1925 to 1933."
Fabio Grobart.
Science and Society, vol. 39, no. 1 (Spring 1975), p. 73-102.
A detailed historical survey of the development of the

Cuban working-class from the organization of the Cuban
National Workers Confederation in 1925 to the revolutionary
general strike of 1933. The article deals specifically
with labor struggles against the regime of Gerardo Machado
(1925-1933.)

838. Despido de obreros y empleados.
Rafael Pérez Lobo.
Havana: Editorial Selecta, 1944. 416p.
An annotated compilation of statutes, decrees, and laws
relating to the dismissal of workers and employees. The
book provides an alphabetical listing of legal grounds for
dismissal.

839. "Economic Significance of Unpaid Labor in Socialist Cuba."
Carmelo Mesa-Lago.
Industrial and Labor Relations Review, vol. 22, no. 3
(April 1969), p. 339-57.
Examines the different types of unpaid labor in Cuba after
the revolution. The essay outlines the way in which Cubans
are mobilized, how labor is utilized, and the contribution
of the unpaid to the general labor input to the economy.

840. El empleo, el sub-empleo y el desempleo en Cuba.
Gustavo Gutiérrez y Sánchez.
Havana: Consejo Nacional de Economía, 1958. 31p.
Presents a brief but valuable profile of employment
conditions during the late 1950s. Its particular value
lies in the portrayal of conditions in Cuba on the eve of
the revolution.

841. Historial obrero cubano, 1574-1965.
Mario Riera Hernández.
Mimai: Rema Press, 1965. 305p. bibliog.
Surveys labor history from the colonial period to the early
years of the revolution. The bulk of the book is devoted
to developments between the 1930s and 1960s.

842. "Institutionalization and Workers' Response."
Marifeli Pérez-Stable.
Cuban Studies/Estudios Cubanos, vol. 6, no. 2 (July 1976),
p. 31-54.
This examination of developments within the Cuban trade
union movement is based on a series of interviews with
union leaders and rank and file workers in 1975. The
subjects include the relations between the leadership and
the workers, the role of local trade unions, incentives,
and the incorporation of women into the labor force.

843. "Labor Conditions in Cuba."
Victor S. Clark.

Bulletin of the Department of Labor, vol. 7, no. 41 (July 1902), p. 663-793.
A comprehensive study of labor conditions in Cuba at the turn of the century. While the author surveys the history of labor from the early colonial period, the principal focus of the article is on late nineteenth and early twentieth century developments. The work is based on extensive research and field trips. An indispensable source for the period.

844. The Labor Force: Employment, Unemployment, and Under-employment in Cuba, 1899-1970.
     Carmelo Mesa-Lago.
     Beverly Hills, California: Sage, 1972. 72p. bibliog.
     A succinct analysis of developments in the Cuban labor forces over three general periods: from 1899 to the late 1920s, the early 1930s to the late 1950s, and 1960 to 1972. The work is based on census statistics, official statistical studies, and government publications.

845. The Labor Sector and Socialist Distribution in Cuba.
     Carmelo Mesa-Lago.
     New York: Praeger, 1968. 250p. bibliog.
     Provides an examination of state planning, and particularly its role in determining distribution.

846. Legislación de accidentes del trabajo de Cuba.
     René Acevedo y Laborde.
     Havana: Imprenta P. P. Prado, 1923. 195p.
     Studies accident law in Cuba, dealing specifically with employers' liability, insurance, government responsibility, and relevant laws and statutes.

847. El movimiento obrero cubano en 1920.
     Olga Cabrera.
     Havana: Instituto del Libro, 1970. 161p. bibliog.
     A study of a critical period of Cuban labor history: a time when workers were advancing towards the organization of national confederation. The work examines the role of the Cuban Communist Party (PCC) in organizing. Focus is on the second national labor congress of 1920.

848. Los obreros hacen y escriben su historia.
     Compiled by Department of Revolutionary Orientation, Central Committee of the Cuban Communist Party (PCC). Havana: Editorial de Ciencias Sociales, 1975.   388p. This collection of essays was originally presented at the first national meeting of the history of the Cuban working class movement in 1972. The essays combine traditional historical narratives with oral histories. Among the topics discussed included labor history to 1868, slavery,

maritime labor, typographical workers' movement, the labor press, and women in the labor movement.

849. Revolutionary Politics and the Cuban Working Class.
Maurice Zeitlin.
Princeton, New Jersey: Princeton University Press. 306p. map.
A study of working class attitudes toward the revolution based on more than 200 interviews in 21 industrial plants across the island in 1962. The workers were classified according to their degree of skill, prerevolutionary employment history, sex, race, attitudes towards communist party before the revolution, and degree of mobility. Zeitlin discovers that support for the revolution was greater among those previously unemployed or underemployed than among those who had stable work.

850. "Some Notes on the Development of the Cuban Labor Force, 1970-80."
Claes Brundenius.
Cuban Studies/Estudios Cubanos, vol. 13, no. 2 (Summer 1983), p. 65-77.
The subjects explored in this analysis include employment, characteristics of the female labor force, and the distribution of employment by economic sectors.

851. Tobacco in the Periphery: a Case Study in Cuban Labour History, 1860-1958.
Jean Stubbs.
London: Cambridge University Press, 1985, 203p. map. bibliog.
The best single account of Cuban tobacco production, both in agricultural and industrial development. Based on archival sources and oral histories, the study examines the inter-relationship between the tobacco farm and the cigar factories over nearly a one-hundred year span.

852. "The Workers' Struggle: 1850-1961."
Hobart A. Spalding, Jr.
Cuba Review, vol. 4, no. 1 (July 1974), p. 3-10.
Surveys Cuban labor history, emphasizing the contribution and participation in the revolutionary struggles of the 1930s and 1950s and the role of the working class in the early consolidation of the revolution.

Education

853. Apuntes para la historia de las letras y de la instrucción
     pública en la isla de Cuba.
     Antonio Bachiller y Morales.
     Havana: Imprenta de P. Massana, 1859-1861. 3 vols.
     A history of the origins and development of the principal
     educational institutions in colonial Cuba. The three
     volumes each deal separately with primary education,
     secondary and professional training, and university
     education.

854. The Basic Secondary School in the Country: An Educational
     Innovation in Cuba.
     Max Figueroa, Abel Prieto, and Raúl Gutiérrez.
     Paris: UNESCO, 1974. 47p.
     A study of the rural secondary education programs, with
     particular emphasis on curriculum, administration, the
     academic year, the structure of the system, and on-going
     research projects.

855. Biografía del colegio de San Cristobal de La Habana.
     Hortensia Pichardo.
     Havana: Editorial Academia, 1979. 229p. bibliog.
     Provides a detailed historical account of one of the most
     important institutions of higher education in colonial
     Cuba.

856. "Changes in Cuban Education."
     Rolland G. Paulston.
     In Educational Innovations in Latin America. Edited by
     Richard L. Cummings and Donald A. Lemke.
     Metuchen, New Jersey: The Scarecrow Press, Inc., 1973.
     p. 150-77.
     Surveys education in Cuba from the early twentieth century

to the late 1960s. The essays deal sympathetically with the advances in educational programs in socialist Cuba.

857. Children are the Revolution: Day Care in Cuba.
Marvin Leiner.
New York: The Viking Press, 1974. 213p.
In this thorough study of pre-school centers in Cuba, the author analyzes key issues of day care programs, including social goals of pre-school care, organization of programs, nutrition and health care, instruction, and the physical setting.   Discussions of child care systems in other countries provides useful comparative perspectives.

858. Children of Che: Childcare and Education in Cuba.
Karen Wald.
New York: Ramparts Press, 1977. 382p.
One of the most comprehensive accounts of primary education and day care in socialist Cuba. The text is accompanied by photographs.

859. Children of the Revolution.
Jonathan Kozol.
New York: Delacorte Press, 1978. 245p. bibliog.
A first person account of the educational programs adopted in Cuba after the triumph of the revolution. The book examines Cuban achievements in such diverse but related areas as the anti-illiteracy campaign in the countryside, adult education programs, and administration of the public school system. The book is based on extensive travel in Cuba and lengthy conversations with Cubans in all areas of public education, from senior administrators to rural school teachers.

860. Código escolar.
Edited by Lisandro Otero Masdeu and Osvaldo Valdés de la Paz.
Havana: Talleres Tipográficos de Carasa y Cía., 1941. 2nd ed. 1941. 1,716p.
A compilation of the laws affecting primary schools, rural education, and private educational institutions during the 1930s and 1940s.

861. Contemporary Cuban Education: An Annotated Bibliography.
Larry R. Oberg.
Stanford, California: Stanford University Libraries, 1980. 76p.
A compilation of titles dealing with education in Cuba after the revolution.

862. La crisis de la segunda enseñanza en Cuba y su posible solución.

Ciro Espinoso.
Havana: Cultural, S.A., 1942. 309p.
Presents a critical study of the secondary school during
the 1930s.

863. Cuba: educación y cultura.
Cuba. Comisión Nacional de la UNESCO.
Havana: Empresa Consolidada de Artes Gráficas, 1963. 81p.
Provides a general statement of purpose of the Cuban
revolutionary government concerning intellectual life and
education in Cuba. It is a useful outline of the stated
educational goals during the early years of the revolution.

864. Cuba, organización de la educación, 1971-1973.
Cuba. Dirección de Producción de Medios de Enseñanzas.
Havana: Ministerio de Educación, 1973. 212p.
Discusses school management and the organization of the
education system. The work also provides background
information on the development of education during the
first fifteen years of the revolution.

865. "Cuban Education and the Revolutionary Ideal."
Samuel Bowles.
Howard Educational Review, vol. 41, no. 4 (Nov. 1971),
p. 472-500.
The essay examines the means by which the new social values
of the revolution are transmitted through the educational
system. Education in Cuba seeks to meet four basic
objectives: economic growth, distance from U.S. hegemony,
attainment of egalitarian society, and the creation of the
new socialist citizen. The article studies the campaign
against illiteracy, the general expansion of schools, and
the extension of educational programs in the fields and
factories to assess how these objectives are being met.

866. "The Cuban Revolutionary Offensive in Education."
Gerald H. Read.
Comparative Education Review, vol. 14, no. 2 (June 1970),
p. 131-43.
Discusses the development of the educational system during
the first ten years of the revolution. Attention is paid
to the grand design of revolutionary education,
particularly in its efforts to universalize schooling,
disseminate Marxist values, and the relationship of
pedagogical theory to practice.

867. "Cultural Revitalization and Educational Change in Cuba."
Rolland G. Paulston.
Comparative Education Review, vol. 16, no. 3 (Oct. 1972),
p. 474-85.
A discussion of theoretical considerations dealing with the

relationship between social development and educational change. The author seeks to examine the process and structure of revitalization movements as manifestations of rapid cultural change in Cuba.

868. "Day Care in Cuba: Children in Revolution."
Marvin Leiner and Robert Ubell.
Saturday Review, vol. 55 (April 1, 1972), p. 54-58.
This description of pre-school care in Cuba, placing emphasis on the educational and medical aspects of day care. Based on a year-long residence on the island between 1968 and 1969.

869. "The Demographic Dimensions of the Educational Problems in Socialist Cuba."
Lisandro Pérez.
Cuban Studies/Estudios Cubanos, vol. 7, no. 1 (Jan. 1977), p. 33-57.
An informative essay assessing the relationship between population growth and primary school enrollment since 1959. The article examines fertility trends after 1959, the increase in primary school enrollment, and the effect of fertility trends on education policy.

870. "La educación en Cuba."
Arturo Montori.
Cuba Contemporánea, vol. 38, no. 149 (May 1905), p. 19-60 and vol. 38, no. 150 (June 1905), p. 121-64.
Provides a detailed survey of the history of education in Cuba from the earliest colonial period to the early twentieth century. Among the topics discussed are the philosophies of leading Cuban educators, provincial education, primary, secondary, and higher education, special vocational and technical schools, and the organization of curriculum and faculty.

871. La educación en el siglo XX.
Emma Pérez.
Havana: Universidad de La Habana, 1945. 126p. bibliog.
A historical survey of education in Cuba in the twentieth century with an emphasis upon the evolution of philosophical trends.

872. Education in Cuba.
Sverin K. Turosienski.
Washington, D.C.: Government Printing Office, 1943. 90p. bibliog.
A survey of Cuban education assessing the historical development of education and the standards of teaching in the elementary, secondary, and vocational schools. Attention is paid to the training and status of teachers,

adult education, and higher education at the University of Havana.

873. Ensayo histórico-estadístico de la instrucción pública de la isla de Cuba.
Pelayo González de los Ríos.
Havana: Imprenta del Tiempo, 1864. 341p.
Represents an invaluable source for the study of public education during the colonial epoch. It provides a vast amount of useful data concerning the numbers of schools and children in school, regional distribution, and educational finances.

874. La enseñanza de la filosofía en Cuba.
Humberto Piñera Llera.
Havana: Editorial Hércules, 1958. 38p.
An overview of the method used in the classroom instruction and study of philosophy. The study was prepared under the auspices of the Cuban National commission of UNESCO.

875. "La enseñanza secundaria en Cuba: reformas que necesita."
Arturo Montori.
Cuba Contemporánea, vol. 27, no. 108   (Dec. 1921), p. 269-315.
Presenting a critique of the condition of the secondary school system, the essay contends that too much of the program does not meet national needs. It advocates the establishment of a sound liberal arts curriculum.

876. Estadísticas de educación, 1965-1966.
Ministerio de Educación.   Departamento Nacional de Estadísticas.
Havana: Ministerio de Educación, 1967. 780p.
This compilation of vital education data, largely for the years 1965-1966. Includes statistics on the number of schools   (primary,   secondary,   and   colleges   and universities), the number of teachers and students, and provides information on special education programs, the education budget, and adult education.

877. El estado actual de la enseñanza primaria in Cuba.
Ramiro Guerra y Sánchez.
Cuba Contemporánea, vol. 27, no. 106 (Oct. 1921), p. 89-105.
A critical survey of the condition of primary education in Cuba during the 1920s. The essay complains of the neglect of the lower grades, the lack of funding, and the general indifference of the politicians to the educational needs of Cuban children.

878. "Exiled Teachers and the Cuban Revolution."

Eugene F. Provenzo, Jr. and Concepción García.
Cuban Studies/Estudios Cubanos, vol. 13, no. 1   (Winter
1983), p. 1-15.
Based on a series of interviews, this study of Cuban
teachers in exile examines their attitudes towards the
education system during the early years of the revolution.
It is particularly useful since it offers a view of the
transition in education from capitalism to socialism.

879. "The Imperial Design: Politics and Pedagogy in Occupied
Cuba, 1899-1902."
Louis A. Pérez, Jr.
Cuban Studies/Estudios Cubanos,   vol. 12,   no. 2   (Summer
1982), p. 1-19.
Discusses the education system during the U.S. occupation
and its use as a medium of cultural imperialism.

880. Influencia de la Universidad de La Habana en la cultura
nacional.
Juan Manuel Dihigo y Mestre.
Havana: Universidad de La Habana, 1924.   114p.   bibliog.
An   historical   survey   of   the   educational   role   and
development of the University of Havana, placing particular
emphasis on the contribution of the university to literary
and artistic achievements.

881. El maestro y la educación popular.
Manuel Valdés Rodríguez.
Havana: Ministerio de Educación, 1950.   396p.
A collection of essays and addresses dealing with a variety
of   educational   issues,   including   teacher   training,
curriculum preparation, and classroom instruction.

882. Manual para maestros.
Alexis Everett Frye.
Havana: n.p., 1900.   165p.
This is a teaching manual prepared by the United States for
public school instructors during the military occupation of
1899-1902.   The work deals with matters of curriculum,
class preparation, and teaching formats.

883. The Nation-Wide Learning System of Cuba.
Carl J. Dahlman.
Princeton, New Jersey: Research Program in Economic
Development, Woodrow Wilson School, Princeton University,
1973.   141p.   bibliog.
A   comprehensive   examination   of   education   in   Cuba
emphasizing   in   particular   its   condition   before   the
revolution and the development of educational policy after
1959.   The study covers informal education (literacy
campaign, adult education), formal education (primary,

secondary, vocational, professional, university), and an
evaluation of the over-all performance of the education
system.

884. "A New Look at the Literacy Campaign in Cuba."
Jonathan Kozol.
Harvard Educational Review, vol. 48, no. 3 (Aug. 1978),
p. 341-77.
Based on a series of interviews conducted in Cuba, the
essay examines the history and development of the literacy
campaign of the early 1960s. Emphasis is given to the
logistical aspects of the program, the recruitment and
training of volunteer teachers, and the development of
instructional methods that were both pedagogically
appropriate and politically correct.

885. La política educacional del Dr. Grau San Martín.
Emma Pérez.
Havana: Ucar García, 1948. 141p.
A sympathetic account of the educational programs during
the administration of President Ramón Grau San Martín
(1944-1948).

886. "Primary Education in Colonial Cuba: Spanish Tool for
Retaining 'La Isla Siempre Leal'?"
Edward D. Fitchen.
Caribbean Studies, vol. 14, no. 1 (April 1974), p. 105-20.
In this study of primary school education in Cuba between
1512 and 1898, the author chronicles the neglect of
education in the colony, arguing that what little formal
education opportunities did exist served principally to
promote the political objectives of the colonial regime.

887. "El problema de la educación nacional."
Arturo Montori.
Cuba Contemporánea, vol. 24, no. 96 (Dec. 1920), p. 329-72.
A critical study of the condition of education in Cuba in
the early decades of the republic. Attention is given to
the scarcity of resources, the lack of trained personnel,
the impact of periodic political disorders on education,
and the state of school administration.

888. El problema educacional cubano.
Aurelio Fernández Concheso.
Havana: Edicion del Instituto Cívico Militar, 1956. 60p.
A critique of the public education system, urging
wide-sweeping reforms.

889. "The United States Military Government: Alexis E. Frye and
Cuban Education, 1898-1902."
Edward D. Fitchen.

Revista/Review Interamericana, vol. 2, no. 2 (Summer 1972),
p. 123-149.
Provides a sympathetic account of the efforts of Alexis
Frye in organizing the public school system during the U.S.
military occupation.

Science, Technology, and Energy

890. "Caribbean Science and Technology."
Wallace C. Koehler and Aaron Segal.
Caribbean Review, vol. 14, no. 3 (Summer 1985), p. 11-15.
Cuban capabilities are examined in a general Caribbean context.

891. "Cuba: the Cybernetic Era."
Ramón Barquín.
Cuban Studies/Estudios Cubanos, vol. 5, no. 2 (July 1975), p. 1-23.
Discusses the development of electronic data processing and computer sciences in Cuba. The article assesses three key aspects of computers in Cuba: the source of technology, Cuban manufacturing of small systems, and the effect of computers on the management of the economy.

892. "The Cuban Nuclear Power Program."
Jorge F. Pérez-López.
Cuban Studies/Estudios Cubanos, vol. 9, no. 1 (Jan. 1979), p. 1-42.
Analyzes Cuban efforts to reduce the national dependency on imported petroleum supplies as a source of energy. The article provides an historical account of the uses of nuclear energy in Cuba and details Cuban plans for future development.

893 "Cuba's Energy Balances and Future Energy Picture."
Rafael Fermoselle-López.
Cuba Studies/Estudios Cubanos, vol. 9, no. 2 (July 1979), p. 45-58.
A survey of energy consumption in Cuba between 1967 and 1976, and offers projections for future needs.

894. "Cuba's Pending Energy Crisis."
Alfred Padula.
Caribbean Review, vol. 8, no. 2 (Spring 1979), p. 4-8.
Studies Cuban dependence upon foreign petroleum imports
within the larger context of the international market in
oil. The author argues that the rising price of oil
imports will require Cuba to adopt nuclear energy in order
to avert serious economic dislocation.

895. "Energy   Production,   Imports,   and   Consumption   in
Revolutionary Cuba."
Jorge F. Pérez-López.
Latin American Research Review, vol. 16, no. 3 (1981),
p. 111-37.
An examination of primary energy production in Cuba,
including petroleum, gas, hydro-electricity, ethyl alcohol,
fuelwood, and charcoal. The author analyzes the source of
energy, the patterns of energy use, and the government
policies that influence energy supply and consumption.

896. Estudio sobre el movimiento científico y literario de Cuba.
Aurelio Mitjans.
Havana: Consejo Nacional de Cultura, 1963. 295p.
This reprint of the 1890 edition discusses the principal
trends in Cuban scientific and literary traditions during
the eighteenth and nineteenth centuries.

897. "Notes on Science in Cuba."
Marcel Roche.
Science (Washington), vol. 169, no. 3943 (July 24, 1970),
p. 344-49.
Discusses the state of science and scientific study in Cuba
based on personal travel and interviews with Cuban
authorities. Particular attention is given to the place of
science and technology in the high school and university
curriculum, research facilities, government support of
research, and the social status of scientists.

898. "Nuclear Power in Cuba: Opportunities and Challenges."
Jorge F. Pérez-López.
Orbis, vol. 26, no. 2 (Summer 1982), p. 495-516.
A study in the development and advancement of Cuban nuclear
power capabilities. The author argues that because Cuba is
poorly endowed with energy resources, and dependent on
petroleum imports, it will need to minimize its oil use and
expand its nuclear energy capacities.

Culture

899. <u>Como surgió la cultura nacional</u>.
Walterio Carbonell.
Havana: Ediciones Yaka, 1961. 131p.
Discusses the origins and development of Cuban culture.
The author gives special attention to the contribution of
Afro-Cubans to national culture.

900. "La cultura caribeña en Cuba: continuidad versus ruptura."
Antonio Benítez Rojo.
<u>Cuban Studies/Estudios Cubanos</u>, vol. 14, no. 1 (Winter
1984), p. 1-15.
An analysis of the interaction between Caribbean cultural
forces and Cuban society. The article's central thesis
challenges the current official view in Cuba that the
revolution has established working-class culture as
national culture and advances the proposition that culture
on the island draws more on pan-Caribbean developments.

901. <u>La cultura en Cuba socialista</u>.
Ministerio de Cultura.
Havana: Editorial Letras Cubanas, 1982. 256p.
This collection of thirteen essays examines the state of
art, literature, and culture generally in the two decades
after the revolution. The subjects include literature,
plastic arts, popular culture, museums and galleries, music,
folklore, dance, and cinema.

902. <u>Evolucion de la cultura cubana, 1608-1927</u>.
José Manuel Carbonell y Rivero.
Havana: Imprenta "El Siglo XX," 1928. 18 vols.
A magnificent multi-volume discussion of all aspects of
Cuban culture over a three hundred year span. The volumes
deal separately with such diverse subjects as lyrical

poetry, <u>bellas artes</u>, revolutionary poetry, oratory, prose, science, and essays.

903. <u>Figuras cubanas; breves biografías de grandes cubanos del siglo XIX.</u>
Salvador Bueno.
Havana: Comisión Nacional Cubano de la UNESCO, 1964. 390p.
A collection of biographical essays dealing with the both outstanding nineteenth century personalities in literature, education, philosophy, politics, arts, science, and music, and the key revolutionary leaders.

904. <u>Formación de la nación cubana.</u>
Carlos Chain Soler.
Havana: Ediciones Granma, 1968. 124p. bibliog.
An interpretative history of the formation of national culture from the early sixteenth century through the end of the nineteenth.   The author examines key elements considered to be decisive in the shaping of Cuban nationality, including race, sugar production, plantation economy, and the wars for independence.

905. <u>Fundadores de la nación cubana.</u>
Emeterio S. Santovenia and Raúl M. Shelton.
Miami, Florida: Rema Press, 1967. 279p.
This collection of fifty biographical essays deals with the principal political leaders, educators, philosophers, soldiers, and scientists who contributed to the shaping of Cuban culture.

906. <u>Grandes hombres de Cuba; estudio histórico-biográfico de la vida de cubanos ilustres.</u>
Carlos M. Alvarez.
Matanzas, Cuba: Librería e Imprenta de Andrés Estrada, 1928. 504p.
Presents a collection of biographies of the most prominent Cuban intellectuals, writers, scientists, educators, philosophers, and public personalities.

907. <u>Las ideas en Cuba y la filosofía en Cuba.</u>
Medardo Vitier.
Havana: Editorial de Ciencias Sociales, 1970.   481p.
One of the most complete studies discussing Cuban intellectual currents in the nineteenth century.   While most of the book is devoted to examining the variety of political philosophies, attention is also paid to economic thought, literary criticism, philosophical currents and pedagogy.   The material is given a thematic unity by the exploration of the role of various schools of thought in shaping Cuban nationality.

908. Los maestros de la cultura cubana.
Ateneo de La Habana.
Havana: Impresores de P. Fernández, 1941.   143p.
Provides a collection of essays examining the role of
several outstanding Cubans in shaping national culture.
The subjects include José Agustín Caballero, José de la Luz
y Caballero, Félix Varela, José Antonio Saco, Domingo del
Monte, Ricardo del Monte, Conde de Pozos Dulces, José
Calixto Bernal, Enrique Piñeyro, Manuel Sanguily, Rafael
María Mendive, and José Martí.

909. Origen y desarrollo del pensamiento cubano.
Raimundo Menocal y Cueto.
Havana: Editorial Lex, 1945.   547p.
A sweeping survey of Cuban intellectual history, examining
the origins of Cubanidad ("Cubaness").   The study begins
with the early years of colonial regime and concludes with
the period in which the book was published.   The author
skillfully places the development of Cuban thought within a
broader   setting,   and   stresses   the   impact   of   the
socio-economic order, specifically slavery and sugar, as
vital determinants of national character.

910. Panorama de la cultura cubana.
Félix Lizaso.
México: Fondo de Cultura Económica, 1949.   155p.
In this survey of Cuba culture, the section dealing with
the colonial period is in the form of "life and times"
sketches of Félix Varela, José de la Luz y Caballero,
Enrique José Varona, and José Martí.   The discussion of
Cuban cultural developments in the republic is arranged
thematically.

911. Patria y cultura.
Rafael María Merchán.
Havana: Ministerio de Educación, 1948.   277p.
An account of the intellectual and artistic currents in
nineteenth century Cuba and their relationship to the
development of a national culture and nationalism.

912. Política cultural de la revolución cubana.
Havana: Editorial de Ciencias Sociales, 1977.   140p.
This collection of materials serve to outline in broad
terms the cultural policies of the Cuban revolution between
1961 and 1976.   Among the contributions are the speech to
intellectuals by Fidel Castro (1961), a declaration of
purpose issued by the first National Congress of Education
and Culture (1971), a report on the role of culture by the
Central Committee of the Cuban Communist Party (1975), a
resolution passed on culture and literature at the 1965
Party Congress, and section four of the 1976 constitution
dealing with education and culture.

Literature

A. General

913. Album poético-fotográfico de las escritoras cubanas.
Edited by Domitila García de Coronado.
Havana: Viuda e Hijos de Soler, 1868. 228p.
An anthology of the writings of women poets.

914. Alejo Carpentier: The Pilgrim at Home.
Roberto González Echevarría.
Ithaca, New York: Cornell University Press, 1977. 307p.
bibliog.
A thorough analysis of the works of one of Cuba's major
fiction writers. The work offers a survey of Carpentier's
narrative work from the 1920s up to the 1970s.

915. Antología del cuento en Cuba, 1902-1952.
Compiled by Salvador Bueno.
Havana: Ministerio de Educación, 1953. 379p.
An anthology of Cuban fiction, including some of the most
prominent authors of the republican years.

916. Bosquejo histórico de las letras cubanas.
José Antonio Portuondo.
Havana: Ministerio de Educación, 1960. 79p.
Studies Cuban literature as it developed during specific
historical periods. The work is organized chronologically
from conquest and colonization through the 1940s.

917. Cincuenta años de poesía cubana, 1902-1952.
Compiled by Cynthio Vitier.
Havana: Ministerio de Educación, 1952. 420p.
A balanced anthology of Cuban poetry. The introduction
provides a good summary of Cuban poetry in the republic.

918. Con Cuba. (With Cuba.) An Anthology of Cuban Poetry of
the Last Sixty Years.
Edited by Nathaniel Tarn.
London: Cape Goliard, 1969. 144p. bibliog.
A collection of Cuban poems in Spanish, with English
translations.

919. "Cuba: poesía entre revolución y exilio."
Orlando Rodríguez Sardiñas.
Revista/Review Interamericana, vol. 4, no. 3 (Autumn 1974),
p. 359-69.
Surveys the bifurcation of the traditions in Cuban poetry
between that which was written in exile and that which was
written on the island.

920. Cuba's Nicolás Guillén: Poetry and Ideology.
Keith Ellis.
Toronto, Canada: University of Toronto Press, 1983. 251p.
Examines the poetry and politics of Guillen and pays
specific attention to the theoretical dimensions of his
work. The study provides an original textual analysis of
Guillen's poetry, stressing the range of poetic modes
through which he expresses concern about Cuban identity,
racial issues, imperialism, class struggle, the revolution,
and socialism.

921. Esquema histórico de las letras en Cuba, 1548-1902.
José Antonio Fernández de Castro.
Havana: Departamento de Intercambio Cultural de la
Universidad de La Habana, 1949. 145p.
A general historical survey of Cuban literature from the
eighteenth century up to end of the nineteenth century.
The book is especially useful in its assessment of the
relationship between literature and the struggle for
independence in the nineteenth century.

922. Estética y revolución.
José Antonio Portuondo.
Havana: Unión de Escritores y Artistas de Cuba, 1963.
103p.
This collection of essays examines various aspects of Cuban
culture, including painting, literature, and literary
criticism, within the context of revolution.

923. "'Generales y doctores' After Forty-Five Years."
J. Riis Ouvre.
Journal of Inter-American Studies, vol. 8, no. 3 (July
1966), p. 371-85.
A discussion of the novel Generales y doctores by Carlos
Loveira (1882-1928), its impact on the literary styles of
the period, and its influence on popular culture.

924. Historia de la literatura cubana.
Salvador Bueno.
Havana: Ministerio de Educación, 1963.   3rd ed. 456p.
bibliog.
Surveys the diverse forms of Cuban literature from the
period of conquest and colonization to the early years of
the revolution.

925. Historia de la literatura cubana.
Juan J. Remos y Rubio.
Havana: Cárdenas y Compañía, 1945.   3 vols.   bibliog.
A comprehensive survey of Cuban literature, following a
general chronological flow as the framework for analysis.
Within each periodization category, the author discusses
the varieties of Cuban literature and their principal
exponents.   Thus, for the nineteenth century, the
examination of romanticism is accompanied by specific
analysis of romantic writers.   The work covers the period
of conquest up to the 1940s.

926. Las ideas en Cuba.
Medardo Vitier.
Havana: Editorial Trópico, 1938.   2 vols.
A detailed history of literary and philosophical
developments in Cuba.   The work centers principally on the
nineteenth century.

927. "'Juan Criollo' After Forty Years."
J. Riis Ouvre.
Journal of Inter-American Studies, vol. 9, no. 3 (July
1967), p. 396-412.
Analyzes the major novel by Carlos Loveira.   The essay
discusses the literary merits of the book and assesses its
value as a reflection of the Cuban social reality and its
impact on that reality.

928. "Lino Novás Calvo and the Revista de Avance."
Raymond D. Souza.
Journal of Inter-American Studies, vol. 10, no. 2 (April
1968), p. 232-243.
Studies the early works of writer Novás Calvo as they
appeared in the early issues of the influential journal
Avance between 1927 and 1930.

929. La literatura costumbrista cubana de los siglos XVIII y
XIX: los escritores.
Emilio Roig de Leuchsenring.
Hanvana: Oficina del Historiador de la Ciudad, 1962.
Analyzes the principal writers associated with the
costumbrista movement.   The twenty-one essays deal with
different authors representing a variety of thematic and

stylistic variations over the better part of a 150-year
span.

930. La literatura cubana. Esquema histórico desde sus orígenes
     hasta 1964.
     Raimundo Lazo.
     México: Universidad Nacional Autónoma de México, 1965.
     256p. bibliog.
     A historical survey of Cuban literature.   The book is
     arranged   in   seven   separate   sections   dealing   in
     chronological order with the development of a national
     literature: the antecedents (1492-1790), the colony
     (1790-1834),   the   period   of   cultural   transformation
     (1834-1868), the struggle for independence (1868-1902), the
     early republic (1902-1940), the end of the bourgeois
     republic (1940-1959),   and the revolution (1959-1964.)

931. Major Cuban Novelists: Innovation and Tradition.
     Raymond D. Souza.
     Columbia, Missouri: University of Missouri Press, 120p.
     bibliog.
     Studies the Cuban novel from the 1850s to the present and
     discusses three of its most prominent contemporary writers:
     Alejo Carpentier, José Lezama Lima, and Guillermo Cabrera
     Infante. The author argues that the emergence of the Cuban
     tradition of the novel is closely related to the
     development of a national awareness and the creation of a
     sense of national identity.

932. El movimiento de los romances cubanos del siglo XIX.
     Edited by Samuel Feijóo.
     Santa Clara, Cuba: Universidad Central de Las Villas,
     1964. 437p.
     An anthology of Cuban romantic poetry from the nineteenth
     century.   A brief introduction sets the context for these
     poems, many of which originally served as an expression of
     Cuban opposition to Spanish rule.

933. La narrativa de Enrique Labrador Ruiz.
     Rita Molinero.
     Madrid: Playor, 1977. 262p. bibliog.
     Examines an important but little known Cuban novelist of
     the 1930s and 1940s. The emphasis of work is on Labrador
     Ruiz's theories of fiction, his method, and literary
     device.

934. Lo negro y lo mulato en la poesía cubana.
     Ildefonso Pereda Valdés.
     Montevideo: Ediciones Ciudadela, 1970.   166p. bibliog.
     The first section of this two-part book is a general study
     of Afro-Cuban influences on national poetry. The second is

an anthology of Cuban poetry representative of Afro-Cuban genre.

935. "La novela en Cuba en el siglo XIX."
Marguerite C. Suárez-Murias.
Revista Interamericana de Bibliografía, vol. 11, no. 14 (June 1961), p. 125-36.
Surveys the development of the novel in nineteenth century Cuba, with particular emphasis on the works of Cirilo Villaverde, José Antonio Echeverría, Félix Manuel Tanio, Anselmo Suárez y Romero, José Zacarias González del Valle, Gertrudis Gómez de Avellaneda, and Ramón Pina.

936. "Las novelas de Carlos Loveira."
Arturo Montori.
Cuba Contemporánea, vol. 30, no. 119 (Nov. 1922), p. 213-39.
A detailed description of the principal novels by Loveira. The essay assesses the origins of the works as well as their style, themes, and character development.

937. Panorama histórico de la literatura cubana.
Max Henríquez Ureña.
New York: Las Américas Publishing Co., 1963. 2 vols. bibliog.
One of the most comprehensive discussions of the history of Cuban literature covering the early days of Spanish colonization to the 1950s. In the nearly 1,000 pages of this 2-volume account, the author examines all the principal literary movements, including essays, journalism, drama, poetry, the novel, historical narrative, and literary criticism, as well as discussing the principal exponents of each movement. An indispensable introductory survey.

938. La poesía contemporánea en Cuba, 1927-1953.
Roberto Fernández Retamar.
Havana: Orígenes, 1954. 131p. bibliog.
Provides a very useful survey of Cuban poets and poetry for the middle third of the twentieth century. Among the themes discussed include social poetry, the influence of race, and the vanguard poets.

939. La poesía lírica en Cuba.
Martín González del Valle.
Barcelona: Tipolitografía de Luis Tasso, 1900. 351p.
A general discussion of Cuban lyric poetry in the nineteenth century, highlighted by a critical discussion of the works of the leading poets of the period.

940. La poesía pura en Cuba y su evolución.

Marta Linares Pérez.
Madrid: Playor, S.A., 1975. 240p. bibliog.
A historical survey of poetry in Cuba, from the early
1900s up to the 1920s. The lives and works of Mariano
Brull, Emilio Ballagas, and Eugenio Floret are examined in
detail.

941. Proceso histórico de las letras cubanas.
Juan Nepomuceno Remos y Rubio.
Madrid: Ediciones Guadarrama, 1958. 303p. bibliog.
Examines the evolution of Cuban literary forms from the
early sixteenth century chroniclers to the twentieth
century writers. The emphasis of the study falls on
nineteenth and twentieth century developments, especially
poetry and journalism.

942. La república de Cuba al través de sus escritores.
Marcelo Pogolotti,
Havana: Editorial Lex, 1958. 208p.
A detailed review of the distinct varieties of Cuban
literature during the twentieth century. The author
examines the means by which Cuban literature served to
reflect both popular moods and political realities in the
republic. The work is an important contribution to both an
understanding of the form of Cuban literature and its
particular function.

943. "A Survey of Cuban Costumbrismo."
Roberta Day Corbitt.
Hispania, vol. 33. no. 1 (Feb. 1950), p. 41-45.
Studes the early nineteenth century literary movement. The
analysis of this development in literature--devoted to the
exaltation of things Cuban--is based on a study of some of
the key representative writers, including Cirilo
Villaverde, Anselmo Suárez y Romero, José Victoriano
Betancourt, Luis Victoriano Betancourt, and José María de
Cárdenas y Rodríguez.

944. Teatro cubano, 1927-1961.
Natividad González Freire.
Havana: Ministerio de Relaciones Exteriores, 1961. 181p.
bibliog.
Surveys three generations of Cuban playwrights, providing
biographical notes on leading dramatists, summaries of the
context and contents of their work, and a general
commentary on the evolution of both the form and function
of Cuban theater.

945. Temas y personajes de la literatura cubana.
Salvador Bueno.
Havana: Empresa Consolidada de Artes Gráficas, 1964.

301p.
A survey of Cuban literature, principally for the nineteenth and twentieth centuries. The work deals with literary movements, individual writers, and the specific literary journals and reviews that exercised influence and shaped the currents of Cuban thought.

946. Los trovadores del pueblo.
Edited by Samuel Feijóo.
Santa Clara, Cuba: Universidad Central de Las Villas, 1960. 684p.
Presents an extensive collection of the lyrics of the Cuban folk music (décima.) The volume has a detailed intoduction, examining the origins of the décima as a form of peasant poetry and a medium of passing along information. The décimas included serve to underscore the variety and versatility of the folk-music in Cuba.

B. Post-1959

947. "Criticism and Literature in Revolutionary Cuba."
Roberto González-Echevarría.
Cuban Studies/Estudios Cubanos, vol. 11, no. 1 (Jan. 1981), p. 1-17.
A thoughtful study of literary criticism in socialist in Cuba that examines both academic and journalistic criticism.

948. "Literature and Revolution in Cuba."
Roberta Salper.
Monthly Review, vol. 22, no. 5 (Oct. 1970), p. 15-30.
A discussion of literary developments in Cuba since the revolution. Beginning with a historical survey of twentieth century Cuban literature, the author places post-1959 writing within a larger revolutionary tradition.

949. Literatura y arte nuevo en Cuba.
Mario Benedetti.
Barcelona: Editorial Laia, 1977. 287p.
This collection of essays deals with a variety of cultural themes, including photography as journalism, mass media, the function of revolutionary Cuba, the social role of the novelist, Afro-Cuban poetry, the role of the intellectual, and the intellectual and the revolution.

950. Nueva literatura cubana.
Julio E. Miranda.
Madrid: Taurus, 1971. 141p.
A discussion of the development of Cuban literature after the revolution. Among the literary forms examined are

poetry, historical narrative, theater, essays, and literary criticism.

951. Prose Fiction of the Cuban Revolution.
Seymour Menton.
Austin, Texas: University of Texas Press, 1975.   344p.
bibliog.
Presents a comprehensive overview of the historical and social forces that shape fictional prose in socialist Cuba. More than 100 novels and short story collections published between 1959 and 1973 are examined with an eye to the social environment in which they were written.   The periodization schema classifies four distinct phases: 1959-1960 (the struggle against tryanny), 1961-1965 (exorcism and existentialism), 1966-1970 (experimentation and escapism), and 1971-1975 (the ideological novel and short story).

952. "Racism, Culture, and Revolution: Ideology and Politics in the Prose of Nicolás Guillén."
Roberto Márquez.
Latin American Research Review, vol. 17, no. 1 (1982), p. 43-68.
A detailed examination of the poetry of Nicolás Guillén as it addresses specifically the issues of the Afro-Cuban experience and the process of national liberation in Cuba.

953. "Recent Developments in the Cuban Novel."
William L. Siemens.
Revista/Review Interamericana, vol. 8, no. 2 (Summer 1978), p. 305-08.
A brief description of the condition of the novel in socialist Cuba, paying attention to the writings of Guillermo Cabrera Infante, José Lezama Lama, and Alejo Carpentier.

954. "Revolución, literatura y religión afro-cubana."
Julio Matas.
Cuban Studies/Estudios Cubanos, vol. 13, no. 1 (Winter 1983), p. 17-23.
An examination of the persistence of Afro-Cuban cults and the problem it poses to the revolution as seen through the fiction of Antonio Benítez Rojo.

955. "Running the Blockade: Six Cuban Writers."
Bell Gale Chevigny.
Socialist Review, vol. 11, no. 5 (Sept.-Oct. 1981), p. 83-112.
Based on extensive interviews, this essay provides interesting portrayals of six prominent Cuban writers: Pablo Armando Fernández, Humberto Arenal, Miguel Barnet,

Reynaldo González, Nancy Morejón, and Manuel Pereira.

956. "The Short Story of the Cuban Revolution, 1959-1969."
Seymour Menton.
Studies in Short Fiction, vol. 8, no. 1 (Winter 1971),
p. 32-43. bibliog.
Examines developments in the Cuban short story during the
first decade of the revolution. Based on survey of twelve
published anthologies of short stories, the essay
categorizes four distinct literary generations: authors
from the 1920s and 1930s, 1940s, 1950s, and 1960s and
1970s. The essay includes an annotated bibliography of the
anthologies examined.

957. "Towards a Theory of Literature in Revolutionary Cuba."
Joseph R. Pereira.
Caribbean Quarterly, vol. 21, nos. 1-2 (March-June 1975),
p. 62-73.
Discusses the development of the theoretical context of
literature in Cuba after 1959. The essay examines the role
of the political leadership in the development of a theory,
and the subsequent founding of various literary journals
and agencies. Particular attention is paid to the role of
the National Council of Culture.

958. Writers in the New Cuba.
Edited by J. M. Cohen.
Baltimore: Penguin Books, 1967. 191p.
An anthology of writers representative of literary
developments in Cuba after the revolution. The collection
contains several short stories, some poems, and a one-act
play.

C. José Martí

959. The America of José Martí.
Edited by Federico de Onís.
New York: The Noonday Press, 1953. 335p.
A selection and translation of the writings of José Martí.
The essays are arranged into four groupings: commentaries
about the United States, works dealing with Latin America,
literary portraits, and political tracts dealing with
issues of Cuban independence. A brief introduction
provides a bio-literary portrait of Martí.

960. Anuario del Centro de Estudios Martianos.
Havana: Biblioteca Nacional "José Martí," vol. 1- . 1978- .
A yearbook devoted to essays on Marti's ethics, aesthetics,
politics, and bibliography.

961. La gran enciclopedia martiana.
     Edited by Ramón Cernudo.
     Barcelona, Spain: Publicaciones Reunidos. E.A. 1978. 14
     vols.
     A collection of Martí's essays, speeches, news stories,
     correspondence, and poetry. The work also includes essays
     on Martí, his life, and his work.

962. Inside the Monster. Writings on the United States and
     American Imperialism.
     José Martí. Edited by Philip S. Foner.
     New York: Monthly Review Press, 1975. 386p.
     This collection of essays deals with various aspects of
     social, economic, and political developments in the United
     States during the last two decades of the nineteenth
     century.

963. José Martí, Architect of Cuba's Freedom.
     Peter Turton.
     London: Zed Books, 1986. 157p. bibliog.
     In part biography, in part critical study, this work gives
     particular emphasis to the ideological formation of Martí,
     underscoring the experiences and philosophical currents
     that contributed to shaping his intellectual development.

964. José Martí, Cuban Patriot.
     Richard Butler Gray.
     Gainesville, Florida: University of Florida Press, 1962.
     307p. bibliog.
     A study of the life and thought of Martí. Of particular
     value is the discussion of the symbolism of Martí in Cuban
     politics and society during the 1940s and 1950s.

965. Martí, Martyr of Cuban Independence.
     Félix Lizaso.
     Westport, Connecticut: Greenwood Press, 1974.   260p.
     A reprint of the 1953 centennial edition. The work is a
     sentimental and sympathetic biography of Martí, with
     emphasis on his revolutionary activities during the 1880s
     and 1890s.

966. José Martí, Mentor of the Cuban Nation.
     John M. Kirk.
     Gainesville, Florida: University Presses of Florida, 1983.
     201p. bibliog.
     Presents a comprehensive examination of the works of Martí
     and his sociopolitical thought. The study pays particular
     attention to Martí's views on politics, social structure,
     economic development, morality, and revolution.

967. José Martí on the U.S.A.

Edited by Luis A. Baralt.
Carbondale, Illinois: Southern Illinois University Press,
1966. 223p.
A collection of essays dealing with the United States
written by Martí. The volume is arranged in three
sections: notable North American personalities, noteworthy
events, and vignettes of life in the United States.

968. José Martí, Revolutionary Democrat.
Edited by Christopher Abel and Nissa Torrents.
Durham, N.C.:   Duke University Press, 1986.   238p.
bibliog.
This collection of essays on Martí deals with a number of
themes, including ideology, revolutionary activity,
treatment of Martí's literary genius, and Martí's views on
the United States.

969. Martí, Apostle of Freedom.
Jorge Mañach.
New York: The Devin-Adair Co., 1950. 363p.
This complete and well-written popular biography is
unabashedly well-disposed to Martí. The book provides a
great deal of information about Martí's efforts in behalf
of the cause of Cuba independence.

970. "Martí, los libros y sus libros."
Fermín Peraza Sarausa.
Revista Interamericana de Bibliografía, vol. 3, no. 3
(1953), p. 245-51.
A bibliographical compilation of the various editions
published of Martí's complete works. It also includes
works by Martí translated into other languages.

971. Martí y su concepción del mundo.
Roberto D. Agramonte.
Río Piedras, Puerto Rico: Editorial Universitaria, 1971.
815p.
This voluminous tome serves as a thematically arranged
compendium of José Martí's ideas. The analytical index
provides an easy to use guide to Martí's thoughts on a
variety of topics.

972. Obras completas.
José Martí.
Havana: Editorial Nacional de Cuba, 1963-1980. 28 vols.
The most complete published collection of the works of
Martí. It includes poetry, fiction, essays, speeches, and
correspondence spanning more than two decades.

973. Our America.
José Martí. Edited by Philip S. Foner.

New York: Monthly Review Press, 1977.   448p.
A collection of essays, speeches, correspondence, and news articles written by Martí between 1878 and 1895 deals with Latin American themes generally and Cuban independence specifically.

Language

974. Diccionario de cubanismos mas usuales. Como habla el cubano.
José Sánchez-Boudy.
Miami, Florida: Ediciones Universales, 1978. 429p.
A compendium of contemporary popular Cuban usage. Its distinctive characteristic is that it includes phrases and constructs that have worked their way into the Spanish spoken among Cubans in exile since 1959.

975. El español en Cuba.
Cristina Isbasescu.
Bucarest: Sociedad Rumana de Lingüística Románica, 1968. 134p.
A study of Spanish dialects in Cuba.

976. El habla popular cubana.
Argelio Santiesteban.
Havana: Editorial Ciencias Sociales, 1982. 366p. bibliog.
A compilation of Cuban colloquialisms.

977. "Influencia de la lengua rusa en el lexico del español en Cuba, 1959-1963."
Jorge Anzardo C.
Islas, no. 64 (Sept.-Dec. 1979), p. 65-109.
This well-developed essay examines the introduction of the Russian words and phrases into Cuban Spanish during the early years of the revolution. Words are analyzed by categories and include economics, science, technology, and food.

978. "Las lenguas africanos y el español coloquia de Cuba."
Sergio Valdés.

<u>Santiago</u>, no. 31 (Sept. 1978), p. 81-107.
One of the better analyses of the impact of African languages on Cuban Spanish. Distinctions are made between the languages spoken in rural and urban Cuba. The essay includes a lengthy bibliography.

979. "A Phonological Study of the Spanish of Havana, Cuba."
Anthony J. Lamb.
Ph.D. Dissertation, University of Kansas. 173p. bibliog.
A detailed examination of linguistic patterns of Havana based on interviews with 30 lower middle class life-long residents of the capital. An interview tape supplement to the dissertation is available for consultation at the University of Kansas Library.

980. "La pronunciación del idioma español in el centro de Cuba."
Ruth Goodgall de Pruna.
<u>Islas</u>, no. 37 (Sept.-Dec. 1971), p. 155-60.
This useful essay on the patterns of spoken Spanish in the central regions of Cuba was based on the speech of two population groups divided by age, with forty being the upper and lower age limit.

981. "Sobre el dialecto cubano y el origen de las razas primitivas de América."
Juan L. Martín.
<u>Revista Bimestre Cubana</u>, vol. 22, no. 1 (Jan.-Feb. 1927), p. 43-62.
Examines the pre-Columbian origins of Cuban dialect and analyzes the contribution of Africanisms and North Americanisms to Cuban Spanish.

982. <u>Las raíces de la lingüística indígena de Cuba.</u>
Juliano Vivanco y Díaz.
Havana: Editorial "El Sol," 1953. 133p.
A detailed account of Indian languages in Cuba and their contribution to the Cuban vernacular.

Visual Arts

983. El arte en Cuba.
Martha de Castro.
Miami, Florida: Ediciones Universal, 1970.   151p.
bibliog.
An illustrated survey account of Cuban art from 1519 to the
1960s.   The work deals with architecture, sculpture, and
painting, as well as briefly surveying minor and industrial
arts.

984. The Art of Revolution.
Dugald Stermer and Susan Sontag.
New York: McGraw-Hill, 1970. 101p.
This richly illustrated and over-sized volume provides one
of the best available collections of Cuban poster art.   The
collection includes representative posters produced by the
Organization of Solidarity with Asia, Africa, and Latin
America (OSPAAAL), the Commission for Revolutionary Action
(COR), Casa de las Américas, and the national film bureau
(ICAIC).

985. Las bellas artes en Cuba.
Edited by José Manuel Carbonell y Rivero.
Havana: Imprenta "El Siglo XX," 1928. 451p.
An excellent collection of essays dealing with all facets
of Cuban cultural development, including literature,
theater, music, painting, sculpture, architecture, and
caricature.

986. Caricatura de la república.
Adelaida de Juan.
Havana: Editorial Letras Cubanas, 1982. 268p.
This presents a history of caricature between 1902 and
1958, with particular emphasis on political function of

this art form.

987. "La caricatura en Cuba."
Bernard G. Barros.
Cuba Contemporánea, vol. 5, no. 3 (July 1914), p. 313-25;
vol. 5, no. 4 (Aug. 1914), p. 458-73.
Presents a history of a popular Cuban art form from the
early nineteenth century to the 1910s. The essay pays
particular attention to the fashion in which caricature
served as a form of political commentary.

988. "Cinema and Politics: the Cuban Experience."
Andrés R. Hernández.
Cuba Resource Center Newsletter, vol. 3, nos. 2-3 (Oct.
1973), p. 19-22.
Surveys the history of Cuban cinema from the end of the
nineteenth century to the revolution. Most of the essay is
devoted to film-making in socialist Cuba.

989. Cronología del cine cubano.
Arturo Agramonte.
Havana: Ediciones ICAIC, 1966. 172p.
Provides a historical study of Cuban film from the late
nineteenth century to the mid-1960s. The book examines
both the technical advances and the artistic achievements
of the national cinema. The varieties of Cuban film are
discussed including commercial drama, documentaries, and
animation.

990. Dos ensayos sobre plástica cubana.
Adelaida de Juan.
Santiago de Chile: Editorial Andrés Bello, 1972. 28p.
Two critical essays examining twentieth century Cuban
painting.

991. Memories of Underdevelopment: the Revolutionary Films of
Cuba.
Edited by Michael Myerson.
New York: Grossman Publishers, 1973. 194p.
This series of essays examines the development of cinema in
socialist Cuba. The volume includes movie scripts,
interviews, a discusssion of the Cuban film institute, and
an analysis of several major and minor Cuban films.

992. "Nuestro arte y las circunstancias nacionales."
Juan Marinello.
Cuba Contemporánea, vol. 37, no. 148 (April 1925),
p. 298-304.
Discusses the emergence of a national style of painting and
sculpture. Author argues that art should serve to uplift
national spirit and promote national pride.

993. "La pintura in Cuba."
Jorge Mañach.
Cuba Contemporánea, vol. 36, no. 141 (Sept. 1924), p. 5-23;
vol. 36, no. 142 (Oct. 1924), p. 105-25.
A two-part essay dealing with the history of painting in
Cuba.   The first part deals with painting from the
sixteenth century to 1900; the second section treats
painting from 1900 to 1924.

994. "Posters From and For the People."
Stephanie Rugoff.
Cuba Resource Center Newsletter, vol. 3, nos. 2-3 (Oct.
1973), p. 23-24.
A discussion of Cuban poster art based on an interview with
the artist Félix Beltrán.

995. "A Short Guide to Old Cuban Prints."
Emilio C. Cueto.
Cuban Studies/Estudios Cubanos, vol. 14, no. 1 (Winter
1984), p. 27-42.
Presents a guide to the most important graphics of Cuban
people and places during the 400 years of the colonial
period.   Some 200 entries are arranged in alphabetical
order, indicating the locations of the originals and the
availability of their reproductions.

Architecture

996. La arquitectura cubana del siglo XIX.
Joaquín E. Weiss y Sánchez.
Havana: Junta Nacional de Arqueología y Etnología, 1960.
126p.
One of the most complete studies of late colonial
architecture.   It is well-balanced in its approach to
public building, private residences, and commercial and
industrial structures.

997. "Contenido de clase en la arquitectura cubana de los años
50."
Roberto Segre.
Revista de la Biblioteca Nacional "José Martí," vol. 17,
no. 3 (Sept.-Dec. 1975), p. 97-126.
A thoughtful essay examining the relationship between Cuban
architecture in Cuba and politics during the 1950s.   The
author outlines in detail the economic sources of Cuban
designs and construction during this period.

998. "Continuidad y renovación en la arquitectura cubana del
siglo XX."
Roberto Segre.
Santiago, no. 4 (March 1981), p. 9-35.
Surveys Cuban architecture from the 1830s to the 1980s.
The author examines the impact of Spanish and North
American styles on Cuba as well as the Cuban expression of
modernism.   Attention is given to the influences of culture
and ideology on Cuban architecture after the revolution.

999. "Cuba: arquitectura y revolución, 1959-1963."
Carmen María Cuevas and José Peláez.
Areíto, vol. 1, no. 4 (Jan.-March 1974), p. 16-22.
After a brief outline of the principal pre-revolutionary

influences on Cuban architecture, this essay examines
the development of new forms and functions after the
revolution. Architectural styles are assessed in their
many expressions--public buildings, housing, parks,
recreational centers, and educational facilities.

1000. Diez años de arquitectura en Cuba revolucionaria.
      Roberto Segre.
      Havana: Ediciones Unión, 1970. 225p. bibliog.
      A survey of architectural form and function in socialist
      Cuba.

1001. Los monumentos de la república de Cuba.
      Emilio Roig de Leuchsenring.
      Havana: Junta Nacional de Arqueología y Ethnología,
      1957-1959. 2 vols. bibliog.
      This survey chronicles the history of the principal
      monuments and public buildings in Cuba.

1002. El pre-barroco en Cuba.
      F. Prat Puig.
      Havana: Burgay y Cía., 1947. 438p.
      A richly illustrated discussion of colonial architecture
      during approximately the first two centuries of Spanish
      rule, examining missions, churches, monuments, public
      buildings, and private homes.   The evolution of the
      details of architecture, such as doors, balconies,
      galleries, upright supports, railings, and ceilings, is
      also assessed, and attention is given to the development
      of   construction   techniques   and   changing   building
      materials.   Richly illustrated with drawings, plans, and
      plates.

Performing Arts

1003. Apuntes sobre el teatro colonial, 1790-1833.
Yolanda Aguirre.
Havana: Universidad de La Habana, 1969. 102p. bibliog.
A study of the development of Cuban theater. Particular
attention is paid to the theater in Havana and the
administration and function of stage productions. The
Afro-Cuban contribution to the development of the
colonial theater is also discussed.

1004. "Dance and Diplomacy: the Cuban National Ballet."
Aaron Segal.
Caribbean Review, vol. 9, no. 1 (Winter 1980), p. 30-32.
A favorable discussion of the Cuban National Ballet and
its role in presenting a positive image of Cuba to the
world. The essay traces the development of the National
Ballet under Alicia Alonso from its origins in 1960 up to
the 1970s.

1005. "Desarrollo de la danza en Cuba."
Aurora Bosch.
Revista de la Biblioteca Nacional "José Martí," vol. 21,
no. 2 (May-Aug. 1979), p. 89-102.
Examines the development of dance in Cuba since the
revolution. The article discusses the National Dance
Company, the National Folklore Group, and the Ballet of
Camagüey province.

1006. Historia del teatro en La Habana.
Edwin Teurbe Tolón and Jorge Antonio González.
Santa Clara, Cuba: Universidad Central de Las Villas,
1961. 163p. bibliog.
A general history of theater in Havana, from the
establishment of theater in the late eighteenth century

through the end of the nineteenth century. The study examines the development of various forms of the Havana theater, including Italian and French operas, comedy, local productions, drama, and ballet.

1007. Introducción a Cuba: la música.
Jose Ardevol.
Havana: Instituto del Libro, 1969.   195p.   bibliog.
A collection of essays dealing with a wide range of themes, all of which are united by the common concern for the social function of music in revolutionary Cuba. The essays examine the development of classical and folk music in Cuba, a discussion of both national and foreign composers, an evaluation of the national symphony, and the role of nationalism in music.

1008. La música en Cuba.
Alejo Carpentier.
Havana: Editorial Luz-Hilo, 1961. 205p. bibliog.
One of Cuba's most prominent writers offers a graceful and informative account of the historical development of music in Cuba. The work deals with the colonial origins of national music, church influences, the influence of romanticism and nationalsm, the Afro-Cuban impact, and the varieties of popular music.

1009. "La música en Cuba durante la etapa revolucionaria."
Sergio Fernández Barroso.
Revista de la Biblioteca Nacional "José Martí," vol. 21, no. 2 (May-Aug. 1979), p. 119-31.
Discusses the development of music during the years of the revolution, including the nature of musical education, the organization of the National Symphony, the establishment of the recording industry, and the manufacturing of musical instruments.

1010. Orbita del Ballet Nacional de Cuba: 1948-1979.
Miguel Cabrera.
Havana: Editorial Orbe, 1978. 148p.
Studies the origins, development, and expansion of the national ballet in Cuba after the revolution. The work documents the role of foreign dancers, the development of the repertoire, accounts of past tours, and biographies of those who are most prominently associated with the company.

1011. "Perspectives on Cuban Theater."
George W. Woodward.
Revista/Review Interamericana, vol. 9, no. 1 (Spring 1979), p. 42-49.
Surveys the development of drama in Cuba after the

revolution. The essay examines state support of theater, the condition of playwrights, and the policy towards production.

1012. Revista de Música.
Havana: Biblioteca Nacional "José Martí," 1960-   .
quarterly.
A journal devoted to the study of Cuban music. Contributions range from works on Afro-Cuban rhythms and to studies on colonial baroque dance.

1013. Teatro cubano contemporáneo, 1928-1957.
Natividad González Freire.
Havana: Sociedad Colombista Panamericana, 1958.   267p.
bibliog.
A general survey of twentieth century theater in Cuba. The author examines several generations of playwrights and their works, with particular attention to the national and international influences on Cuban drama.

1014. "Theater and Political Criteria in Cuba: Casa de las Américas Awards, 1960-1983."
Paul Christopher Smith.
Cuba Studies/Estudios Cubanos, vol. 14, no. 1 (Winter 1984), p. 43-47.
Analyzes the interaction between changing ideological developments and shifting artistic modes of expression.

1015. "Transforming Theater."
Cuba Review, vol. 7, no. 4 (Dec. 1977), p. 3-24.
Presents a special issue dedicated to the development of the theater in socialist Cuba. Among the themes explored are children in theater, popular theater, rural theater, and interviews with several Cuban actors and playwrights.

Sports

1016. Caza y pesca en Cuba.
A. Carlos Pérez Ramos.
Havana: Editorial Lex, 1945. 247p.
This discussion of the game and fishing laws in Cuba
includes a compilation of the principal laws and decrees
dealing with fishing and hunting and the municipal
responsibilities involved in upholding these laws.

1017. "El deporte como factor patriótico y sociológico: las
grandes figuras deportivas de Cuba."
José Sixto de Sola.
Cuba Contemporánea, vol. 5, no. 2 (June 1914), p. 121-67.
This assessment of the competitive aspects of sports as a
means of exalting nationality leads into a more general
discussion of sports in Cuba, such as baseball,
gymnastics, boxing, boating, tennis, and basketball.
Cubans who have attained sporting distinctions receive
brief biographical attention.

1018. Manual del cazador y del pescador fluvial.
Cuba. Ministerio de Agricultura. Dirección de Montes,
Minas y Aguas.
Havana: Imprenta "Editorial Neptuno," 1942. 54p.
A compilation of fish and game laws and fishing regulations.

1019. "Thinking Politically About Sports."
Norm Diamond.
Cuba Review, vol. 7, no. 2 (June 1977), p. 3-9.
Examines the development of sports in a political
context. The emphasis is on Cuban efforts to establish a
sports system for the population at large as a means both
for reasons of health and international competition.

Libraries and Archives

1020. <u>Biografía del Archivo Nacional de Cuba</u>.
Joaquín Llaverías y Martínez.
Havana: Publicaciones del Archivo Nacional de Cuba,
1954. 59p.
An account of the history, organization, and development
of the Cuban National Archives by one of its most
prominent past directors.

1021. <u>Boletín del Archivo Nacional</u>.
Cuba. Archivo Nacional.
Havana: 1902-   . irregular.
The principal publication of the Cuban National Archives,
containing published document collections, research
articles, and inventories of the archival record groups.
It is published irregularly, often on a semi-monthly
basis, sometimes as one annual issue.

1022. <u>Catalog of the Cuban and Caribbean Library</u>.
University of Miami. Coral Gables.
Boston: G.K. Hall, 1977. 6 vols.
Provides a useful guide to one of the larger and most
complete Cuban collections in the United States. It is
an indispensable research tool.

1023. "Cuba Materials in the Bureau of Insular Affairs Library."
Louis A. Pérez, Jr.
<u>Latin American Research Review</u>, vol. 13, no. 1 (1978),
p. 182-88.
A compilation of the materials housed in the BIA Library
in the National Archives. The collection contains
newspapers, unpublished manuscripts, and rare books.

1024. <u>Cuban Acquisitions and Bibliography</u>.

Edited by Earl J. Pariseau.
Washington, D.C.:   Library of Congress, 1970.   164p.
Provides an indispensable research guide to the book
holdings, manuscript collections, and archival records
held in various libraries and archives in the United
States, the United Kingdom, Spain, and Germany.   Also
surveyed are the strong Cuban holdings of major research
libraries in the United States and Europe. Its principal
shortcoming is the absence of information concerning
research facilities in Cuba.

1025. Cuban Periodicals in the University of Pittsburgh
      Libraries.
      Compiled by Eduardo Lozano.
      Pittsburgh: University of Pittsburgh Libraries and
      Center for Latin American Studies, 1976.   2nd ed.   68p.
      This is a useful guide to the periodical holdings at one
      of the major depositories of Cuban materials in the
      United States.

1026. Directorio de archivos y museos de Cuba.
      Compiled by Fermín Peraza Sarausa.
      Havana: Anuario Bibliográfico Cubano, 1945.   3p.
      A guide to the archives and museums in Cuba.

1027. Guide to Materials on Latin America in the National
      Archives of the United States.
      George S. Ulibarri and John P. Harrison.
      Washington, D.C.:   National Archives and Records Service,
      1974.   489p.
      An invaluable and comprehensive research guide to records
      on Latin America.   The Cuban materials represent one of
      the larger collections available for use.

1028. "The Holdings of the Library of Congress on the
      Population of Cuba."
      Lisandro Pérez.
      Cuban Studies/Estudios Cubanos, vol. 13, no. 1 (Winter
      1983), p. 69-76.
      Presents a review of the Library of Congress holdings
      relating to demography.   The essay includes titles for
      the colonial period, the years 1899-1958, and the post-
      revolutionary period.

1029. Inauguración del edificio del Archivo Nacional.
      Cuba. Archivo Nacional.
      Havana: Archivo Nacional, 1944.   57p.
      Presents a commemorative publication containing an
      inventory of archival holdings in such diverse areas as
      maps, engravings, and record collections.

1030. List of Books Relating to Cuba with Bibliography of Maps.
Compiled by A. P. C. Griffin and P. Lee Phillips.
Washington, D.C.: Government Printing Office, 1898.   61p.
A brief bibliographical compilation of the materials
housed in the Library of Congress at the end of the
nineteenth century. An appendix includes a catalogue of
relevant manuscripts.

1031. Materials in the National Archives Relating to Cuba.
Seymour Pomrenze.
Washinton,   D.C.:   National   Archives,   Reference
Information Circulars, no. 34, 1948. 12p.
Provides a useful guide to the Cuban holdings of the U.S.
national   archives.   The   guide   to   the   material   is
organized into three periods: pre-1895, 1895-1902, and
post-1902.

1032. The National Archives of Latin America.
Roscoe R. Hill.
Cambridge, Massachusetts: Harvard University Press,
1945. 169p.
A general description of Latin American archives, their
histories,   a   brief   inventory   of   their   holdings,
regulations for use, and available inventories.   The
discussion of the Cuban National Archives (p. 64-81) is
useful, but somewhat dated.

1033. "Record Collections at the Cuban National Archives: A
Descriptive Survey."
Louis A. Pérez, Jr.
Latin American Research Review, vol. 12, no. 1 (1984),
p. 142-56.
Provides an inventory of the principal manuscript
collections, record groups, and published holdings of the
Cuban Archives.

1034. Research Guide to Central America and the Caribbean.
Edited by Kenneth J. Grieb.
Madison, Wisconsin: University of Wisconsin Press, 1985.
431p.
Includes chapters describing the Cuban National Archives
and the National Library of Cuba.

Mass Media

1035. Cuban Communications.
James W. Carty, Jr.
Bethany, West Virginia: Bethany College, 1976. 72p.
A collection of articles previously published in Times of the Americas dealing with mass media in socialist Cuba. Most of the essays deal with the press, magazines, radio, and television.

1036. Diario de la Marina.
Havana: 1835-1960. daily.
A conservative daily newspaper which dealt with national and international news, entertainment, sports, culture, and society. Its publication was suspended in 1960.

1037. Gaceta de La Habana.
Havana: 1848-1902.
The official publication of the colonial government throughout the latter half of the nineteenth century. It published decrees, legislation, new statutes, and all announcements of an official character.

1038. La Gaceta Oficial de la República de Cuba.
Havana: Ministry of Justice, 1902- . irregular.
The principal means by which the government communicated the passage and promulgation of new laws, decrees, and legal codes.

1039. Granma.
Havana: 1965- . daily.
The official newspaper of the Cuban Communist Party (PCC). Materials include national and international news, sports, entertainment, and feature columns.

1040. Havana Post.
Havana: 1900-1963.   daily.
One of the oldest English-language newspapers of Cuba.

1041. Hoy.
Havana: 1940-1965.   daily.
The official newspaper of the old Communist Party of Cuba
(PSP), covering news, editorials, sports, and articles on
ideology.   It merged with Granma in 1965.

1042. Juventud Rebelde.
Havana: 1965-   .   daily.
Published by the Union of Young Communists, this
newspaper is oriented toward Cuban youth.   It deals with
national and international news, sports, entertainment,
and material of general interest to youth.

1043. El Mundo.
Havana: 1901-1969.   daily.
A Havana daily containing general news articles, feature
columns,   sports,   and   entertainment.   It   suspended
publication in 1969.

1044. "Public Opinion and the Press in Cuba."
Ernesto E. Rodríguez.
Cuban Studies/Estudios Cubanos,   vol.   8,   no.   2   (July
1978), p. 51-65.
An examination of the nature of public opinion in
revolutionary Cuba as expressed in 166 readers' letters
published in Granma, the official publication of the
Cuban Communist Party (PCC).

1045. Revolución.
Havana: 1959-1965.   daily.
The official news organ of the 26 of July Movement.
Contains   news   articles,   sports,   and   editorials.
Indispensable for research on the early years of the
revolution. Merged into Granma in 1965.

1046. Times of Havana.
Havana: 1957-1960.
A short-lived English-language Havana daily.

Professional Journals
and Periodicals

1047. Revista Cubana de Medicina.
Havana: 1972- . bi-monthly.
Published by the National Center of Medical Information,
this is a professional journal devoted to articles on
general medicine. The contributors include national as
well as foreign authors and articles are reprinted from
medical journals outside Cuba. The publication includes
book reviews and bibliographies and provides summaries of
the articles in English.

1048. Bohemia.
Havana: 1908- . weekly.
A popular weekly magazine dealing with current events,
sports, entertainment, culture, and international news.

1049. Casa de las Américas.
Havana: Casa de las Américas, 1960- . bimonthly.
A periodical devoted to art, literature, and cultural
activities. While the principal focus is on Cuban
developments, considerable attention is also paid to
Latin America.

1050. Cine Cubano.
Havana: 1960- . monthly.
Devoted to developments in Cuban cinema, including
analyses of directing, acting, and film making.

1051. Cuba Azúcar.
Havana: 1966- . monthly.
Published by the Ministry of Sugar, this magazine is
devoted to developments in the sugar industry. Most
material is technical, for which English language
summaries are provided.

1052. Cuba Internacional.
Havana: INRA, 1959-   . monthly.
A richly illustrated monthly magazine devoted to
archaeology, history, economics, culture, education, and
politics.   Issues are often devoted to single special
themes.

1053. Cuba Socialista.
Havana: Sept. 1961-Feb. 1967. monthly.
Published under the supervision of the Cuban Communist
Party, this was an important publication during the early
years   of   the   revolution,   devoted   principally   to
economics,   ideology,   politics,   and   international
relations.

1054. "A Guide to the Location of the Nineteenth-Century Cuban
Magazines."
Ivan S. Schulman and Erica Miles.
Latin American Research Review, vol. 12, no. 2 (1977),
p. 69-102.
A valuable guide to Cuban periodical literature.   The
compilation establishes the availability of a large
number of magazines in Cuba, Spain and the United States
and the extent of these holdings.

1055. Islas.
Santa Clara, Cuba: 195-   . triannual.
Published by the Central University of Las Villas, this
journal contains articles of general interest, including
history, essays, poetry, and documents.

1056. Mambí.
Santiago de Cuba: 1960-   . monthly.
Published by the Young Communist Union and Federation of
University Students of Oriente Province, the periodical
contains articles of general interest to university
students, including national and international news,
entertainment, fashion, and education.

1057. Pensamiento Crítico.
Havana: 1967-   . monthly.
Published by the Center of Latin American Studies in
Havana, this versatile periodical is devoted to social
and   political   thought.   Emphasis   is   given   to
investigation of the process of revolutionary change in
Africa, Asia, and Latin America.   The journal often
reprints articles from other publications.

1058. Revista de Arqueología y Etnología.
Junta Nacional de Arqueología.   1938-1940; quarterly;

1941-   irregular.
Professional journal of Cuban archaeology and ethnology.

1059. Revista de la Biblioteca Nacional "José Martí."
Havana: 1950-   . triannual.
Published by the National Library, the periodical
provides an important scholarly articles on history,
literature, and bibliography.

1060. Trabajo.
Havana: 1960-   . bi-weekly.
A popular magazine published by the Ministry of Labor.
Devoted to labor issues, including information on wages,
industrial safety, production, trade unions, and
management.

1061. Unión.
Havana: 1962-   . quarterly.
Published by the Writers and Artists Union, the
periodical is devoted to literary topics including
fiction, literary criticism, poetry, and articles on art.

1062. Verde Olivo.
Havana: 1960-   . weekly.
The official magazine of the armed forces published by
the Ministry of the Revolutionary Armed Forces (MINFAR).
The publication examines issues directly relevant to the
education and training of the military, including
weaponry, history, culture, and international
developments.

Encyclopedias and Directories

1063. <u>Cuba en la mano. Enciclopedia popular ilustrada.</u>
Compiled by Esteban Roldán Oliarte.
Havana: Imprenta Ucar, García y Cía., 1940. 1,302p.
maps. plates.
A comprehensive one-volume reference work on Cuba,
covering topics such as local geography, botany, zoology,
history, education, culture, tourism, communication,
sports, politics, military affairs, ships, and industry
and commerce. Many of the essays were contributed by
leading specialists in the field.

1064. <u>Cubans of To-day.</u>
Compiled by William Belmont Parkes.
New York: G. P. Putnam's Sons, 1919. 684p.
A compilation of biographical sketches of prominent Cuban
men and women in the early republic. They represent all
sectors of national life, including politics, education,
journalism, literature, commerce, and diplomacy.

1065. <u>Diccionario biográfico cubano.</u>
Compiled by Francisco Calgano.
New York: N. Ponce de León, 1878. 727p.
A biographical compilation of prominent Cubans and
Spaniards of the late nineteenth century.

1066. <u>Directorio administrativo y judicial de Cuba.</u>
Compiled by Francisco Muñoz Bonal.
Havana: Imprenta Alemana, 1925. 383p.
A directory of Cuban attorneys.

1067. <u>La enciclopedia de Cuba.</u>
San Juan, Puerto Rico: Enciclopedia y Clásicos Cubanos,
1975-1977. 14 vols. bibliog.

Each of the fourteen volumes of this collection deals with distinct themes and categories: 1. poetry; 2. theater;   3. the   novel;   4-5. history;   6. war; 7. architecture, music, and plastic arts; 8. geography, folklore, education, economics; 9. Pinar del Río and Havana;   10. Matanzas;   11. Las   Villas   and   Camagüey; 12. Oriente; 13-14. government.

1068. La enciclopedia de Cuba.
      Edited by Vicente Báez.
      Madrid: La Enciclopedia de Cuba, 1975. 12 vols.
      A multi-volume collection dealing with virtually all aspects of Cuban history, art, literature, politics, economy, education, and society. The essays include works by some of the most prominent Cuban scholars in exile.

1069. Enciclopedia popular cubana.
      Havana: Editorial Lex. 1948. 3 vols.
      An encyclopedia of things Cuban--history, biography, geography, culture, economy, foreign affairs, and government.

Anthologies

1070. Cuba, Castro, and Revolution.
Edited by Jaime Suchlicki.
Coral Gables, Florida: University of Miami Press, 1972.
250p. biblio.
The collection includes essays which deal with historical antecedents of the revolution; pre-revolutionary social structures; economic politics; the revolution and intellectuals; Cuban-Soviet-Latin American relations; and Cuban ties with Latin American communist parties.

1071. Cuba in Revolution.
Edited by Rolando E. Bonachea and Nelson P. Valdés.
Garden City, New York: Doubleday and Company, Inc., 1972. 544p.
A collection of more than twenty essays dealing with a large number of issues of the Cuban revolution. The contributions include North American and Cuban writers in exile as well as from those in Cuba itself. The subjects covered include the revolutionary war (1953-1958), bureaucracy, mobilization, economic policy, sugar production, labor, health, education, and culture.

1072. Cuba: Internal and International Affairs.
Edited by Jorge I. Domínguez.
Beverly Hills, California: Sage Publications, 230p.
Five essays ranging over the domestic and foreign policies of the Cuban revolution. The specific topics include the politics of the revolutionary elite, mass media, economic planning, the evolution of Cuban foreign policy, and U.S.-Cuban relations.

1073. Cuban Communism.
Edited by Irving Louis Horowitz.

New Brunswick, N.J.:   Transaction Books, 5th ed. 1980.
576p.
This collection of sixteen essays deals with a variety of
themes touching upon all aspects of the Cuban revolution.
Among the subjects treated are race and class, education,
military, agriculture, urban planning, economic policy,
and foreign policy.

1074. Cuba: the Logic of the Revolution.
Edited by David P. Barkin and Nita R. Manitzas.
Andover, Massachusetts: Warner Modular Publication,
1973. 192p.
A compilation of essays dealing with antecedents of the
revolution,   social   class-egalitarianism,   economic
development and consumption, economic organization and
incentives, educational developments, urban planning,
political culture, and Cuba as a model for other Latin
American countries.

1075. Cuba: Twenty-Five Years of Revolution, 1959-1984.
Edited by Sandor Halebsky and John M. Kirk.
New York: Praeger, 1985. 466p.
A   quarter-century   retrospect   includes   essays   on
education, medicine, nutrition, women, religion, popular
culture, cinema, literature, economic planning, labor,
foreign policy, U.S.-Cuban relations, and historiography.

1076. Fidel Castro's Personal Revolution in Cuba: 1959-1973.
Edited by James Nelson Goodsell.
New York: Knopf, 1975. 349p. bibliog.
Essays and excerpts from books dealing with various
aspects of the Cuban revolution, such as politics,
economics, culture, and foreign policy.

1077. Man and Socialism in Cuba: the Great Debate.
Edited by Bertram Silverman.
New York: Athenum, 1971. 382p.
The "great debate" is about the efficacy of moral
incentives over material incentives. This collection
brings together a variety of opinions on the subject,
including those from top officials in the Cuban
government, European economists, and North American
academics.

1078. The New Cuba: Paradoxes and Potentials.
Edited by Ronald Radosh.
New York: William Morrow and Company, Inc., 1976. 248p.
A collection of essays dealing with the Cuban communist
party,   culture,   U.S.-Cuban   relations,   and   economic
development.

1079. <u>Revolutionary Change in Cuba</u>.
      <u>Edited</u> by Carmelo Mesa-Lago.
      Pittsburgh: University of Pittsburgh Press, 1971. 544p.
      Eighteen essays arranged in three parts: polity,
      economy, and society. The themes examined in the first
      part include the role of the communist party, the
      consolidation of power, role of foreign countries, and
      Stalinism in revolutionary politics. The section on the
      economy discusses central planning, labor, international
      economic relations, and growth policies. The third
      section, looking at society, covers social structures,
      education,   religion,   art,   theater,   cinema,   and
      literature.

Bibliographies

A. General

1080. Anuario bibliográfico cubano; bibliografía cubana.
Compiled by Fermín Peraza Sarausa.
Havana: Anuario Bibliográfico Cubano, 1937-66. 30 vols.
This massive bibliographical series provides a guide to
vast range of Cuban materials. This compendium is an
indispensable guide to the literature, particularly in
the social sciences and humanities.

1081. Bibliografía cubana del siglo XIX.
Compiled by Carlos Manuel Trelles y Govín.
Matanzas, Cuba: Imprenta de Quirós y Estrada, 1911-1915.
8 vols.
Perhaps unparalleled in its completeness, this multi-
volume work is indispensable for all research dealing
with nineteenth century Cuba. The periodization of the
work organizes the nineteenth century into eight periods,
with a volume for each. Each volume has annotations,
notes, and brief biographies.

1082. Bibliografía cubana de los siglos XVII y XVIII.
Compiled by Carlos Manuel Trelles y Govín.
Havana: Imprenta del Ejército, 1927. 2nd ed. 463p.
Provides a comprehensive bibliographical guide to works
published during the colonial period. The entries are
arranged in five categories: materials written by Cuban
residents and exiles; the colonial press; manuscript
collections; materials written by foreigners; and
cartography. Its use outside Cuba is limited by the
unavailability of many of the cited works.

1083. Bibliografía cubana del siglo XX.

Compiled by Carlos Manuel Trelles y Govín.
Matanzas, Cuba: Imprenta de la Viuda de Quirós y
Estrada, 1916-1917.   2 vols.
A comprehensive bibliographical compilation of Cuban
materials published between 1900 and 1916.

1084. Bibliografías cubanas.
Compiled by Fermín Peraza Sarausa.
Washington, D.C.:   Government Printing Office, 1945.
58p.
A general bibliography of Cuban bibliographies.

1085. Bibliografía de bibliografías cubanas.
Compiled by Tomás Fernandez Robaina.
Havana: Instituto Cubano del Libro, 1973.   340p.
This comprehensive compilation of Cuban bibliographies.
The book arranges the material by nineteenth and
twentieth century order, and within each includes general
bibliographies, specialized compilations, library
catalogues, and guides to newspapers. It includes
materials published both within Cuba and abroad.

1086. The Complete Caribbeana, 1900-1975: a Bibliographic
Guide to the Scholarly Literature.
Compiled by Lambros Comitas.
Millwood, New York: KTO Press, 1977.   4 vols.
Over 2,000 pages of bibliographic entries dealing with
the humanities, social sciences, natural sciences, and
business. It provides an indispensable guide.

1087. Cuba, 1953-1978: a Bibliographical Guide to the
Literature.
Ronald H. Chilcote.
White Plains, N.Y.:   Kraus International Publications, 1986.
2 vols. 1,387p.
This vast bibliographical compilation--2 volumes, 10
parts, 68 chapters, and nearly 20,000 separate entries--
comes as close to a definitive guide as one can
reasonably expect. The work includes citations of books,
articles, and newspapers in about a dozen languages from
nearly 50 countries--dealing principally with the twenty-
five years after the attack on Moncada barracks in 1953.

1088. "Cuba Libre? Social Science Writings on Postrevolution-
ary Cuba, 1959-1975."
Irving L. Horowitz.
Studies in Comparative International Development,   vol.
10, no. 3 (Autumn 1975), p. 101-23.
Provides an annotated examination of the principal
English-language works dealing with the Cuban revolution.

1089. The Cuban Revolution: a Research-Study Guide (1959-1969).
Compiled by Nelson P. Valdés and Edwin Lieuwen.
Albuquerque, New Mexico: University of New Mexico Press,
1971. 230p.
One of the most complete bibliographical guides available
for the period, including references on all aspects of
the revolution: politics, international relations,
economy, culture, and a variety of social topics.

1090. Handbook of Latin American Studies.
Hispanic Foundation, Library of Congress.
Cambridge: Harvard   University   Press,   1935-1951;
Gainesville, Florida: University of Florida Press,
1952- . annual.
An on-going and indispensable annotated guide to the
general literature dealing with Latin America. From vol.
27 onwards in 1965 the guide divides the entries into
annual alternating volume for the humanities and social
sciences.

1091. Revolutionary Cuba: a Bibliographical Guide.
Compiled by Fermín Peraza Sarausa.
Coral Gables, Florida: University of Miami Press,
1966-1968. 3 vols.
A comprehensive compilation of the materials published
both within Cuba and abroad which deal with the
revolution.

B. Topical

1092. Alejo Carpentier, Bibliographical Guide.
Compiled by Roberto González Echevarría and Klaus Muller-
Bergh.
Westport: Greenwood Press, 1983. 271p.
A compilation of nearly 3,200 entries dealing with works
by and about Carpentier. The entries are not annotated.

1093. "Bibliografía   comentada   de   estudios   lingüísticos
publicados en Cuba, 1959-1980."
Iraida López-Iñíguez.
Cuban Studies/Estudios Cubanos, vol. 13, no. 1 (Winter
1983), p. 69-76.
A compilation of more than 200 works published in Cuba
after the revolution dealing with linguistics.   The
topics covered include grammar, phonetics, syntax,
semantics, lexicography, dialects (Spanish and non-
Spanish), and general studies.

1094. Bibliografía crítica de la poesía cubana. Exilio 1959-
1971.

Compiled by Matías Montes Huidobro and Yara González.
New York: Plaza Mayor Ediciones, 1972. 136p.
This selective annotated bibliography of books written by
sixty-seven Cuban poets in exile. The introductory
essays provide a useful survey of Cuban poetry in exile.

1095. "Bibliografía de autores de la raza de color de Cuba."
Carlos Manuel Trelles y Govín.
Cuba Contemporánea,   vol. 43,   no. 169   (Jan.   1927),
p. 30-78.
A compilation of references of literary works by and
about Afro-Cubans. The material is arranged in sections
dealing with   slavery   and   post-slavery,   Afro-Cuban
newspapers, works by white authors about blacks, and
works   dealing   with   Afro-Americans   in   the   Western
Hemisphere.

1096. Bibliografía de la guerra chiquita, 1879-1880.
Compiled by Miriam Hernández Soler.
Havana: Instituto Cubano del Libro. 265p.
A guide to materials dealing with the ill-fated and
short-lived   separatist   uprising.   The   bibliography
included references to published works, manuscripts, and
newspaper accounts.

1097. Bibliografía de la guerra de independencia, 1895-1898.
Compiled by Araceli García Carranza.
Havana: Instituto Cubano del Libro, 1976. 746p.
An important annotated guide to the literature covering
the political, military, social, literary, and diplomatic
aspects of the war of independence. The bibliography is
arranged into four large sections dealing with the Cuban
insurgency, the U.S. intervention, biographies of the
participants, and literature.

1098. Bibliografía de la guerra de los diez años.
Edited by Aleida Plasencia.
Havana: Biblioteca Nacional "José Martí," 1968. 388p.
An enormously useful compilation of materials relating to
the first Cuban struggle for independence (1868-1878).
The   annotated   items   include   general   works,   autobio-
graphical   accounts   from   participants   on   both   sides,
document collections, and newspapers.

1099. Bibliografía de poesía cubana en el siglo XIX.
Biblioteca Nacional "José Martí." Departamento Colección
Cubana.
Havana: Biblioteca Nacional "José Martí." 1965. 89p.
A bibliographical guide to Cuban nineteenth century,
arranged in the chronological order of the original
publication. Partially annotated.

1100. Bibliografía de los suelos de Cuba.
Compiled by Juan de Días Tejeda y Sainz.
Santa María del Rosario, Cuba: Editorial Var, 1943. 77p.
A bibliographical compilation of works dealing with the
varieties and composition of Cuban soils.

1101. Bibliografía del teatro cubano.
Compiled by José Rivero Muñiz.
Havana: Biblioteca Nacional, 1957. 120p.
A bibliographical compilation of Cuban drama, including
works by, and on, Cuban playwrights.

1102. A Bibliography of Cuban Belles-Lettres.
Compiled by Jeremiah D. M. Ford and Maxwell I. Raphael.
Cambridge, Massachusetts: Harvard University Press,
1933. 204p.
A guide to studies dealing with Cuban literature. The
bibliography is organized into four parts, dealing with
general works, specific works of literature, anonymous
and collected works, and periodicals. Many of the
entries are annotated.

1103. "A Bibliography of Cuban Creative Literature: 1958-1971."
Edited by Lourdes Casal.
Cuban Studies Newsletter, vol. 2, no. 2 (June 1972),
p. 2-29.
A comprehensive compilation of entries of novels and
short stories, plays and poetry by Cuban authors both in
Cuba and in exile.

1104. A Bibliography of United States-Latin American Relations
Since 1810.
Compiled by David F. Trask, Michael C. Meyer, and Roger
R. Trask.
Lincoln, Nebraska: University of Nebraska Press, 1968.
441p.
This comprehensive compilation of materials deals
generally with inter-American relations. Many of the
annotated entries deal with U.S.-Cuba relations. The
1968 bibliography was augmented by the Supplement to a
bibliography of United States-Latin American relations
since 1910 which was compiled by Michael C. Meyer
(Lincoln, Nebraska: University of Nebraska Press, 1979.
193p.)

1105. "A Bibliography on Cuban Women in the Twentieth Century."
Nelson P. Valdés.
Cuban Studies Newsletter, vol. 4, no. 2 (June 1974),
p. 1-31.
One of the most complete bibliographical surveys
available on the subject of women's studies in Cuba.

Although now somewhat dated, this is an important work to consult for all research up to the mid-1970s.

1106. Biblioteca geográfica cubana.
Carlos Manuel Trelles y Govín.
Matanzas, Cuba: Imprenta de J. F. Oliver, 1920.   340p. maps.
A useful bibliography of works related to travel and description, geography, cartographical subjects, and maps.

1107. "A Briefly Annotated Bibliograhy of Fidel Castro's Works: 1959-1970."
Rolando E. Bonachea.
Cuban Studies Newsletter, vol. 3, no. 2 (June 1973), p. 1-65.
A very useful guide to the published transcriptions of the speeches, interviews, and pronouncements of Fidel Castro.   The materials include coverage of politics, economic policy, social programs, and foreign relations. Its usefulnesss is enhanced considerably by the inclusion of a subject index.

1108. Cuba, viajes y descripciones, 1493-1949.
Rodolfo Tro.
Havana: n.p.,   1950.   188p.
A detailed and annotated bibliography of travel accounts.

1109. Cubans in the United States: a Bibliography for Research in the social and Behavioral Sciences, 1960-1983.
Compiled by Lyn MacCorkle.
Westport, Connecticut: Greenwood Press, 1984.   227p.
Presents bibliographical compilation of 1,600 references to English- language materials dealing with education, economics, public administration, psychology, health, politics, sociology, and demography.   The entries are not annotated.

1110. "The Cuban Novel, 1959-1969:   An Annotated Bibliography."
Lourdes Casal.
Abraxas, vol. 1, no. 1 (Autumn 1970), p. 77-92.
Provides a useful compilation and description of novels published in the first decade of the revolution.

1111. The Cuban Revolution of Fidel Castro Viewed from Abroad: Annotated Bibliography.
Gilberto V. Fort.
Lawrence: University of Kansas Libraries, 1969.   140p.
A compilation of works published largely in English, Spanish, and Portuguese dealing with the Cuban revolution. The publications, which include books, pamphlets, and

general studies that devote at least one complete chapter to some aspect of the revolution, appeared in print between 1959 and 1967. The materials are arranged in chronological order.

1112. The Cuban Revolutionary War, 1953-1958: a Bibliography.
Louis A. Pérez, Jr.
Metuchen, New Jersey: The Scarecrow Press, Inc., 1976.
225p.
A compilation of materials dealing with the years of armed struggle against the regime of Fulgencio Batista (1952-1958).   The bibliography encompasses the period between the attack on the Mondada barracks (July 1953) and the victory of the revolutionary forces (January 1959).

1113. Cuban Studies/Estudios Cubanos.
Pittsburgh: Center   for   Latin   American   Studies,
University of Pittsburgh.   1971-1985.   semi-annual.
1986-   . annual.
Perhaps the single most important journal devoted to Cuban studies published outside Cuba.   It contains feature articles,   research   notes,   book   reviews, professional news, and an extensive on-going biblio-graphical inventory.   An indispensable publication for all work on Cuba.

1114. "Cubans in the U.S.: A Survey of the Literature."
Lourdes Casal and Andrés R. Hernández.
Cuban Studies/Estudios Cubanos, vol. 5, no. 2 (July 1975), p. 25-51.
A comprehensive review of the major trends relating to treating Cuban exiles.   The major categories of discussion include causes of emigration, demographic origins, exiles as sources of information, assimilation and acculturation, political attitudes and behavior in the United States, family changes and sex roles, mental health, occupational adjustment and social mobility, youth, attitudes towards other racial and ethnic minorities, and the Cuban impact on the United States. The article contains an extensive annotated bibliography.

1115. Historia del movimiento obrero en Cuba: bibliografía.
Biblioteca Central Rubén Martínez Villena.
Havana: Universidad de La Habana, 1973. 48p.
An important bibliography of working class politics and organization, spanning the nineteenth and twentieth century.

1116. Historiography in the Revolution: a Bibliography of Cuban Scholarship, 1959-1979.

Louis A. Pérez, Jr.
New York: Garland Publishing, Inc., 1982. 318p.
A compilation of books and articles dealing with Cuban
history which were published during the first twenty
years of the revolution. The bibliography is divided in
two principal sections, on a chronological format (1492-
1952) and the other thematic. The latter includes
materials dealing with women, labor, communism, slavery,
peasantry, and foreign relations.

1117. "The Making of a Revolutionary: a Fidel Castro
      Bibliography (1947-1958)."
      Nelson P. Valdés and Rolando E. Bonachea.
      Latin American Research Review, vol. 5, no. 2 (Summer
      1970), p. 83-88.
      A compilation of the principal writings by Fidel Castro
      during his formative political years.

1118. "La obra escrita de don Fernando Ortiz."
      Juan Comas and Berta Becerra.
      Revista Interamericana de Bibliografía, vol. 7, no. 4
      (1957), p. 346-71.
      A bibliographic compilation of the published works of the
      prolific ethnologist Fernando Ortiz Fernandez.   The
      material is arranged in the order of books, articles, and
      his introductions to other works. The listing follows a
      chronological order.

1119. "Prose Fiction Criticism and Theory in Cuban Journals:
      an Annotated Bibliography."
      Terry J. Peavler.
      Cuban Studies/Estudios Cubanos, vol. 7, no. 1 (Jan.
      1977), p. 58-118.
      A comprehensive compilation of literary sources published
      in Cuba after 1959.   The categories include general
      literature, literary criticism, literary theory, and
      specific authors and works. Also included are citations
      dealing with Cuban critical writings on literature in
      other Latin American countries and the United States.

1120. "United States Doctoral Dissertations on Cuban Studies in
      the Twentieth Century."
      Compiled by David S. Zubatsky.
      Cuban Studies Newsletter, vol. 4, no. 2 (June 1974),
      p. 35-55.
      A useful compilation of dissertations written in the
      twentieth century on all aspects of Cuban studies. The
      article contains information on ordering copies that are
      available through University Microfilm.

Index

References are to item numbers, not page numbers.

Architecture. 79, 89, 211, 983, 985, 1067
    colonial. 1002
    20th century. 998
    1950s. 997
    post-1959. 999-1000
    churches. 1002
    class content. 997
    Havana. 243
    history. 996, 1002
    ideology. 998
    monuments. 1001
    Spanish influences. 998
    United States influences. 998
Archives. 1026, 1034
    Cuban. 72, 321, 1020-1021, 1029, 1033
    directory of. 1026
    Latin American. 1032
    publications. 1021
    United States. 1023, 1027, 1031
Arciniegas, Germán. 172
Ardevol, José. 1007
Area Handbook for Cuba. 2
Areíto. 25
Arenal, Humberto. 406, 955
Argüelles, Lourdes. 478
Argüelles Valcarcel, Félix M. 490
Arisso, Ana María. 445
Armas, Ramón de. 299
Armed forces. 2, 71, 228, 565, 585, 615-31, 1062-63, 1073
    colonial. 262, 269, 622
    republic. 615
    post-1959. 227, 382, 614, 616, 619-21, 625, 628-29, 655
    Afro-Cubans. 630
    and Autentico party. 624
    and Fulgencio Batista. 624
    and communist party. 617-18
    and José Miguel Gómez. 631
    and Gerardo Machado. 624
    militarism. 626-27
    Rebel Army. 19, 333-34, 616, 619-20
    Rural Guard. 631
    statistics. 750
    and United States. 615
Army Politics in Cuba, 1898-1958. 615
Around the Corner to Cuba. 105
Arqueología indocubana. 149
La arquitectura cubana del siglo XIX. 996
Arrendamientos urbanos. 468
Arredondo, Alberto. 424, 764
Art. 21, 23, 136, 211, 305, 312-13, 321, 903, 1049, 1068